BLESS THE BITTER AND THE SWEET

For Paul,

2016

"Go Forth"

and

"Fear Not"

!!! ♡♡ℓ6 ♂♀

BLESS THE BITTER AND THE SWEET

*A sabra girl's diary from the last days of
British rule and the rebirth of Israel*

Naomi Harris Rosenblatt

For my husband, Peter;

For our children,
Therese and Marshall, Daniel, David and Laurie;

For our grandchildren,
Zachary, Samuel, Jacob, Abigail, Benjamin, Nathaniel, and Caroline

And for those who come after...

I do not want to die taking these chronicles with me to the grave, not having paid homage to the land in which I was reared, to my demanding Hebrew Reali School, *to my nurturing youth movement, to a love story, and, most of all, to my mother and father who remain at the inner core of my being. I want our children and grandchildren and all the generations that follow to know the rock from which they were cut and the quarry from which they were hewn.*

This story was brought to life

in June 1946 after the famous "Night of the Bridges." It was just a year after the end of World War II and two years before Israel's Independence. The tension was palpable. Curfews paralyzed ordinary life and powerful searchlights swept the night sky seeking out those whom the British rulers called "illegal immigrants"—the wretched, traumatized remnant of European Jewry. The "Night of the Bridges" was a defiant response to British policy and the world's silence. Fourteen courageous Palmach boys, members of the strike team of Israel's nascent underground army, lost their lives that night on the A-Ziv Bridge.

It was a time of powerful emotions and amazing deeds. It was a time of death and romance, joy and grief—the stuff of dreams. The story depicts day-to-day life in a sabra girl's coming of age during the last years of British colonial rule, Israel's rebirth in a bloody war and the first years of its independence. During these times, she is introduced to a young visitor from New York's Upper East Side and their love affair blossoms during the summer school holidays and military service.

Cover: Dressed for Shabbat on Panorama Road overlooking the bay of Haifa, 1950.

Look to the rock from
which you were cut
and to the quarry from
which you were hewn…

—Isaiah 51:1

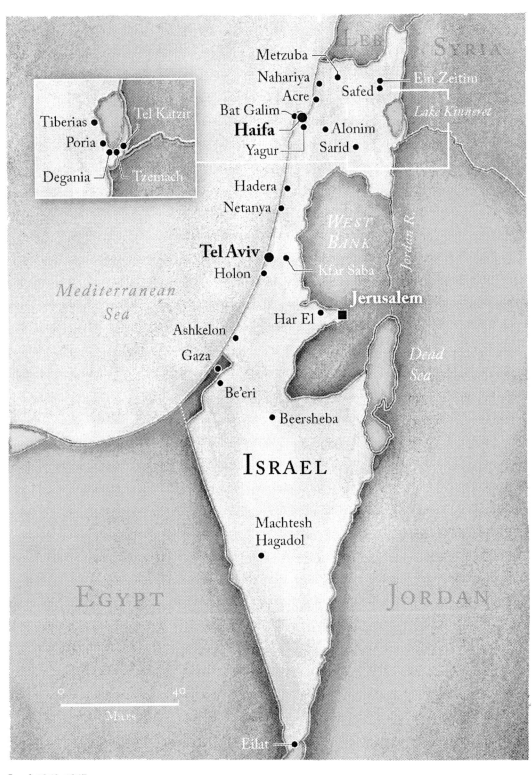

Israel, 1948–1967.

Preface

It is difficult—65 years after the first entry—to know just why I began to keep
a diary, especially since at the time, my parents had to stand over me with a
daily admonition "Naomi, do your homework!" Why would I have spent hours
writing down my thoughts and feelings during such distracting and hectic times?
Why did I even start?

The first entry came just as the first anniversary of the "Night of the Bridges"
approached—an important milestone in the lives of those living in Palestine,
or "the Land of Israel," as its Jewish inhabitants called the area even before Israel
was officially an independent state. The Scouts to which I belonged commemorated
significant events, and this one was fresh in all our minds and hearts. The Night
of the Bridges, as it came to be known, took place in June 1946, just a year
after the end of World War II and two years before Israel's Independence Day.

So much was happening in our lives. I was 13 at the time, and becoming acutely
aware that the air all around me was heavy with tension. Powerful searchlights
constantly intruded, sweeping across the ceiling of my bedroom, seeking out those
whom our British rulers referred to as illegal immigrants—wretched refugees
from the Holocaust in Europe. Those wounded souls who had somehow managed
to escape the death camps—and were left only with their mind-numbing tales
of horror and aching losses, were trying to find refuge and a home in the Land
of Israel. Curfews were imposed, with menacing warnings of the consequences
if the curfew was not adhered to.

Although Germany, the common enemy, had been vanquished, the Yishuv—
the Jews living in Palestine before Israel became a state—felt deeply disappointed
with the heartless rules and the obstacles set up by the British Mandate to stop
the Jewish community from saving the Jews being held indefinitely in displaced
person camps in Europe. The Yishuv was changing its policy toward the British.
Cooperation between the two sides practically ceased. Lines were drawn and the
different sides dug in. The Haganah—and its elite fighting force, the Palmach,

which later served as the core of the Israel Defense Forces—led an all-out struggle to save the European Jewish remnant. With quiet courage and resolve, the Palmach helped smuggle these people in unseaworthy boats through the British blockade, settling them into the Land of Israel. Most of the Jews had lost close relatives—whole families or even communities—in the Holocaust. The Yishuv realized they were alone in the world and could not depend on the mercy of others. Saving those who had survived was part of the DNA of the community, part of the responsibility of Jews going back to antiquity. In fact, I had stared for years at the saying from the Talmud on our classroom walls, absorbing its meaning: "The children of Israel are responsible one for another."

The Night of the Bridges marked a change of direction for the Haganah, from aiding "illegal immigration" alone to an offensive against British rule in Palestine under the Mandate. The Bridges operation itself seemed to mark that tipping point with an abrupt shift from the Yishuv's relatively quieter time when we and the British were fighting the same enemy, the Germans. The new direction ended our World War II alliance with the British and began a period of open hostility. The Palmach set out to blow up 11 bridges linking Palestine, or the Land of Israel, to its neighbors in order to disrupt British communications with those countries. Fourteen Palmach boys lost their lives at the one bridge, the A-Ziv, where the operation failed—the one and only bridge where there were casualties.

I had been deeply stirred by the heroism of these young, brave boys, most of whom were kibbutz members. I remember the profound effect it had on me at that time, when I resolved that the 14 must never be forgotten. Learning more about that night, as I did during the activities surrounding the anniversary commemoration, gave me a greater sense that I was part of something larger than myself. I didn't want to forget, nor did I want those boys to EVER be forgotten. It signaled for me the beginning of a time when I no longer felt neutral toward our British rulers, even though as Israeli Prime Minister Golda Meir later said, British policy was heartless and cruel, but as rulers go they could have been much worse.

The prevailing mood of the Jews in the country at the time is reflected perfectly in the words carved into two modest plaques that mark the spot of the tragedy; the words speak of the Night of the Bridges as among the most important operations in the resistance movement prior to the establishment of the State of Israel. The operation, a defiant response to British policy and to the world's silence, is described in detail and signals that "If the Jews have no entrance to their own country, there will be no entrance to anybody else."

This emotional time, with its powerful mix of pain and pride, might have helped jump-start my diary, provoking reflections on and feelings about what had happened—and what I was going to do about it. I was determined that we were not going to be victims anymore. A new Jewish identity was being forged. The first anniversary of such a historic event in my life and my land galvanized me to begin and keep a diary. My diary soon ranged across the panoply of issues and events in the life of an active adolescent in a land about to be reborn.

So it is that what began as a spontaneous effort not to allow the memory of the 14 to fade from history grew into this diary handwritten in Hebrew and kept sporadically for the next five years. I always knew it was there, lying somewhere around the house, unread for so long. Somehow I could not bear reading it earlier than I finally did for fear it would bring on a bout of homesickness. It was decades later that I picked it up again, thinking my children (then grown with children of their own) might find the story of their mother as a young girl interesting. I translated it into English, trying hard to be true to the original, to maintain the integrity of the language and the accuracy of what was written all those decades before.

In an effort to flesh out some of the background and context of the diary I have written an introduction to the people and events that were major features of my youth. Some of the subjects run into each other—life does not move in an orderly fashion. I also kept a page of the diary blank, because I was not able at the time to write about the battle in which my beloved cousin Danny fell at the very outset of the 1948 War of Independence. It was too painful to record then. The introduction also supplements the diary's accounts of my service in the fledgling Israeli Navy and my meeting and romance with a 15-year-old American visitor to whom I am married today, 62 years later. This is my personal account of those times.

A special thank you to Evelyn Small whose wise suggestions, guidance and knowledge were indispensable; to my assistant Peshie Chaifetz, whose skill and companionship I fully appreciate; and of course...to Peter who is always at my side!

*I*N THE BEGINNING

Part I

From Scotland and Canada, They Went Forth and Feared Not.

SARA ABRAHAMSON's hair was auburn and curly. She had a high forehead, wide-set dark-brown eyes, a strong jaw line and prominent cheekbones. She was born and brought up on a farm 40 miles north of Winnipeg, Canada. A blurb in her 1920 University of Manitoba yearbook said of her: "Born and educated in Winnipeg, Sara decided to follow in the footsteps of her family and study law. We know that she will be an ornament to the profession, as she invariably makes a success of anything she undertakes." Indeed, she became a professional woman, a lawyer, but sometime shortly after her graduation in the early 1920's, Sara, along with her two older sisters, Mary and Esther, moved with their parents to the Land of Israel, and never saw Canada again.

My beloved grandmother Nechama Abrahamson in Canada, with Mary, baby Esther and Simon. My mother, Sara, was not born yet.

Ephraim "Eph" Harris was tall and slim. His glasses rested on an aquiline nose of which he was proud, remarking that in profile it looked Roman. He was born in Manchester, England, and brought up in Glasgow, Scotland. He graduated from the University of Glasgow with a master's degree in German, Russian and Italian literature.

He was fluent in Hebrew in addition to all three of those languages, and also knew Latin and Greek. He landed in the lovely Mediterranean port town of Haifa in 1920 and lived there for the rest of his days.

Sara and Eph were my parents. They reached the Land of Israel separately and for different reasons. My father was a graduate student in Rome studying the classics, preparing to assume a teaching position at a Scottish university away

Opposite: Me as a young child, already posing.

Father in Glasgow, Scotland, in his kilt, at age 14.

Sara and Ephraim Harris—my mother and father on Herzl Street in Haifa in the late 40's.

from the confines of family and the small Jewish community in Glasgow. His family had fled Spain during the Inquisition, found refuge in Padua, Italy, produced two chief rabbis, moved to Holland and came to England in the 17th century. This was at a time when England, under Cromwell, had reopened her doors to Jews, having expelled them late in the 13th century, one hundred years after the massacre at York. My four-greats-grandfather, Hershel Meyer, was Chief Rabbi of London from 1790 to his death in 1801. I've been told that he lived close to the synagogue so as to be able to walk to services on the Sabbath.

In Rome, my father encountered a group of idealistic Russian Jewish intellectuals with round metal-rimmed eye glasses and unruly hair on their way to Palestine, then a British mandate. He was intrigued by them and their destination. The fact that the country was under British rule, made the idea of going to Palestine all the more interesting to him.

Once he touched its shores, he fell in love with the quality of life there and even more so with Jewish history—with the continuous logic of its teachings, with its unbroken bond with the ancient land, with its aspirations and longings. He returned to Glasgow to visit his family every couple of years, except during World War II, of course. He called these visits "home leave" and as often as possible he would retreat on his own to his beloved remote Isle of Skye, off the western coast of Scotland, accompanied only by his manual typewriter.

Mother's path to Israel, then Palestine, was less direct. Her father, my Grandfather Moses

Abrahamson, whom I unfortunately met only when I was a small child, had left Kovno (now called Kaunas), Lithuania, at 17, and headed off to England. The story goes that one day in London, he lost his way and stopped a mounted policeman for directions to Threadneedle Street, in broken English of course. Lo and behold, the policeman jumped off his horse, walked with him for a block, and pointed him in the right direction. My grandfather was overwhelmed. A policeman going out of his way for a poor Jewish immigrant boy? What a contrast to the autocratic Czarist Russia from which he had come! To savor the experience fully, he would stop a policeman every few blocks, and the sweet pattern would be repeated.

It was at that point that his lifelong love for England was kindled, though he did not remain there. He felt it was much too cohesive a society for a foreigner to fully assimilate. So Moses Abrahamson picked up his wife and the two children they had at the time—Simon, the elder, and Mary—and went off to homestead in western Canada, where he acquired a working farm. Soon after the family of four got comfortably settled in Winnipeg another daughter, Esther, was born, followed by my mother, Sara.

Canada proved accommodating. Moses Abrahamson ran for and was elected to Winnipeg's Board of Education at age 46 on December 23, 1913. According to the *Manitoba Free Press*, he became a candidate for the school board "as a result of a strong desire among the foreign element to have a representative who could discuss school affairs in their own languages." According to the paper he campaigned in six languages. It was an amazing feat for a candidate whose passionate speeches were in

The four Abrahamson children in Winnepeg, Canada. L-R: Sara, my mother, Mary, Simon, and Esther.

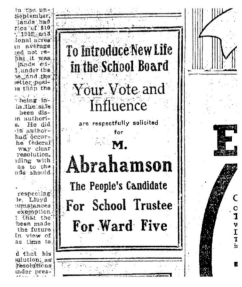

The Manitoba Free Press *announces my grandfather, Moses Abrahamson's candidacy for the Board of Education.*

English, but when at a loss for a word Yiddish was unapologetically thrown into the mix. Some of the voters mistook the Yiddish for Hebrew.

In November 1917, a year before the end of World War I, the Foreign Secretary of the United Kingdom issued the Balfour Declaration, publically endorsing the establishment in Palestine of a national home for the Jewish people. There and then, Moses Abrahamson decided that if Britain, the country he so loved, favored helping rebuild the historic home of the Jews in the Land of Israel, he would rally to the call.

Mother, then in her early 20s, decided to join her parents and her two sisters. Their brother, Simon, who had earlier become Canada's first Jewish Rhodes Scholar despite coming from a Yiddish-speaking family, was by then a highly respected lawyer. Simon's response to his father's decision was: "If you think England will hand over power without blood and tears, you don't know history." He elected to settle in California, creating a deep, painful schism in the family that took years to heal.

Who knows what motivated my mother to leave the familiar and comfortable future of a professional woman? It could have been any or all of a number of reasons: getting away from the cold of western Canada to a Mediterranean climate, curiosity, or her capacity and desire to will a dream into reality.

My grandfather, Moses Abrahamson, during the early years in Tel Aviv in an elegant linen suit.

As Grandfather waited on the station platform for the train to leave Winnipeg with his wife and three daughters, the small Jewish community came to say goodbye and to see him off. He was asked, in Yiddish, "Moses, where are you going?" His answer: "I'm going home!" The family arrived in the Land of Israel in 1920, settling in Tel Aviv, where my grandfather built one of the very first houses, at 6 Nachlat Binyamin, a section of the city close to the sea.

According to Mother, Moses Abrahamson was a handsome man who sported a red handlebar mustache. He was brilliant, charismatic, and articulate, with passionate ideas and strong opinions about various issues. On Sabbath afternoons, after his nap, he held court with a small group of companions hanging on his every word. He could be difficult, but he was a man of foresight, an early Zionist, and he was willing to take risks to pursue a vision.

He had no secular education to speak of, nor did he speak the King's English. He had been educated in Lithuania in the *cheder*, a small, single-room religious school, and later on went to a yeshiva, a school for Jewish rabbinic and religious studies. It was in these institutions that he gained his wisdom, strengthened his values, and honed his analytical skills. A story runs in the family that when my grandfather was a young boy in Russia, he loved playing outdoors and climbing trees, his cheeks aflame with excitement. His mother, alarmed, would gaze up toward heaven and fervently pray that her son would eventually evolve from a wild, ruddy-cheeked peasant boy to a tame, pale, scholarly "*cheder* angel."

Another story told to me is that Grandfather used to say: "A toothless old man, bald and incontinent, who craves closeness is often left alone longing for the human touch. But a hairless, toothless and incontinent baby, on the other hand, holds the attention of the entire family." That was his way of seeing life and looking at the world—realistically, savoring the irony of it all, yet never losing his idealism. In one lifetime Moses Abrahamson moved from Russia to England to Canada, and eventually settled for good in the Land of Israel where he was able to live out his vision.

In Eastern Europe, the custom was to marry poor rabbinical students to the daughters of the well-to-do leaders of the small community. My maternal grandmother, Nechama, was the daughter of comfortable merchants, and Moses Abrahamson was a poor but brilliant rabbinical student. As the custom dictated, he was a guest at Nechama's family's lunch table every Monday and Thursday. As time passed, that weekly ritual led to their arranged marriage. No one asked if they were in love. It was a match, the nucleus of a brand-new Jewish household.

My grandmother was called "Nechama die Kluge," which everyone took to mean "Nechama the wise." She was deeply loved by her three daughters and renowned for her wisdom and goodness. Unfortunately, I remember very little of her. She died in Tel Aviv in 1937. I was only four years old, and in those days travel from Haifa to Tel Aviv was a considerable undertaking, often accompanied by casualties caused by sniping from Arab villages along the route. I do remember clearly walking down "Mountain Road"—the steep hill from our

My mother and I on the Simchat Torah holiday, on a rare visit to Tel Aviv.

house—with my mother walking and sobbing as she headed to the train station to go to my grandmother's funeral in Tel Aviv.

Over many years, Mother filled me with stories about her mother, and those who knew them both say that my mother and grandmother were very similar. In Tel Aviv, across the street from Nechama's home, a good-natured poor Orthodox Jew and his wife ran a small kiosk. The couple was blessed with ten children. The husband suffered from stomach cancer and was consumed with worries about supporting his vast family. Every day, no matter how hot the day, my grandmother Nechama prepared and carried out to the little kiosk, bowls of chicken noodle soup—healthy and easy to digest. This, I was told, went on for months until the man died and the kiosk was sold.

The other story I recall about my maternal grandmother in 1920s Tel Aviv concerns a young woman in her late 30s. The woman was an immigrant of modest means with no family. Grandmother took it upon herself to settle the girl in a secure marriage. It was deemed a duty in Jewish communities to be responsible for poor, unmarried women and to provide them with a dowry to help set up their household. This was done first out of compassion and a strong sense of communal responsibility, and, second, because of the age-old commitment and concern for Jewish continuity.

Grandmother came up with an excellent prospect for the single woman: she found a shy, pimply 32-year-old accountant, also a new immigrant, also without a family of his own, and also poor. Somehow Grandma got the date on the woman's birth certificate altered to make her 30 years old, a little younger than the accountant. Grandmother wanted no cause for resistance by the accountant, so in this case the end justified the means. The two got married and set up a household. To everybody's amazement, the accountant made some very shrewd investments, and it was not long before the poverty-stricken bride came visiting my grandparents bedecked with jewelry and sporting a brand-new address in the burgeoning new housing section of north Tel Aviv.

Sadly, I never knew much about my paternal grandparents, Henry and Leah (née Silverman) Harris. The first time I met them, when I was six, was in 1939. My parents and I visited Glasgow during the summer holiday just before I started first grade. We left to go back home on a ship I remember being called the *Auford*, supposedly the last ship to leave England for Palestine before World War II broke out. My family later heard a rumor that the ship was sunk by the Germans on the return to England. I do know that Grandfather Henry Harris was a huge man. When entering a taxi, he caused it to tilt, or so it seemed to me. He taught me to dance the fandango, and a good time was had by us both. I heard from my mother that Grandfather Harris loved Charles Dickens and so did she. Their common appreciation for the great author created a lively subject for conversation, and a bond evolved between my reserved Scottish grandfather and his emotional and animated daughter-in-law. He was tough on my father in a rather typically Victorian way. Perhaps he had been influenced by his own father, the headmaster of a Jewish boys' school in Manchester, England. When my father, aged eight, won first prize for a play he wrote in Latin, his father's only response was, "Of what use will that be in your life?" That story angered me when I was a child, and it still saddens me today when

My paternal grandparents Leah Silverman Harris and Harry Harris, on holiday in Nice.

I think of how it must have upset my father. Grandfather Harris believed that one should not "wear one's heart on one's sleeve." His Scottish reserve and his innate philosophy combined to produce the frequently stated warning that one "should leave room for the deluge"—save emotion for real crises. His bent toward being unemotional was in vivid evidence in a small episode right after World War II when my father returned to Scotland for the first time after the war. After not having seen his son for five or six years, Henry Harris took one look at him as he walked in the door and greeted him with, "Oh, Ephraim, take off that dreadful hat." Father told this story ever after with a mix of criticism, incredulity, and some irritation, but definitely with a sprinkling of humor.

My grandparents in Scotland, with their daughter, my aunt Helen.

I was, however, deeply insulted and always felt hurt on my father's behalf. I blamed British Victorian attitudes for my grandfather's behavior—without, of course, knowing all that much about the subject.

I remember little about my father's mother, my Grandmother Leah. The years of the war, the geographic distance between us, and the lack of modern-day communication made it virtually impossible to get to know each other. Correspondence was censored during the war years and slow; telephoning was prohibitively expensive and out of the question. What I do know is that while my grandfather was a scholar, she was a businesswoman and the manager of a very posh—or, as we now call it, high-end—ladies' clothing boutique. I didn't discover this until much later, when I was an adult. In part I think this was because it was not entirely admirable for a woman to be in business, so her particular skills and expertise weren't much talked about, though they might have been indispensable.

NEITHER OF MY PARENTS was the prototypical Jewish pioneer escaping persecution and poverty. It's not that they did not love Scotland and Canada, but they simply felt more deeply committed to the Land of Israel. Once my mother reached the Tel Aviv of the 1920s, she never looked back. She fell hard for the simplicity of the life there, moonlit walks on the Tel Aviv seashore, the struggles, hopes, and goals of a highly motivated Jewish community, and, not least, the Sunday tea dances with British officers on their way to India, then part of the British Empire. The officers' upper-class "Oxford" accents, typical of their class, contrasted with the broad Canadian accents with which she had grown up. The whole atmosphere was exhilarating and romantic. Both Mother and Father socialized with the small English-speaking Jewish community, and it was no doubt at some gathering of this community where they met. They fell in love, married, and eventually begot me.

Me at age four.

The only home I ever knew as a child was in Haifa, to which my parents had moved sometime before I was born. Haifa was—and is—a spectacularly beautiful town built on the slopes of Mount Carmel, overlooking the long curve of what is known as the Bay of Haifa along the Mediterranean coastline. Even at the time I was growing up there, Haifa was principally a port city, developed in part because the British had recognized the area as being strategically important and created a deep-water port there. It was then and remains the third-largest city in the country, and always the most important city in the north. The port area at the foot of the mountain lent the city an international flavor—and still does. The view from the top of Mount Carmel—the docks, the ships, the beauty of the bay, the lights at night—is unforgettable. Jerusalem has always been unique—a city like no other. In my youth, Haifa was referred to in Hebrew as *ir hapoalim*, the town of the working people, but I viewed Haifa then and still do now, especially in comparison with Tel Aviv, as quieter and superficially less sophisticated.

View of Haifa in 1951, looking toward the oil refinery.

My house was in a pretty neighborhood opposite the lush, manicured Bahá'í Gardens halfway up Mount Carmel. Ours was a lovely, comfortable, airy apartment. The living room was always flooded with light, with windows and doors opening out to a balcony surrounding our entire flat. The furniture was upholstered in blues and reds, and a predominantly blue Persian rug covered the living room's stark white tiles. Watercolors, etchings and shelves full of books lined the walls. Behind Father's desk hung two stark etchings by Goya depicting brutal hangings. The men's trousers were bunched around their feet, and their faces hung down. My father bought these prints of the etchings at the British Museum when he was a student. I don't know why, but I was drawn to those powerful, grim portrayals and have been attracted to Goya's art ever since.

Our first floor balcony looked onto a quiet tree-lined walk. I spent much of my childhood and adolescence on that balcony, from which I could vault myself over the parapet and into the yard at a moment's notice. Even my vigilant father, ever concerned about my homework, could not catch me before I disappeared with a waiting friend.

Sitting on deck chairs on our balcony, we would gaze out at the Persian Gardens, meticulously laid out, cascading down Mount Carmel. I've always been thankful to those of the Baha'i faith for expressing aspects of their religion through magnificently laid out gardens. Tall, dark-green cypress trees stood out proud and straight against the light summer sky. At sundown the heavy, intricate gold-accented black iron gates of the Baha'i gardens slammed shut until the next morning.

From one corner of our balcony, we could see the blue Mediterranean, full of ships coming and going. When I was little and the ships let out a deep, bellowing sound, my father told me they were bidding me goodbye. I believed him, of course. I always believed him. He never misled me.

Every morning Mr. Spinney, a mustached, stout Englishman invariably wearing a Harris tweed jacket, walked past our balcony from the French Carmel, a section of Haifa named for a French order of nuns who lived in a convent up the hill from us, toward Haifa's German Colony, so called because it had been settled by German Christians in the early 1900s. We never saw a single soul come in or out of the convent and grounds; I was always curious and fascinated by the mystery of their lives behind those high walls. Mr. Spinney was a large man with ruddy cheeks. Though he did not know me, he would acknowledge my presence on the balcony with a loud, cheery "good morning!" jauntily swinging his walking cane. He owned Spinney's, a big grocery shop with an outdoor café dotted with green leafy trees under which huge— at least they seemed huge to a little girl—towering

Ruth Chissik, who gave me my first Vogue *magazine, with me at age 5 on the Matzdorf balcony.*

Sudanese waiters with smooth black skin and tribal cuts on their cheeks served tea and cucumber sandwiches. They wore long white cotton robes, broad red sashes around their waists, and tall, tubular, dark-red tarbushes with a black tassel, traditional Turkish hats. When my mother took me there for afternoon tea, I felt ever so sophisticated. The café was packed with Jews, Arabs, and Brits. The diversity of Haifa's various communities added worldliness and a touch of mystery to the place. Mother and I observed the crowd and savored second-guessing people's relationships and backgrounds.

At home we always sat down for a three-course lunch: soup, main course and fruit, all accompanied by plenty of thick, brown bread. Slicing the crusty bread with a heavy carving knife was my father's task. Even on the hottest days of summer, I was expected not to leave the table until I had finished my lentil soup, despite the fact that my forehead was dotted with beads of perspiration. Being forced to finish hot soup on a hot day produced terrible rows with me refusing to finish and escaping into the yard and up the hill, leaving my father fuming and furious at my impertinence. This kind of conflict between us was probably even more unsettling for my father because it represented a clash of cultures: he, of course, never permitted himself to be rude to his father. He certainly would never have disobeyed or talked to his father that way. No doubt, the contrast with my obstinacy and rudeness made those trying times even more frustrating for him.

OUR NEIGHBORHOOD was a lovely and lively one. It was in the area immediately surrounding our flat that I met my very first friends, and it was here, at least early on, that our neighborhood was centered. The whole area came to a standstill for the mid-day siesta. Our German Jewish neighbors kept the rule meticulously. There was a sign in Hebrew and in German on many of their doors: "No knocking, no ringing between two and four"—*nicht klopfen, nicht klingen*. If one of us young children playing outside raised his voice, he'd be doused with water by an irate neighbor on the second or third floor above us and the rest of us hurriedly scampered away.

Our family friends were all English-speaking, by and large from England and South Africa. The neighbors were mostly "Yeckes"—Jews from Germany. There was also a smattering of Romanian and Hungarian Jews. The neighbors mostly spoke the language of the country of their birth in their homes and Hebrew in public. After the 1948 War of Independence, with a growing Israeli-born generation, Hebrew became the norm. We children, of course, all spoke Hebrew.

Our neighbors came from solidly bourgeois backgrounds. Their furniture was heavy, central European in style. The bed linens, the white embroidered tablecloths brought in crates called "lifts" and the beautiful Rosenthal china all spoke of well-run, comfortable European households and easier times in the past. Their many picture albums were full of photos of holidays in the Alps, with stern nannies in starched white uniforms and nurses' caps looking over Rolls Royce–like baby carriages.

When I was growing up in Haifa in the early 1940s, the Arab and Jewish communities of the town were socially autonomous and peaceful. Commercially, there was a great deal of interaction between the Jews and Arabs. Fresh vegetables, fruits, and chickens often came from surrounding Arab villages. We studied Arabic in school. Neither community, however, sought out social interaction. Certainly there was no wish to have one's children intermarry—each group was content with its own identity, integrity, and community. However, this is not to say that all was calm. In the late 1930s and especially after the end of World War II, travel on the roads became increasingly hazardous as sniping from Arab villages became frequent. I was too young to be aware of the countermeasures taken by the Haganah and the Palmach.

Even during and after the 1948 War of Independence, I never heard cries for slaughter or fiery tirades against the Arabs. My parents would refer to the massacres of Jews in Hebron in 1924 and 1926, but their comments were never—ever—accompanied by shouts for cold-blooded revenge. Instead it was more about feelings of anger, grief, and loss—quite a contrast with my mother's loud tirades about German atrocities during World War II against the Jews, often accompanied by a declaration that if she caught Hitler she would drop him into a cauldron of boiling oil.

Our next-door neighbors were the Matzdorfs, a family to whom I felt close; Doctor Kurt Matzdorf ("Kurtchen" to his wife), our family doctor; his wife Frau Gerda Matzdorf; their son Ezra; their daughter Hannah; and Mrs. Matzdorf's elderly mother, referred to as "Oma," German for grandmother. They were living proof of the qualities of the German Jews who had immigrated to the Land of Israel. The values embedded in them were indispensable in trying times. Dr. Matzdorf had been in charge of a large hospital in Breslau, Germany, before the family fled in the late 1930s, just before the gates slammed closed and all hell broke loose. They came with little money and no knowledge of spoken Hebrew or English. We suspected that Mrs. Matzdorf, at least in the early days of their arrival, cleaned people's houses in the mornings. She was no silent martyr; in her case it was simply a matter of what had to be done. She accepted her circumstances, grateful to have escaped from the burning caldron of Europe.

The living room of their apartment served as the doctor's waiting room and was transformed miraculously every morning from what had been a bedroom the previous night. The other room was shared by the children and their 80-year-old grandmother. The third room was devoted to the doctor's office, a sort of down-at-the-heels place with furniture in need of paint, but immaculate and well-scrubbed. A faint odor of disinfectant hung in the air. The doctor was a kind man, portly, of medium height, with a small black mustache and the cleanest hands and nails I had ever seen. Observant Jews, they were worldly, well-educated, and cultured.

Hannah was a few years older than I was, and I looked up to her, but our friendship was relegated to visits on each other's balconies every so often. Perhaps because of the age difference, we grew apart as we grew up. Ezra, her brother, was my age, and we played together a great deal when we were young. When we were about six years old, I recall quite well that we were playing a sort of soccer game with a group of children in our backyard. The ball rolled deep into the bushes. We both fell right into the bushes as well, trying to retrieve it. Six-year-old Ezra grabbed the moment to ask me if I'd marry him. I had to think quickly about how to say no without hurting his feelings, while getting out of the thorny bushes in one piece. I told him I'd love to, but that we should wait a little while.

Every late afternoon the Matzdorfs sat down to coffee and sandwiches on their balcony, next to an attractively laid out tea trolley. This teatime might also have served as an early supper for them—never mind that they were ever so frugal and the sandwiches and cold cuts were miniscule. The Frau Doctor would take ages to chew with tightly closed lips and eventually would swallow the food down. It never occurred to them—nor did I expect it—to offer me a sandwich, though I was warmly welcomed to visit with them. They addressed each other with decorum and their manners at the table were impeccable. Had they been served tea at Buckingham Palace, they would not have had to alter their behavior one iota. Even in the worst of economic times, they would take a bus up to Mount Carmel and rent chairs for a couple of hours in a pine forest in order to breathe the clear air and enjoy the beauty of nature. Mrs. Matzdorf called it *erholung*— a term denoting recreation and relaxation, a kind of R&R.

Oma would also take the bus up to Mount Carmel and spend time painting watercolors of the Haifa port on small white tiles. Her clothes were ancient, neat, and freshly pressed. She wore a cameo brooch at her throat, and her white hair was gathered into a tidy bun. Oma's life and standard of living had been shattered by Hitler's Germany. She lost all semblance of privacy, status, or financial independence. She only spoke German, and was too old to learn Hebrew. I don't remember ever chatting with her, just smiling broadly and slightly bowing my head to her. Yet, circumstances over which she had no control did not conquer or humiliate her. She and her family never compromised their civilized standards of behavior, even in the most difficult of circumstances.

Oma's daughter, Mrs. Matzdorf, assessed all humans by three criteria: *Tüchtigkeit* (diligence), *Sparsamkeit* (frugality), and *Beziehung* (upbringing), the last being most important to her. This kind of thinking characterized the German Jews. A bittersweet story went around after the war when more was known about the horrors of the camps. It told of two doctors, German Jews in Theresienstadt, who kept bowing and deferring to each other over and over again as to who should go first to pick up scraps of food out of a garbage can.

Mother was always admonishing me to learn life lessons from "those" German Jews, especially given their self-discipline and sense of decorum even during trying days. For my mother, character and strong inner resources were the two most important qualities to strive for. Beauty, youth, and money could—and would—disappear; only one's character and inner resources could be relied on for the long run. It was her way of advising me not to be dependent on the external world for defining who I was or would become. Her grounded wisdom stood me well in later life, and I rely on it in good times lest my head swims, and in bad times lest I despair.

On Friday evenings, Erev Shabbat, I would hang around the Matzdorfs until they would have to invite me for Kiddush, the Friday night blessing over the wine and candles. It was of no account that the doctor was hardly making a living and that his wife may have been cleaning other people's houses. Herr Doctor sat at the head of the table, getting all the respect as head of the family, and his wife, Frau Doctor, took her place at the other end. On these nights, the family seemed transformed; the children were in immaculately ironed clothes. I watched Mrs. Matzdorf fish out a gold necklace and bracelet from the depths of her wardrobe. The table was laid with their best white linen and German china. Dr. Matzdorf led the traditional blessings over the wine, the braided challah bread, and his children. Mrs. Matzdorf lit the candles and said the blessings over them. The Sabbath eve was different from all other evenings, as everyday life was shut out and the telephone fell silent. The family was together, a cohesive unit. A sense of spiritual gratitude pervaded the room and the family. They thanked God for having been chosen to enact the Friday night tradition and hallow it.

Also around the oval table every Friday night were a pretty 20-year-old, dark-eyed, orphaned niece who had lost her entire family in a death camp and old Aunt Judith, Tante Yudit. Ezra and Hannah were not crazy about their spinster aunt. A severely crippled hunchback, she resembled a gargoyle on the roof of a medieval cathedral. She always looked ancient to us. Her black-purple dyed hair was pulled up in a tight chignon, and a few hairs grew out of a mole at the corner of her chin. Deep lines ran across her forehead and around her eyes. They must have been the result of the strain and toll from her ever-present limp. She lived in one small room on Ben Yehuda Street, at the foot of Mount Carmel. On Friday night there was no public transportation, and, even if there had been, she would not have broken the law and ridden on the Sabbath. Thus, on the sixth day of every week, before the setting of the sun, she would limp up the steep hill to the Matzdorfs' flat for the Friday evening festive meal. If not for the ancient Sabbath eve tradition, she would never have been invited anywhere. But to Doctor and Mrs. Matzdorf and their children, it would have been inconceivable, even sacrilegious, not to have included Tanta Yudit.

Tanta Yudit's life changed dramatically with German reparations some years after World War II. She began spending the hot summer months in Switzerland and started to wear colorful, floral-patterned silk dresses. Her clumsy black orthopedic shoes were upgraded to very fine leather. She enjoyed again a basic standard of comfort and financial security. The reparations were due in part to the working relationship of two unusual leaders, David Ben-Gurion, Israel's first prime minister, and Konrad Adenauer, the chancellor of Germany. These two courageous men, in an emotional time raw with the open wounds of the Holocaust, were able to come together and decide on positive ways of forging an association between the two countries to last for years to come.

Most of our family's friends ranged from mildly religiously observant to not at all, but the experience of generations pointed to the wisdom of the Sabbath tradition. Even in the most left-wing, secular kibbutzim, young people would stream into the communal dining room on Friday evenings, faces scrubbed clean, white shirts on the boys and folk dresses on the girls. A special atmosphere hung in the air. All parts of the community came together. Around 4:00 on Friday afternoons Haifa would begin to slow down, with buses full of men coming home early carrying flowers, in particular gladiolas. A hush would fall on the city and on our neighborhood. There was a sense of people coming together in a celebratory atmosphere and staying home after dinner. Our work and school week was six days, Sunday through Friday, so the Sabbath was precious. Calm and an air of a quiet holiday prevailed, with no rushing to be somewhere else. I always felt the Sabbath was a special time, even though my family did not observe the Friday night rituals and light the candles. We did, however, always stay home, just being with each other around our dining room table and having a special meal together that was more elaborate than our usual fare. From what I observed among my friends and my parents' friends, the Friday night tradition protected and strengthened the family. One did not have to reinvent the wheel every Friday evening; this ancient religious tradition was incorporated even into secular Jewish life.

In the building opposite our flat was Margo and Heinz Leibowitz's apartment, consisting of three rooms that they shared with Dr. and Mrs. Ambach, Margo's parents. The young Leibowitzes were elegant and dashing. The parents had gotten out of Germany just before 1939 when war broke out. They joined their children in Haifa and thus survived. Mrs. Ambach's old mother was seized by the Nazis and taken to Theresienstadt, the supposed transit camp that became an endpoint for many Jews, where she perished. When Mother and I dropped by for chocolate cake and coffee after the afternoon nap, the conversation inevitably turned to how the Ambachs managed to escape by the skin of their teeth. Mrs. Ambach was haunted by incessant guilt at having left her old mother behind. It was then Mother's turn, through logic and genuine feeling, to convince Mrs. Ambach that she really had no other option. It was either their survival or all three of them would have stayed behind and ended up in ashes. When on my own, I wept and prayed to God to never, ever put me in a similar situation like that of Mrs. Ambach and her mother. That fear and that prayer have remained with me till this very day. My mother was quick to point out to Daddy and me how discreet and tactful Dr. and Mrs. Ambach were while having to share the cramped space with their adult children and how responsible the children felt for their parents. The Ambachs were careful never to be around when their daughter and dashing son-in-law were entertaining the British Army. They weren't alone. My Aunt Mary, who lived in Tel Aviv, noticed older couples sitting in the parks on Sabbath mornings. She concluded that parents who shared small apartments with their married children were being tactful and giving the young couples some privacy and time to themselves. During World War II and right after, these living arrangements were replicated all over the country.

My mother and my witty Aunt Mary in Tel Aviv.

Like the Matzdorfs, the Ambachs were refined and cultured. They had escaped Germany with hardly any money. Every day after the mid-afternoon nap, they would go past our first floor balcony to Café Sternheim where they met their German-speaking friends. Dr. Ambach usually wore a double-breasted Chesterfield coat with a Persian fur collar, with Mrs. Ambach in a beautifully tailored gray or dark-green suit with a slouching felt hat to match, a la Marlene Dietrich. Mother would be on our balcony, complimenting them as they walked by on how very elegant they looked. Dr. Ambach would tip his hat to Mother. Mrs. Ambach, slim and erect, would laugh

The balcony played a huge part in my childhood and youth. Mother and Mrs. Ambach talking across the balconies.

and tell us how old the clothes really were. The quality of their clothes spoke of another time, another place in their lives. Mrs. Ambach had been the tennis champion of Würzburg, Bavaria, in the "good days."

Mrs. Ambach and my mother thought highly of each other even though they were worlds apart. Lively conversations across their two balconies took place during the daily morning ritual of putting the bedding out to air on the balcony parapet. My family's blankets were straightforward brown wool. The Ambachs, on the other hand, had huge puffy eiderdowns encased in dark maroon covers, brought with them from Germany; they were the kind a bride got with her trousseau along with silver or fine china, all made to last forever. Mother spoke to Mrs. Ambach in English, and she would answer in German, which my mother understood enough of to make sense of Mrs. Ambach's points. One running argument between them focused on whether Shakespeare or Goethe was the greater writer. It's hard to believe, but those two understood each other and got their points across.

Though Germany spat out families like the Ambachs and the Leibowitzes the way whales expel fountains of water, the Ambachs moved back to Germany, the scene of the crime, right after the establishment of the state in 1948. We felt betrayed and hurt because Israel was a refuge for them when they so badly needed one and where many people had risked their lives to save them.

My friend Esther Marcus and me in school uniforms in front of our scout hut in Haifa.

FRIENDS FROM MY NEIGHBORHOOD—all of whom appear in various diary entries—included Judita (we pronounced it Yudita) Marcus an Italian girl. I loved her flat with its beige-white tiles, cool to the touch and highly polished. Her hen-pecked father shuffled around the apartment with dusters tied to the soles of his shoes to add polish to the tiled floors. Everything was very neat and nice and quiet, including her parents, who always invited me to join them for lunch on their balcony. They spoke Italian among themselves while Judita and I chattered away in Hebrew. We invariably ate pasta in different shapes, smothered in tomato sauce. I recall liking the seashell-shaped ones the best, but everything was good and new to me because we never had pasta in our house.

Esther Marcus, to whom I was very close, was Judita's cousin. We spent many an afternoon in each other's flats, talking and playing school for hours. Her father owned a printing shop and brought home masses of colored paper in all sizes, which because of the war was strictly rationed. We loved it and put it to good use in our pretend school. She had shiny auburn hair always on the verge of unraveling from loose braids. They bounced around her shoulders and back as if they had a life of their own. Her movements were so graceful, and she often would burst into peals of contagious laughter. Esther was not beautiful but very appealing and was enviably self-confident with the boys. Although she was a year older than I was and therefore not in the same class at school, we were very close companions, but our friendship was more a part of neighborhood life than school life.

Victor Porjolt, known as Vicky, lived upstairs from me in our same building. He was older than I was by a couple of years, and much more worldly. A first-class musician on the accordion, he was musical in every way. He had come from Romania with his family in his early teens and seemed very European, certainly much more polished than the schoolboys in my class. Vicky's mother was strikingly pretty and spent a great deal of time tanning and oiling herself. His father was several years older than she, and my dominant impression of him is that he was grumpy. I think Vicky was lonely within his family. When I was fairly young, Ezra and I used to follow an unsuspecting Mrs. Porjolt up the hill, where she would meet a particular English soldier. They would walk together for some distance and then disappear out of sight and into the woods. We also saw lots of unused condoms strewn on the ground between the pine trees. We knew enough of whatever was happening not to mention any of this to our parents. We collected a few of the unused condoms, brought them home, filled them up with water in my bathroom sink and watched them blow up like little balloons.

I used to visit Vicky in his flat and he would show me albums of their family life in Bucharest—high hedges, baby carriages being pushed by nannies in starched uniforms, country houses with folk furniture painted over with colorful flowers. In some ways, as I grew older, I didn't altogether trust Vicky. He was a little too polished for my taste, and I preferred the bluntness of my classmates. However, he was an excellent dancing partner. He would guide me through tangos with a sure hand on my back, wearing a mild expression of humor, encouragement, and affection. The whole world seemed to melt away when we danced. He helped me improve my style over the years. The relationship between us, especially as I entered adolescence, was slightly flirtatious but it never had any depth to it. He liked my mother and had long conversations with her about life and its discontents.

My friend Nitza Sachs and me, 1946.

Daniel Annisfeld was another close neighbor, living in the apartment building next door. He was handsome; he liked the girls and the girls liked him. Our relationship survived because it was anchored in a meaningful companionship. We spoke a lot to each other, with no expectation of a romantic involvement. I certainly kept mine realistically under control. With boys in general, I kept firmly in mind a favorite quotation of my Aunt Esther's, which may not be true to the original but which I remember as "What care I if they be fair, if they be not fair to me?" I never permitted myself to lose my heart if I didn't feel it would be reciprocated.

There were other girls in the neighborhood as well. Nitza Sachs was a very good friend, but for the most part our friendship didn't carry outside of our neighborhood and as we grew older our lives went in different directions. I knew her parents well, but I didn't particularly like going to her flat. Her father, a very nice man, had been born in Palestine and was a functionary in city government. He always looked unhappy, especially when I would see him walking home from the bus with his shoulders hunched and his head lowered after the long day's work. I don't think her parents' marriage was a happy one. Nitza's mother was a large, statuesque woman with thin braids wrapped around her head, Russian style. The braids had thinned after years of combing and pulling them tightly from a part down the middle. She was born and brought up in Bucharest. Nitza regaled me with stories about her mother's beauty in her youth, and how all the young men of Bucharest threw roses in her path when she was on her way to the opera.

Oddly, my friend Ora also spoke of her mother in this way. Ora's mother was small and round like a pear, with pretty features and exceptionally even teeth, highlighted by a silver one on one side. Whereas Nitza's mother, as I recall, had attended university, Ora's mother came from a small shtetl. In Ora's version of the story, it was shy Yeshiva boys who fell in love with her mother in droves. I don't recall whether roses were part of the narrative.

I remember running home to tell Mother about the popularity of my friends' mothers and the scores of gentlemen callers. Every time I would recount one of these stories, Daddy would snicker, but my mother would smile and gently say she didn't remember anyone throwing roses in her path in Winnipeg. She told me that we didn't seem to have these kinds of stories in our family history. She did say that in her youth she loved dancing, and especially in the '20s in Tel Aviv and Jerusalem, there were lots of tea dances. Because she was a tireless dancer, she was naturally very popular on the dance floor with the British officers serving the Mandate. Her stories made me even more curious about what she was like as a young single woman.

There were also other young neighbors whose lives were more on the periphery but nonetheless memorable. One was a mentally handicapped boy, Amud Nebenzahl, whose mother my mother especially respected. Mother went out of her way to give Amud lots of attention and praise him to his doting mother. He had a habit of throwing cushions and chairs from their second floor balcony, and we would pick them up at the end of the day and take whatever he'd thrown over it back to their flat, never making anything of the incident.

When I was quite young, during the first years of World War II, I'd spend hours in my pajamas tiptoeing on the cool tiles, peering through my bedroom's dark-green shutters at the goings-on outside and in the neighbors' apartments. I was always put to bed earlier than any other child I knew. I was not tired, and it was still warm and bright outside. My father thought it was uncivilized to keep children up late. The minute he shut my bedroom door I would spring to my feet, run to the shutters, open the slits ever so slightly, and peer out, transfixed and fascinated by what I saw. Margo, Mrs. Ambach's daughter, slim in a tailored skirt and sweater to match, her hair beautifully swept up into an elegant chignon and her tanned face perched on a long graceful neck, was often flirting good-naturedly with marvelous-looking British officers. The officers appeared to be straight out of central casting. They sported wonderful, large mustaches and rocked with lots of loud, hearty, masculine laughs. Whiskey flowed like water. Their polished Sam Browne belts shone across their chests, and gold insignia glistened on their epaulettes. Their accents were lovely to listen to—words like *baaath* and *Indiyaaa* with their stretched-out As seemed to trail off into the heavens. I would stand watching for what seemed like hours, ignoring any cramp in my feet or calves. At times, Margo's husband, Heinz, or one of the officers would spot me, wave cheerfully, or wink. I was mortified. I closed the slits of the shutters a little bit more and went on peering, gazing, staring, completely rapt.

Across another alley was a handsome three-story apartment house built of large local stone. Spacious balconies surrounded the flats. The house looked as if it would last forever. Two flats were taken up by the families of British Police. One of them was the Tarlings. Their young son, Ronnie, and I played "doctor" on our balcony, crouched behind a worn deckchair, during the excruciatingly hot, lifeless, boring siesta hours. His hair and skin were tanned the color of dark honey. From time to time, Ronnie Tarling would lower his khaki shorts, and I saw for the first time what a male member looked like. The game, however innocent, did not please my father, who discovered us. He was vigilant about not letting anybody or anything disturb my mother's nap, but the minute she woke up, he sought her help. As usual, she was definite but tactful. She told us not to go on with the game because we might "harm" ourselves. We did not question her about the nature of the harm. I have always been grateful that she stopped the game and saved face for both Ronnie and me.

Maureen was the six-year-old daughter of the other British Police family. She had the disconcerting habit of covering me with the thick blackout curtain that we used to cover our windows against the threat of Italian air raids in the early years of World War II. She darkened the room, drew the curtains, slammed shut the shutters, and whispered to me to wait for the Second Coming of Jesus. This scene always took place at about two in the afternoon. Outside the sun was bright and blazing. I, on the other hand, was in the pitch black, hermetically sealed room, stiflingly hot, petrified, and waiting for something awesome to occur. I was about six or seven then and did not have the faintest idea who Jesus was or what he represented, or how long I would have to wait in that uncomfortable position for this mysterious second coming to take place.

As for my extended family, we didn't see much of them, although the distances were not great. My mother's two sisters were both living in Palestine, but complicated transportation—few cars and buses, no telephones, very few roads and most of all a lack of security on the roads—was a big factor preventing our getting together. My Aunt Mary, the eldest of the three Abrahamson sisters, lived in a tiny and charming flat in Tel Aviv. She had bright red hair, a color she never lost, even in old age. Like both her sisters, she was a brilliant conversationalist, witty and perceptive. I well remember visits with just the two of us sitting on her balcony overlooking Fishman Street, talking for a long while as the sun went down.

She was married, fairly briefly, to an Egyptian Jew from a prominent Cairo family. They had two children, Ruthie and David, who were about ten or more years older than I was. During World War II, Mary joined the Auxiliary Territorial Service, essentially the women's branch of the British Army. Mary was always a bit of a hippy, quite unconventional, an original character. After the war, when she was in London she liked to go to Hyde Park and stand up at Speakers' Corner, lecturing the British about this and that, including their poor cooking. She spoke with humor and passion about women being paraded in beauty pageants and lamented that men were not scrutinized in the same way. A member of the Belgian royal family happened to hear her one day and was so taken by her wit that he offered her tickets to the theater, and she found herself sitting not far from him that very evening. He turned out to be the future king of Belgium. One thing about her that I will always remember is that she raved about my father's erudition, and how he and my mother had such a rich companionable relationship. She admonished me to force my mother to rest more because she thought Mother was not physically strong. Everything Aunt Mary said was nine parts true and one part exaggerated.

Mother's other sister, my Aunt Esther, had coincidentally, like Mother, also married a Scottish Jew. I used to love to visit them in Jerusalem, a very special place for me always. Going there in and of itself was a special event. It took more than four hours from Haifa, driving up winding roads with lovely hills on either side, a beautiful ascent. My excitement grew as we got nearer. The city had an air of other-worldliness to it. Even the air seemed purer there. I wondered aloud about the uniformity of Jerusalem's stone buildings, some a very light pink. It all spelled elegance to me.

Aunt Esther and Uncle Tommy Coussin lived with their only child, Danny, in the Greek Colony, a charming Jerusalem neighborhood bordering the German Colony, whose lands had been bought up in the early 20th century by wealthy members of the Greek Orthodox Church community. I loved the entire area, with its solid stone houses, its mellowness and air of mystery and dignity, and especially loved their house, with its garden full of old, leafy, tall trees surrounded by a stone wall. The British Officers' club was across the street. I spent many an hour perched on Aunt Esther's garden wall with my Jerusalem girlfriend Tamara Levin watching the gymkana—where British soldiers on horseback were galloping around in some kind of elaborate ceremony that the British had imported from India—and giggling at the sight of them from afar. The officers shot quick glances at us and must have thought the two of us were older than we really were.

My aunt's living room was very cozy, all in brown, yellow, and soft rust color. They had an old record player called a Victrola, which I'd crank up and listen to Rimsky-Korsakov's "Scheherazade." Then I would pretend I was a veiled Salome. My dance would start from behind a loosely woven beige curtain, and from there, undulating my nearly non-existent hips and twisting my hands this way and that way, I would emerge from behind the curtain all seduction and mystery to my invisible audience. This performance took place during the ubiquitous, boring siesta time when no one was around to talk to.

I particularly remember time spent with Aunt Esther. I loved her in part because she talked to me as an adult, did not mince her words and did not go out of her way to spoil or mollycoddle me. An excellent example of how she dealt with me had to do with Dr. Albert Schweitzer. I knew that both she and my mother had a great deal of respect for him and his humanitarian work in Africa. To counter their effusive admiration, which for some childish reason irritated me, I once intruded on their conversation by saying, "Well, he is no different from you or me—he also uses the lavatory!" Aunt Esther immediately shot back, "Yes, Albert Schweitzer and you both use the lavatory, but he also builds hospitals and you don't." End of discussion. I never forgot the lesson.

Aunt Esther and I took long walks up and down the hills of Jerusalem. We always made sure to pay a visit to an ancient Scot who lived in the Old City of Jerusalem in one light-filled, airy room absolutely devoid of material goods. I distinctly remember the room with its thick, whitewashed walls and high arched windows. He had regular features, lovely white hair, a long white flowing beard, a thick Scottish brogue, and lots of natural charm. He always offered us the very best brewed strong English tea (no tea bags) in slightly chipped cups and saucers. Like so many in Jerusalem who have come before and after him, he believed he was the Messiah. He was charismatic enough that people around the world—in small towns as far away as New Zealand and Australia—believed he was as well. I was in awe of him and of those visits, and of the special atmosphere throughout Jerusalem, which made the city so unique. When the man died, my Uncle Tommy spent lots of time sending back to his far-flung disciples all of the gifts—knitted sweaters, socks, scarves, and small amounts of money— his believers, unaware that he had died, had sent him. I have often wondered if Esther and Tommy helped him a little along the way. After all, he was a fellow Scot.

Another walk Aunt Esther and I often took passed a high-walled impenetrable convent that I was told housed terminal patients with leprosy. We walked past intriguing European monks from various denominations in cassocks and sandals, many wearing round wire-rimmed glasses; nuns dressed in the habits of their order, their starched head coverings hiding most of their faces; ultra-Orthodox Jews with fur-brimmed wide hats, black shiny robes, and long side locks, some with knee-high white socks, and their children, with high, pale foreheads, large eyes, and side curls

My aunt Esther walking the hills of Jerusalem.

as well—all scurrying around the twisting narrow paths of the Old City. All of them, groups and individuals, seemed always to be in a hurry. I remember once seeing a father and his son on the eve of the Sabbath hurrying to the Wall. The father held tightly to his son's hand. The son, dressed like his father except for the hat, appeared to be a replica, a smaller version of his father. In retrospect, it seems right out of a Chagall painting. Father and son reminded me of Abraham and Isaac and the line in Genesis: "*so they went both of them together.*" They belonged to each other, they grew out of each other.

At one point, while my aunt and I were strolling through Mea Shearim, one of the oldest Orthodox neighborhoods in Jerusalem, a very old Jew, literally on the verge of being biodegradable, side curls and all, pointed his cane at my aunt's modest neckline, shook his head, and muttered disapproval. Aunt Esther responded in Yiddish, pointed her walking stick right back at him, and told him that if he was so religious he should be gazing up at heaven and not concentrating on her neckline!

I will never forget two episodes that happened when Mother and I visited Jerusalem before 1948. We went to the Western (Wailing) Wall—or as in Hebrew, *Kotel*, in the Old City of Jerusalem, the only remaining part of the ancient retaining wall that surrounded the Jewish Temple. As we were leaving we had to pass by the British guard house. On the tin wall was scratched "Palestine to the Arabs." My mother took one look at it and with all the confidence of a well-educated, English- speaking woman, turned to the very young pink-cheeked British soldier and started with, "Young man, I am old enough to be your mother. Let me tell you a little about the history of this country and of the Jews, which I assume you don't know much about... ." She thus gave him a piece of her mind in her unique, articulate way. He listened politely, amazed and interested. He apologized for the graffiti, and we bid each other goodbye. I was relieved to be gone.

The second episode took place in Jerusalem on Ben Yehuda Street. Mother and I were walking when I noticed my mother becoming upset. She had seen a little Arab boy of about eight walking behind a small donkey up the street and prodding the animal with a nail. My mother loved animals. Our library had many Penguin books about animals and insects, such as *The Life of Bees* and *Ants*.

My father, Uncle Tommy, and me age two.

Wanting to be considerate after she had asked the little boy to stop and he didn't, she looked for an Arab policeman rather than a Jewish or British one. She found one and he was most obliging. To our horror, rather than talking to the little boy, with one fell swoop he picked the boy up by the ear, shouted "*Yalla*"—meaning scram or get out of here—and threw him across the sidewalk. We both were left devastated.

Uncle Tommy, too, was memorable on these visits. Like my father, he came from Glasgow.

His son, Danny, often called him "Sir Thomas."
He had come to Palestine in 1917 with the British
Army commanded by General Allenby, which
expelled the Turks and took Jerusalem, ending
400 years of Turkish rule and leading in 1922 to
the British Mandate. Tommy joined the British
mandatory police, eventually rising to Lieutenant
Colonel and paymaster of the British Police.
Tommy had reddish cheeks and cornflower blue
eyes. When he spoke Hebrew, his Scottish accent
was so heavy that one would think he was still
speaking English. He was an avid gardener and
was known for his decency, charm, and warm
hospitality. Whenever we visited them, Uncle
Tommy brought Mother and me a cup of
strong English tea to our beds in the morning,
and woke us up with the cheeriest of "good

*My uncle Tommy, Aunt Esther, my mother and
me in front of our apartment in Haifa, opposite
the Persian Gardens.*

mornings." The only inconvenience—which I'm sure was an irritation solely to
me and not to Mother—was that he insisted on walking into our bedroom
before dawn, with the sun only starting to rise, and we were, after all, on holiday.
Mother fell all over herself, commenting on how considerate Uncle Tommy was.

Most memorable of my visits were those when I was a bit older and my cousin
Danny was home with his parents, back from serving in the Jewish Brigade in
Europe during World War II. Danny, seven years older than I was, was like a brother
to me. Although we did not see each other on a regular basis, I saw him more
frequently after the war, when he was serving in the Palmach and working on a
kibbutz. He'd appear unannounced for a visit at our house and walk in with his face
tanned, hair unruly, dusty from driving an open kibbutz truck in the high sun.
A visit from him was always a minor celebration, especially because he never
stayed for long. He loved his Aunt Sara, my mother, and she adored him. He
would pick her up and swirl her around, all the while sporting his mischievous
but charming broad smile. He was forever famished, and Mother would rush to
the kitchen to prepare hot cocoa and a sandwich, fussing over him throughout
his visit. His life was dangerous and demanding. My father knew not to ask him
questions, but my mother couldn't help herself. He never answered her directly,

but just joked around. He knew I was in the scout youth movement and he'd asked me with a wink if I had a boyfriend, which of course I didn't. He spoke in perfect English to my parents and joked in Hebrew with me. Somehow that signified to me that we were even more connected because we were both sabras, native born in the Land of Israel.

Danny seemed to sense how deeply my mother loved him and how proud she always was of him. Somehow she was able to get him to talk, to break through his usual reserve. For however long his visits to us lasted, all seemed right with the world. We were so happy to see him come and so sad to see him leave. My heart ached with love, Mother's ached with worry, and Daddy wore a stiff upper lip.

———————————————

Tea, sympathy and British Soldiers. Values and faith.

My father and me near our apartment on Tel Chai Street in Haifa.

FROM MY EARLIEST MEMORIES, my parents were always there for me. I don't remember ever coming home to an empty flat. I was confident in their love for me and took it quite for granted as the natural state of affairs. I admired and respected them, even when I was upset, angry, and rude. I knew they were devoted to each other despite disagreements and disparities in their temperaments which inevitably caused blow ups. However, I was never worried nor did it ever occur to me in my wildest dreams that either one of them would walk away, leaving the other—and me—alone. Their solid relationship underlay my sense of place in their lives, and remains an integral part of who I am.

Mother was lively and a brilliant conversationalist. Quotations from great writers were an integral part of her conversations: Shakespeare's "Uneasy lies the head that wears a crown" or "There is a tide in the affairs of men…," were her way of summing up in a few wise words an existing situation. Although Mother quoted Shakespeare a great deal, she never forgave him for his cruel treatment of Shylock. "How could a man of Shakespeare's caliber, a student of the human condition, be so insensitive?" she would wonder aloud. She felt deeply disappointed, profoundly resenting the anti-Semitic myths that Shakespeare's image of Shylock perpetuated.

Another favorite quotation of hers was "When you have children, you give hostages to fortune," by which I think she meant to reinforce the idea that children have a profound effect on parents and that one's personal happiness depends on one's children's happiness. She believed that parents are bonded emotionally—and forever—to whatever life brings to their children.

Mother was interested in all living creatures and full of empathy for them. She never met a person whose personal story she did not find interesting. She was entranced by the complexities of human relationships, especially the male/female dynamic. For what seemed like hours, she and I would discuss the marital and romantic relationships of family, friends, and neighbors. This happy gossiping carried on throughout our lives. Just a few years before she died, we concluded with all seriousness that despite his marriage to Jacqueline Kennedy, Aristotle Onassis would never have the depth of passion for her that he had and would always have for Maria Callas.

The one and only time I recall Mother giving me a spanking—a time I'll never forget—was when I derided one of the British officers, Alan Champion, who came a lot to our house. Maybe I was jealous of the attention my parents, and especially she, gave him. He had something wrong with his back, and I commented to the effect of "He's nothing but a hunchback." She flew across the room and warned me to never, ever speak about him or anyone else in that way, with that kind of name-calling. This was the only time she disciplined me harshly and it made a deep impression.

For the most part, Daddy left my mother to deal with all the dramas of their maturing daughter. He was reserved and moody, qualities that I was only able to begin to understand as I grew older. When I was young, I found it difficult to relate to him, especially when he was withdrawn. But I also remember him being charming with people with whom he had a subject in common—art, cinema or history. Loving any rare touch from my father, I'd beg him to let me sit on his knees while he read his book. With a pained expression, which I deliberately ignored, and after he was gently pushed by my mother with "Oh, Eph, let her sit on your knees," he would

Captain Alan Champion, a regular at our home during tea time in the 1940's.

reluctantly let me jump up on his lap. His restlessness always discouraged me from staying on his knees for too long, but while there, I loved the feel of his rough Harris Tweed jacket on my face and the sweet smell of his pipe. He was not given to displays of affection, and I don't recall him ever hugging or kissing me or using terms of endearment. I was cautious with Father but never afraid. I felt utterly secure in his presence. Mother was an armchair socialist; Daddy was somewhat more conservative. Both were genuine intellectuals who reveled in ideas, read incessantly, and talked to each other about what they read—even to a point that when Mother had the door to the lavatory closed he'd stand outside the door reading aloud to her the end of the article they'd been discussing. He was devoted to her but rarely demonstrative. At times when he was in a good mood he'd say that Mother's high forehead reminded him of Marlene Dietrich. I do remember seeing him embrace and kiss her on the mouth, in the far corner of our hall where no neighbor could spy on them, and when I was little, I would do my best to squeeze in between them.

Interesting ideas and lively conversations were discussed and argued over around our dining room table, covering everything from religion and politics to cinema and the arts. They became an integral part of my general education, for which I remain eternally grateful.

English was the language we spoke at home, and most of our books and newspapers came from England. Family in Glasgow sent the latest book reviews and editorials from the London *Times,* the *Observer*, and *Punch*, but I grew up in a Hebrew-speaking culture, especially at school and with all my friends. I was mortified whenever Mother loudly and articulately spoke in English when we were in a public place and where we could be overheard.

As early as 1936, my father began writing for the English-language newspaper then known as the *Palestine Post*, which later became the *Jerusalem Post*. He wrote articles and reviews on art and cinema, covering Haifa and the north for nearly 50 years until his death in 1984—always posting his copy on time. Every Saturday evening after returning home from the cinema with Mother, he'd sit down and type out his review. Daddy would then ask Mother to read over the article. She invariably would suggest a small change. He would get upset, and she would say, "Well, why did you ask me?" He then invariably incorporated her suggestion. This ritual was repeated each week, and I could hear their irritated back-and-forth from my bed.

When he was with PICA, a Jewish land settlement group funded by a leading member of the Rothschild family, my father worked according to colonial hours and was home between 3:00 and 4:00 most afternoons. Friends would drop by around 5:00 for tea and ginger snaps, and they'd talk until it grew dark. There was always a strong mixture of pride, concern, and anxiety running through their conversations, reflecting what was going on within the Jewish community and, of course, reflecting the war raging in Europe. Thanks to strict rationing, visitors never stayed for supper.

Money was never a subject of conversation at our house, and I had no idea how much or how little money my family had. I don't recall my parents articulating a pressing need for money, and I never felt I lacked for anything. Yet, I do know that I used the same very small brown leather schoolbag I got as a present when I was six years old in first grade until I graduated at age 18, twelve years later.

My father believed strongly that basic comforts in life were essential, especially the older one got. Maybe that is what is meant by the statement that an Englishman's home is his castle—however modest the home. Both of my parents appreciated good taste and natural elegance, neither of which was ever assessed by price. I do remember one night, while I was tucked in bed waiting for the light to be turned off, watching Mother get upset and anxious as she rummaged nervously in the top drawer of the cupboard, searching for some small change she had misplaced. I was quietly hoping, praying that she would find it. In retrospect, I guess we could have used a little extra money at the time, but the only time I recall her doing some work outside of our home was when I was about five or six. She began to give weekly English lessons to a Professor Baer, an assimilated Viennese Jew of the Dr. Freud generation and sensibility. I have my doubts about how much English the professor learned, but I do know they had long conversations which Mother thoroughly enjoyed and learned from. She admired his breadth of culture, level of learning, and old-world manners. Neither Daddy nor I ever met the professor.

Despite the stable life we three enjoyed together, all was not always easy in our house. There were also some rows. My parents only ever got angry with me when I acted in a way they considered irresponsible, which, in my father's case, usually had to do with paying too little attention to my studies. He was often irritated with what he considered my flightiness and not being studious enough. As I grew into adolescence, my rebelliousness focused more on him than on my mother, especially when he would accuse me of being rude and impertinent. He particularly disliked it if he felt that I was filling my head with inconsequential thoughts, especially about boys. I never failed to rise to the bait and one time I hit back where I knew he was most vulnerable—loyalty to his British background.

I shot back that I did not want to be like *his* intellectual English women, like "those dried-up bluestockings" in Oxford or Cambridge. Those women, according to my uninformed facts, had to wear brooches on their chests to tell their fronts from their backs. I continued to say that I was delighted not to have grown up in an always-damp town like Glasgow—a town he loved. I went on and on, pushing against so many things he valued.

Once, driving back to Haifa from a trip to Tel Aviv, Daddy, whose knowledge of history was vast, pointed out that the country road we traveled was an ancient Roman route. I knew he admired many aspects of ancient Rome, but I disliked Rome because the Roman army had brutally destroyed Jerusalem in 70 A.D. after fierce battles, and because it reminded me of the British, who justified everything they did in the name of "law and order." Thus I piped up from the back of the car: "Was that Roman emperor good or bad to the Jews?" Daddy was exasperated with my cheekiness: "For God's sake, can't you forget the Jews for once?" Of course I couldn't. How could I after what the Romans had done to us? My father was disgusted, and the combative dialogue came to an abrupt end.

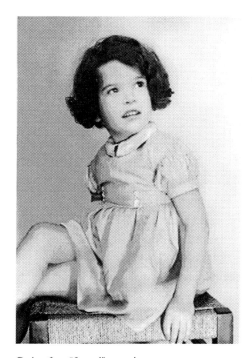

Posing for a "formal" portrait.

On Sabbath mornings when I was six or seven years old, Daddy would take me to art exhibition openings. I loved crossing the street with him because that is when he'd let me hold his hand; in fact, he insisted, and I felt triumphant, safe, and proud. At the exhibits, where the paintings were hung high above my head, I'd get restless very quickly. I'd nudge him to tell me which ones were the best so I could get the viewing over with quickly and move on to enjoy watching the crowd filling the room. He would never help me out by telling me which works were the ones to which I should be paying attention. His answer was always the same, and thus I learned my first lesson in art appreciation: I had to make up my own mind and not merely follow popular trends. The second lesson I learned was to be "wary of a derivative style." Daddy went out of his way, on foot or by bus, in the blistering heat of summer or on the damp days of winter, to visit far-off kibbutzim or out-of-the-way galleries to encourage young Israeli artists. He was never unkind in his criticisms. An appreciation written by his editor Meir Ronnen in 1984, at the time of his death, titled "A Critic and a

Gentleman," commended him for his "own unique brand of appreciation and probity" and for rarely saying something was particularly bad or good, but contenting himself with "pointing out the best of what an artist had to offer."

I was proud of my father—the breadth of his knowledge, his appearance, even his reserve. I was well aware of the profound respect he got from artists and the general public. During exhibits, I would prod him to be friendlier, more forthcoming with this one or that one and to be more effusively thankful when receiving praise and applause after one of his lectures, but to no avail. I've often thought of how lost he'd be in today's aggressive and loud "me, me, me" self-promoting culture.

During and after World War II, there was a period of austerity, or *tzena* in Hebrew, with strict rationing of food, electricity, gasoline, water, and other necessities. My father supervised the water boiler and monitored the assigned times for its use. As a child, with both our electricity (for heat) and water severely restricted, on non-bath days I was perched on a high stool in the bathroom facing the sink and scrubbed vigorously with a cold damp washcloth, all the time shivering and dying to get off the stool and dive into the comforting, well-worn, brown bathrobe hanging on the hook at the back of the bathroom door.

Mother and I shared a leisurely bath on Fridays in the late afternoon. When Mother sank into the

Me at age six, my cousin Danny at age 14 in Haifa with Uncle Tommy in his Army uniform during WWII.

Hugging my mother on our apartment balcony in July 1952. The balcony still reveals the neglect of years of war.

warm water, she would get a heavenly look on her face and mutter "What a *mechaye*!" a Yiddish term conveying "what a life" or "what a reviving feeling." I, too, loved that moment and find myself repeating her phrase whenever I lower myself into a warm bath. I still miss her greatly. I remember her white skin gleaming and unblemished.

Her face, in contrast, bore lines reflecting the tension of those years. Later, when

I first saw Lucian Freud's painting of a nude woman with blue veins shining through luminous skin, it struck me that this was so like what I remembered about my mother.

I loved those bath days. I'd urge Mother to sing to me. She sang a lot and I loved it. She would sing wonderfully spirited songs, often "The Maple Leaf Forever" with its lines about "Canada's fair domain"—songs from World War I or earlier that she had learned in Canada before coming to the Land of Israel. I became familiar with "Roses of Picardy," "When Johnny Comes Marching Home Again," "Rule Britannia" (can you believe it?), "It's a Long Way to Tipperary," and "Daisy Bell," with its popular refrain, "Daisy, Daisy, give me your answer, dear." She seemed to know all the verses of so many lovely songs. I still recall whole lines from the "Skye Boat Song" ("Speed bonnie boat, like a bird on the wing, onward the sailors cry") and from one whose name I don't remember but some of whose lines I memorized. They've stayed with me all these years: *I'm on my way to Heligoland to get the Kaiser's goat, in a good old Yankee boat, down the Khiel Canal we rode. A son of a gun, if I see a Hun, I'll make him understand. I'll knock the Heligo into Heligo, out of Heligoland!*" She also regaled me with lively stories about scores of Canadian cousins and her long walk to school and back in the 40-below-zero temperatures of the Canadian winter. When she was small and suffering a toothache, she would slip in among the cows and lean her cheek on their warm bellies for comfort.

I would occasionally sing Hebrew songs from school or my youth group to her as well. Mostly I'd sing when we were in the kitchen together, while she was preparing the tea and I had her full attention. She especially loved a beautiful and poignant song about a workingman coming home from the fields after a long day of plowing and sowing. It has a lovely lyrical quality, all about protecting our land and its people. Mother actually got teary at times on hearing the lyrics, which I remember as: *"Rest and tranquility descends over the fields of the Valley of Jezreel. Dew below and the moon above, from Beit-Alfa to Nahallal. What is the night whispering? What is it telling us? Go to sleep you magnificent valley. We are here to guard and protect you."*

Mother was deeply touched by many of these songs, but especially that one about the Valley of Jezreel. Another song she loved was "Around Us the Storm Howls," the spirited song of the Palmach—the strike unit of the Haganah. We often sang this song on long hikes: *"All around us the storm howls, but our heads will not bend. We the Palmach are always the first on call, we are the Palmach! We are the first, in the light of day and in the darkness of night, we are always ready for the call, we are, we are the Palmach!"*

During the early war years Britain was, of course, fighting for her life, and my parents would tune into the radio for the latest news. The signature tune of the BBC's Radio World Service, "Lilly Bolero," would come on, signaling that the news was next. We would turn silently and with great anticipation toward the wireless, listening intently for word on the war. My parents would often actually stay standing by the 43 radio, my mother quietly cheering on the brave British pilots. While Rommel and the "invincible" German army were advancing eastward, marching through the North African desert toward the tiny Jewish population in Palestine, one line in "Rule Britannia"—"Britons never will be slaves"—was relevant and deeply moving to us. Thank God, the German army was vanquished before it could reach us.

Each year on the first raw, rainy day of winter, Daddy would march out onto our balcony, vigorously and happily rub his arms together, and report to us how the weather reminded him of Scotland generally and Glasgow specifically. From 1941 to 1943, he served in the Palestine Volunteer Force, organized to increase security on the home front. The windows of our apartment

Me and Laurie Price, a British soldier, at the beginning of WWII.

were shut and heavily taped against the possibility of air raids. Our faces and necks dripped with perspiration in the summer's stifling heat. When we heard the warning sirens, Mother and I would hurry to the air-raid shelter. It had no electricity, and we kids would giggle and whisper jokes in the dark. It felt good to be surrounded by neighbors rather than alone. My father, not surprisingly, refused to join the group gathered in the shelter, preferring to stay back in an interior hall of our apartment.

Throughout the early years of World War II, the women of Haifa volunteered their time in the Army Garrison Club on Pevzner Street, where British soldiers and officers could relax, eat, and meet the locals. Many stationed in Haifa lived far better lives than their families back home in wartime England. A few of the officers became regulars at my parents' home.

The officers who frequented our neighbors the Leibowitzes' were of the fishing, shooting, and hunting variety, and drank seemingly unendingly. Those who came to our house were more intellectual and drank a lot less. While stretched out on our living room Persian carpet, they would read aloud T.S. Eliot's poetry: "In the room the women come and go / Talking of Michelangelo," and "I have measured out my life with coffee spoons." The images from these verses became as familiar to me as the name of our local newspaper. My mother used to comment that only the British could crouch on the carpet balancing a cup of tea and soundlessly eating an apple, while still carrying on a conversation.

Good manners were on display at all times. Many times I'd come into the living room, just home from school, a little girl with ink-stained hands and knobby knees, and be greeted by four or five British and Australian officers who sprang to their feet as I entered. How delicious it was to be female! We had no help at the time, and they never left without volunteering to take the endless cups of tea into our kitchen, but my mother always refused their help.

My father kept one bottle of whiskey in the dark corner of the buffet in our dining room. A shot of whiskey—neat—would be offered on special occasions. It never occurred to anybody, least of all to her, that Mother should be offered a drink, too. One day Mother, Daddy and I were walking home late in the evening after celebrating Passover at a friend's house. The weather was mild, the streets deserted and dark. Mother kept muttering the whole way home that Daddy had had too much wine and seemed to her to be a little tipsy. My father's irritated response was, "For God's sake, how can anybody get drunk on four small glasses of sweet Passover wine?" The only place one could buy liquor in Haifa was in extravagant gift shops filled with chocolates, mouthwatering marzipan, and other fancy candy.

Everybody loved the Aussies. They were brave, straightforward, and good-natured. They drank like fish and wore their easily identifiable wide-brimmed "jungle" hats with one side of the brim folded up. Once, merry with wine and carried away by the local celebrations on the eve of the Jewish New Year, they blocked the main road between Haifa and Tel Aviv with a row of chairs—I can't recall anybody having gotten angry with them! They, too, dropped in for tea and lively conversations, and were offered the ubiquitous chocolate tea cake that always came out of the same round, reddish-yellow tin box with its exotic Chinese scenes. I loved that cake and would have been crushed had a richer cake been substituted for it.

Some of the regiments stationed in Haifa were of the Scottish Black Watch. Their heavy, pleated green-and-black tartan kilts swung gracefully from side to side as they walked. The rumor among us children was that they were stark naked under their kilts. We schemed to bend low to the ground when they climbed onto the bus and thus check, but to the best of my knowledge the actual plan never materialized and I never did find out the truth. At times I'd accompany my mother to meet her lady friends for afternoon tea on the veranda of the Lev HaCarmel hotel on Mount Carmel. Down the street was the Piccadilly, a nightclub with lively music and dancing—mostly British soldiers and respectable Haifa women. It was then that I confided to my mother that my life's ambition was to grow up, wear dresses made of Georgette, that wonderful sheer fabric, and dance away the days at the Piccadilly. One night, after having gone for afternoon tea at the hotel, my parents were preparing for bed. I overheard my mother whisper her concerns to my father, "You know, Eph, thank God Naomi is not 18. What a problem we would have with her and the British Army." In my mind's eye, I could see my father nodding in agreement while getting his legs, one after the other, into his pajama pants.

Padre Hill, a regular visitor at the Harris household in the early 1940's.

Padre Hill was one of the British Army clerics stationed in Haifa. A Methodist minister, he grew up in a mining community, as his Welsh family had for generations before him. His hair was auburn, thick, and cut short. He wore round steel eyeglasses and talked in a deep, deliberate way. He always wore the white clerical collar. He was one of the regulars at afternoon tea and once told my parents of a case in which a young soldier on the Italian front was found under a bed in the fetal position, frozen with fear. Padre Hill told us the soldier had been court-martialed for desertion and was either shot or severely punished. A long, heated discussion ensued about discipline in time of war. My mother was horrified at Padre Hill's seeming lack of compassion for the young soldier and I found it difficult to get over the image of the young petrified soldier curled up like a ball under the bed.

One afternoon another young officer, wearing civvies that day, came to say goodbye. He was off to the Front in Italy. I was probably six or seven, wearing a Mother Hubbard dress of muslin material with tiny orange flowers. We were sitting next to each other on the sofa while my mother went to the kitchen to bring in tea and ginger snaps. The soldier very gently put his hand under my dress. I turned into stone and did not move. When he heard my mother coming back down the hall with the tea tray, he jumped up and leaned on the bookcase pretending to look for a book. I never said a word to Mother so as not to upset her. We heard soon after that he had been killed in battle. I ran to my bedroom and wept copiously for him while Mother tried to console me. I never uttered a word.

I used to pelt Mother with questions, one of them being: "Whom should I marry? A rich builder, or a poor university professor?" And she replied: "Choose the one you would most want to be with when you close the bedroom door at night." I also once asked her, "Mummy, why did you marry Daddy?"—a seemingly innocent question that might have been interpreted as curiosity, but for the fact that it followed an impatient reprimand from my father. She never fell for it. Even though we were so close she never encouraged an alliance between us against my father. Instead, she tried to interpret him to me. Her answer to my question was always the same: "You'll be lucky if you marry a man as erudite, decent, kind and loyal as Daddy." Her consistent response taught me to appreciate the values of loyalty, responsibility, and kindness in marriage. It helped me through the years to cope with my father's difficult moods, to learn to understand him rather than remain angry.

Mother also introduced me to books like Charlotte Bronte's *Jane Eyre*, Jane Austen's *Pride and Prejudice*, D.H. Lawrence's *Sons and Lovers*. Men like Mr. Rochester and Mr. Darcy were deemed to be the right husband material. She said it was easy to find a simple, cute guy to get married to, but it was the especially interesting ones who were complicated and much more of a challenge to handle and to maintain their attention and affection —in other words, don't expect them to be easy. The vibrations around the subject of marriage were always positive and supportive. Mother felt that both genders needed each other. Marriage was not about competition or control. It was about cooperation, consideration, tenderness, affection, and loyalty. She greatly admired women who created harmony between the various members of a family. She constantly pointed out women who were role models from whom I should learn. Had she lived in England or America she could have easily been a suffragette, but she harbored no hostility or negativity toward men. She was sympathetic to their issues and needs as well. In fact she liked men and enjoyed their company. She believed that men and women thought differently and had different approaches to life and to relationships, and she respected those differences.

Mother also felt that the best husband material for me would be Jewish and from an English-speaking culture, Israel included—not because Jews or English speakers were better people but because in the long-haul of marriage, we would share rich traditions and would be familiar with each other's values and expectations. In times of conflict we would share the same concerns and reference points. Her opinions on these subjects, always grounded in compassion, greatly influenced me. Mother's responses to human predicaments were invariably a combination of tough realism, empathy and kindness. For example, her understanding and concern for Oscar Wilde, and the anger she expressed over the tragic end of his life, was repeated over and over again as she shared her insights with me while I was still young. I still stand by them and regard them as decisive in my becoming a psychotherapist.

Mother's feelings about religion were conflicted. On one hand, she envied and admired those with the capacity to believe. On the other hand, she could not, in her heart of hearts, reconcile a child crippled by polio with the existence of God. I could not bear seeing her unhappy and searched for a resolution. I told her that the fact that she talked so much about it was in itself an act of faith, and that God was not interested in blind faith. Her questioning reflected compassion and caring, which served God's purpose more than pious words ever could.

My father never answered me directly when I badgered him about whether he believed in God. "I don't know," he would answer impatiently. He did not make it easy for me, nor was he lured into offering me a pat response that could ever adequately address the enormity of my spiritual question. It was frustrating at the time, but looking back, his reply paved the way for me to grapple with the issue and develop my own ideas, my own relationship with Providence and the Bible. My father often commented that his problem was that he was too rational, too intellectual, and so it left him grappling with issues of faith and reason and their seeming incompatibility. He was well versed in the Hebrew Bible and believed in its emphasis on day-to-day ethics, compassion and social justice. Biblical archaeology and Biblical history were two of his loves. In our conversations about faith, what he did volunteer was: "It was brilliant of the Jews to simplify and pare down their religion, morality, and spirituality to one God, a transcendent, continuous, and an organizing principle in history." He also said that the fact that the God of the Hebrew Bible had no personal story or mythology encouraged the long Jewish tradition of intellectual pursuits and questioning. He believed that the Jews, like migratory birds, had a homing instinct for the Land of Israel from time immemorial.

Although he certainly was not an observant Jew, my father knew well the wisdom and stories of the Bible. I recall many years into my adulthood, when my mother died, I offered the kind of two-bit advice that any therapist knows often works in times of grief, suggesting he'd feel better if he allowed himself to cry. To my surprise, he quickly responded, "Naomi, you think you know the Bible. Don't you remember King David, who wept over his sick child but stopped his lamentations when the child died, saying he wasn't going to weep anymore because he knew he couldn't bring the child back again? He said "I shall go to him, but he will not return to me." I was touched and impressed.

Daddy and I had few one-on-one conversations. Those we did have—mostly while he took care of me on the rare occasions that my mother was away—were short, to the point, and philosophical in nature. My father's statements remain with me, including "Democracies are slow to wake up to a crisis until they are on the brink." I also remember him saying at one point, as early as 1946, that Europe was tired and overly refined, and Europeans were having fewer and fewer children. He predicted that the hungry Third World would eventually sweep over the continent with large numbers of children, all willing to do the work that the Europeans were staying away from. These two ideas I heard again and again as a teenager, around our dining room table.

As a culture critic, he often wrote his ideas into his articles. I know I picked up some random thoughts of his from overhearing my parents' conversations. One observation of his that I recall is that no first-rate play or film could or should offer unrelenting tragedy. It must be balanced with a light touch, or audiences would find it hard to tolerate. At another rare time of his being alone with me at supper, I asked him what he'd been reading. He said it was Alfred North Whitehead. When I wanted more of an explanation of what Whitehead was writing about, he pointed to the wall and asked me what color it was. When I said white, Daddy proceeded to explain to me how two people can see the same color and yet perceive it differently. That idea, too, has remained with me. His comments and insights contributed a lot to enriching my sensibilities and broadening my general education.

Emotionally, Daddy was a conservative, but intellectually he was a liberal.

Our conversations, few as they may have been, almost always contained seminal ideas from which I have borrowed ever since leaving home. For example, he said it was important to study one form of art, and that it really didn't matter which you chose, because you could always apply ideas from one discipline to another. We had no piano and therefore I was sent to a modern dance class instead of taking music lessons. My father said that I could borrow ideas from the dance class and transfer them to music and vice versa. In my life I still use this cross-fertilization concept in my work in psychotherapy and Bible study—both deal with the human condition but from different angles.

How I wish Daddy and I had had many more conversations—and that I had written down the ones we had. A particular one I will always recall came long after my childhood, when I was visiting my father when he was in his 80s. It was getting late in the evening, and I, then a grown woman with young children, dared to ask him the broad, philosophical, big questions with which I was preoccupied: "What do you think is in the far-off future of the Jewish people?" In his factual, no-nonsense style that I so trusted, he said he did not imagine the Arabs or rather their leaders would ever grow to accept the reality of Jewish life in the Land of Israel. They would always want to make trouble. He was not at all pessimistic or fearful—merely realistic. Another time during a similar visit I asked him if General Moshe Dayan's reputation as an active ladies' man affected his role as a commander and leader. My father said it had no effect. He also said that evening that women under the age of forty were not interesting, thus eliminating the majority from consideration. For my father, companionship and good conversation were essential. I also asked him why he and Mother had had only one child. "Oh," he said, without a moment's hesitation, "Mummy and I thought a child would be good for our marriage." I've never been sure what he was driving at, and it has remained for me an unanswered question.

The Sabbath eve was different from all other evenings…as everyday life was shut out and the telephone fell silent. the family was together, a cohesive unit. A sense of spiritual gratitude pervaded…

Dressed up for the Purim holiday with the Matzdorf children:
Hanna as Queen Esther, me as a clown and Ezra as a girl.

Aunt Esther, Mother, me and our army friends on our balcony.

Entertaining British officers during the first years of WWII.

Me, Ehud Mandelblitt and Esther Marcus on a "glamourous" holiday to Tel Aviv by bus, 1947.

Esther Marcus and me in Holon, near Tel Aviv, 1947.

"What the Lord requires of you: only to do justly, and to love mercy, and to walk humbly with thy God."

—Micah 6:8

My class outside of the Reali School, most in Scout uniform.
I'm in the second row, second from right. On my right: Arza, then Ora.

58

My close friends Riva and Arza with me in the schoolyard at Reali.

Dressed up in Aunt Esther's hat and shoes in Jerusalem for Purim—a flight of fantasy.

founded 1913

בית הספר הריאלי העברי בחיפה
THE HEBREW REALI SCHOOL IN HAIFA

My school badge, featuring the school's motto: "Walk Humbly."

WHATEVER I GOT from my parents in the way of education, conversation and wisdom has stayed with me throughout my lifetime, as has much of my more formal education. My experience at the Reali School in Haifa was remarkable from beginning to end, with a powerful and lasting impact. My parents were both set on sending me to the best academic school, and I'm confident it was a financial burden. I am forever grateful for the decision they made.

Avraham Biran, the world-famous archaeologist, once described the school as the Eton of the British Mandate. Well, not exactly. I wouldn't go that far, but I certainly agree with his implication: the school was first-rate academically and demanding, with a strong commitment to teaching self-discipline, responsibility and leadership. One of the phrases ingrained in us was the motto "walk humbly," a quotation from the prophet Micah 6:8: "What the Lord requires of you: only to do justly, and to love mercy, and to walk humbly with thy God." This motto was embroidered in white below a sketch of our school at the bottom edge of our school insignia, sewn on to our school uniforms. Although I cannot swear how many of us practiced this lofty ideal to the fullest, we wore it proudly.

Because students came to Reali from all over Haifa, the school was an important source of new friends. Reali was co-ed, but my closest friendships at school were with girls. Ora Yarkoni, Arza Rabinovitz, and Riva Plotnik were my closest friends in late adolescence. Our friendships added richness to my life, into which I still tap today. Although I spent a good bit of time with Arza and Riva, both of whom were unique personalities and an integral part of my youth, my relationship with Ora Yarkoni was probably the longest, deepest and closest of all. She and I shared so many thoughts, especially during our teenage years. Many of the insights gleaned from our conversations remain relevant and are with me still. We spent hours talking about life in general and about the nature of personal relationships in particular. We would analyze boy–girl relationships, and I so clearly remember her saying that she'd rather have fewer admirers than many. She thought that fewer relationships meant each one would be more meaningful. It never occurred to her that any of her admirers would break up with her or get bored with her. I remember her once saying something to the effect of "When a boy falls in love with me, it's like a piece of wool stuck to my sweater; it never lets go."

Ora was exceptionally attractive and incredibly popular. I distinctly remember one Shabbat morning when we were all about 15, and several friends came over to my place. The boys were in immaculate white shirts, short khaki pants, and sandals, and the girls in white blouses and blue or white shorts. But Ora was wearing white sandals and short-shorts to match, which in the style of the day were gathered in elastic around the tops of her thighs. The white of her perfect, starched clothes contrasted with her face and her long suntanned legs. As usual, she was very striking. It's funny that I can still close my eyes and picture her at different times in different places, exactly as she looked then. Another time I recall

With Riva and Arza in the schoolyard at the water fountain.

A cartoon from my diary showing how overwhelmed I felt by the weight of my responsibilities running the group's cultural activities.

she had on long blue woolen slacks and a hand-knit gray sweater in a thick cabled pattern. She paid a lot of attention to her grooming and would wash her thick, wavy hair and comb it out carefully and slowly. She used only Adin soap, considered somewhat of a luxury, for her face. She was self-confident and spontaneous. She moved with grace, her posture straight, her carriage erect.

Ora adored her family and hero-worshiped her older brother, Yudah, who was in the Palmach. Her parents were nice, good people, and a devoted couple. Her father was a humble tailor, but, in her inimitable way, she was proud of him. To hear her hold forth about him, or show off some item of clothing he'd sewn for her, you would have thought he was Armani or Dior. On her marvelous figure, her father/tailor-made slacks did indeed look spectacular.

She was a serious student and very ambitious about her studies, which I decidedly was not. She had an excellent command of the Hebrew language and her puns were witty. She interpreted all that happened to her and to those she loved in the most glowing terms. Some of my friends found it irritating; my mother however, thought it was an admirable characteristic. In short, my friend

My classmate Rafi Freund napping beside his neat cot in his hut made of bales of hay after a day of hard work at our work camp at Kibbutz Beeri in summer of 1950.

Ora was endlessly beguiling, amusing, and clever. She exuded vitality, and I loved her. It broke my heart when she died in her 20s from bone cancer.

She had married Rafi Freund, one of our classmates, for whom I once had had a soft spot. Ora had become a zoologist and Rafi a geologist. When I visited her in the Shaarei Tzedek hospital in Jerusalem, she was lying in bed, one leg heavily bandaged after an amputation above her knee. I asked her how Rafi was doing, and did he have somebody to talk to during this difficult period. She looked at me and, somewhat surprised, said, "He's got me. He does not need anyone else."

When I was at Reali, the school's students were fortunate to have as headmaster the esteemed Dr. Arthur Biram, who had founded the school in 1913 and led it since its inception except for a period during World War I when he, a German Jew, was drafted into the German army and was awarded the Iron Cross for his service. Dr. Biram was a student of the great German biblical historian Eduard Meyer and instilled in us a deep respect for the tie between Biblical history and archeology. He believed that the study of the Bible with its history and heroes was basic to Jewish identity. The unbroken bond with the Land of Israel was and is rooted deep in the Biblical narrative. He taught us that the

My closest friend, Ora, polishing her shoes in front of our tent at Ein Zeitim during summer camp. Her posture was unfailingly erect.

Bible brings the past right into the present. From him, we learned, for example, that a 2,500-year-old wall in Megiddo in northern Israel—the remains of the city's fortifications mentioned in the Bible—supports the Bible's account.

My love affair with the Bible started when I was a six-year-old schoolgirl and has never abated. Early on I understood that if I studied the Bible I would know everything about adult life without ever having to leave my neighborhood. I used to jump off the bus and run home to tell my ever-attentive mother what I had learned that day. One time, I breathlessly recounted, in broken English (as Hebrew was my mother tongue), what I had learned from Genesis: "Mummy, you'll be sick of your children." This was my poor translation from the Hebrew of Genesis 3:16: "I will greatly multiply thy pain and thy travail; in pain thou shalt bring forth children... ." Despite my mistranslations, she never ceased to be impressed with the timeless wisdom and realism of the Biblical stories.

My Biblical studies began in earnest in the first grade at Reali and went on for the next twelve years, with the material becoming more difficult each year. Our study of the Bible and the way we were taught made it clear that if we were to be educated adults, it was incumbent upon us to be knowledgeable about the Hebrew Bible, regardless of our level of observance or faith in God. Learning this history and these stories was all part of being and becoming an educated Jew. The school's approach to Biblical studies emphasized the moral, spiritual and historical. Our teachers presented the Bible as the chronicle of Jewish life from the moment that Abraham and his wife, Sara, said no to pagan culture and followed the command to go to a land they had never seen. It recorded the first 2,000 years of a people—my friends and I were merely links in a long historical chain going back to ancient Israel.

We studied the prophets in our late teens. When I read aloud in class in its original magnificent Hebrew the story of Isaiah's anguish at the eternal themes of injustice, indifference to the have-nots and abuse of power, or memorized his hopes and dreams for a loving, law-abiding, peaceful world, I sensed with every fiber of my being that this was sublime, powerful, and authoritative stuff. We argued and wrestled over contemporary interpretations and studied the insights of rabbinical commentary. We were encouraged to ask questions and to raise original interpretations. We needed no translation because the Bible was written in Hebrew, our mother tongue. We talked about Sara, David, Ehud, Samuel, Abigail, and Daniel in the present tense. Their language was our language, the land they walked on was the land we walked on, hiked, loved, and promised to protect.

By the time we graduated and were ready to begin our military service, we knew the Book in the Biblical sense of "knowing" a woman—intimately, lovingly, respectfully, and at times even humorously. It became bone of our bones and flesh of our flesh, and its verse and narrative dotted our language and references.

Reali was not a religious school. Nevertheless the boys donned *kippot* (skullcaps) during Biblical studies, out of respect for thousands of years of tradition. The minute the bell rang, they'd shove their *kippot* into their back pockets, stumble over each other to get out of class, and head straight onto the playing field. Then they'd come back, their cheeks flushed, sweaty from the rough and tumble of recess, fish out their crushed skullcaps, slip into their desk chairs, and in one fell swoop transform themselves from the wild abandon and roughness of soccer to students analyzing and questioning the eternal issues and motives of human nature as it came into conflict with the will of God. Sometimes, like all adolescents, we'd snicker at erotic sections. We found many references titillating—breasts like "two fawns" or "clusters of grapes" in the Song of Songs—and would collapse into barely suppressed gales of laughter.

Geography teacher Professor Braver, who was killed in a convoy on the way to Jerusalem during the siege in 1948.

Dr. Yosef Schechter and Dr. David Neiger were my great Bible teachers. Both loved the Book and transmitted to us its grandeur, its humanity. Dr. Schechter was roly-poly, with corn-blue eyes and red cheeks. He'd walk up and down in front of the blackboard waving the Book while conveying an idea. His emphasis was on the eternal meaning and purpose of human life found in the Bible, for both individuals and peoples, and he illuminated that which was timeless in its teaching. He saw no disconnect between the moral values and the national concerns of Amos, Micah and other prophets, or the Biblical kings such as David. The matriarchs and patriarchs of Genesis wrestled with the web of family relationships just as we students and our parents did. Above all he was interested in infusing his students' lives with an inner sense of purpose, meaning and belonging. I lapped up his lessons, although I was not one of his star pupils and I don't think he ever knew how respectful I was of his teachings, nor could he have imagined that his impact would last throughout my lifetime, my teaching and my two books.

Dr. Schechter taught the Talmud with the same passion as the Bible. I decided early on that the Talmud was not for me. The class was essentially an hour of aggressive discourse that left me cold, and I felt very much left out. I was angry, restless and resentful. The class fostered a macho atmosphere of intellectual rivalry as each boy challenged the others' interpretations and argued for his own. I did not try to compete, nor was I interested in keeping up in this aggressive atmosphere, which I resented. I quickly found my escape staring out of the window to the left of my desk and out to the street, choosing to daydream about future boys in my life and the approaching delicious languid summer holidays.

Dr. Neiger had an angular, handsome face, dark hazel eyes under bushy eyebrows, and a voice deep, granulated, and authoritative. Both men taught the senior grades. Much time was devoted to the teachings of spiritual and moral giants like Isaiah, Amos, and Ezekiel. The prophets taught us that callous behavior toward

Dr. Neiger with my friend Yossi in front of the Reali School.

the poor, the dilution of Biblical beliefs, and ignoring the Covenant were cataclysmic in their consequences and dangerous for our survival as a people. We were "chosen" all right, but for what? We were chosen for the responsibility of living up to the Biblical expectations of us!

In our senior year, we were divided into science and literature departments. I was in the literature department, where Bible studies and world literature, from Thomas Mann's Buddenbooks to the Forsyte Saga, were emphasized and taught by those stellar teachers. They never lowered their standards just because we were young students. The expectation was that we would rise to the challenge. Therefore the quickest and most responsive students got the most attention and respect. I drank it all in, and while I loved those classes, sadly, I don't think my illustrious teachers really realized how engaged I was. I never achieved above a B+. I took in all of this Biblical and literary study with the same spirit in which it was taught. After all, I concluded, if I'm to be a person of consequence in this life, then it follows that each and every one of my actions is potentially loaded with consequences.

The prophets expected of us, in the name of God, compassion and fidelity coupled with action—this was not up for negotiation. The prophets' grave words implied that I, Naomi, had the capacity and, equally important, the obligation, to rise to their high expectations. Their pounding words, set in powerful language and rich images, conveyed to me a strong sense of my worth and responsibility. On the other hand, Sara's jealousy of "the other woman," Hagar; Rebecca's terrible choice as to which of her twins should receive the birthright; the perils of sibling rivalry; King Saul's depression; King David's adulterous affair with Bathsheba; his son Absalom's rebellion and the rape of his half-sister, Tamar; Jacob's difficult and conflicted nature—all these stories taught me compassion for the intricacies of life, its contradictions and human vulnerabilities. I was addicted. There were no illusions, no fairy tales. The Bible was about tough love: stark reality on one hand, with hope, love, purpose, and faith on the other. All were integrated into one whole.

Other teachers at Reali were as memorable as my Bible teachers. Our French teacher, Mrs. Kalugai, had a most peculiar appearance. Her legs were very bowed, her eyes wide apart, intelligent and bulging. Her hair was sparse to the point that I feared she was going bald. She always wore it combed back into a bun, and bits of glistening skull showed through. She spoke French in a most precise way. She was a superior teacher who was highly regarded and respected by all. She rarely, in fact raised her voice above a whisper and always held our attention. She had written a book of poetry about women in the Bible. Some of the verses spoke of the beauty of the female breast and about women in love and longing. When looking at her, it was impossible to imagine those kinds of thoughts crossing her mind.

Arabic was always difficult for me, so much so that Mother even hired a tutor for me at one point. Arabic class was taught by the brilliant and eccentric Dr. Kiester. He announced his arrival in class by kicking the door open with his shoe, pointing at a student, and barking out an Arab verb to be conjugated without delay by the victim he had pointed to. At times, a bit of spit escaped and preceded him into the room. My classmates who were good at the language and confident loved his method of teaching, but I was petrified of him. Kiester, as we called him, took no prisoners. God help those who couldn't keep up! Somehow, with the aid of my tutor, Shulamit, I survived his class.

MANY OF MY LONG-LASTING VALUES GREW out of my life in the youth movement, the Scouts, or *Tzofim*, as it is in Hebrew. Reali and the Scout movement were closely tied. Dr. Biram, who had been familiar with the evil of politicized youth movements that were popular in places like Germany and Russia, was adamant about separating the Tzofim from any specific political party. At the same time he insisted on incorporating into the Movement the values of responsibility, love of country, and the importance of settling on the land.

My father, a historian and a product of Scotland's educational system, was an admirer of his philosophy and approach to educating the young.

Youth scout camp in 1946.

Youth movements in the Land of Israel provided critical opportunities that fostered close and enduring friendships, and, above all, a sense of belonging. Even as a grown woman when I was a guest at the White House—even at the very moment President Lyndon Johnson strode into the East Room to the first stirring bars of "Hail to the Chief," I never experienced anything like the excitement and trepidation I felt as I readied my young self to enter the room where our Scout group met on Saturday nights. These evenings were usually social, light in content, with lots of folk dancing and group singing, usually accompanied by an accordion or harmonica. I most often wore a dark blue pleated crepe skirt that swung slightly as I moved and a meticulously ironed Yemenite blouse of white cotton or silk with red embroidery around the cuffs of the short, puffed sleeves and around the jewel neckline, and white sandals. Other nights I wore a sarafan, a dress made of heavy crepe-like material, thickly gathered around the waist, with a top like a tight-fitting sleeveless bolero. A third choice was a royal blue dress with a small pattern of flowers, puffed short sleeves, a form-fitting top, and a full gathered skirt. None of the clothes that my girlfriends and I wore would work for contemporary anorexic-looking models because the clothes emphasized femininity, fullness and grace. Today's more unisex styles would have been abhorrent to my generation of young girls and their admirers. I used to fret to my poor mother that I was not "full" enough for these peasant styles, especially the tight bodice effect. Mummy, who could spot my moods from the far corner of a room, purposely waved away my concerns with a restless expression of impatience and reassured me in strong terms that one day I'd be delighted, even grateful not to be so buxom. I was absolutely aware of what she was trying to do and never believed her anyway. Nonetheless, I would leave the house somewhat comforted.

On Tuesday afternoons, my Scout group held a more serious and businesslike meeting, whose purpose was to prepare us for leadership and responsibility. When I was in charge of developing meaningful and entertaining programs for our group meetings, I was never totally satisfied and never felt I'd done a good enough job. For these meetings, we wore Scout uniforms, with the girls in khaki skirts and blouses and the boys in khaki short pants and shirts, reserving their clean white shirts for the Saturday night events. The boys' short pants were very short and hung low on the hips—all the better to show off long torsos and strong brown legs ending in sandals. In the hot summer, we girls wore shorts, too, in blue, white, or khaki, gathered tightly with elastic at the tops of our thighs. Because all of our meetings consisted of boys and girls together, we gave much attention to our appearance, however simple and predictable.

The group at Kibbutz Beeri 1950. Peter at top left.

Girls and boys were aware and attracted to each other and also fell in love. Some relationships were serious and long lasting—some even culminated in marriage, such as Ora and Rafi's—but the communal aspect of our group was always there. Thus, one did not have to have a boyfriend or girlfriend to go out with; there were always wholesome and healthy group gatherings and a sense of belonging to fall back on and be a part of. I never stayed home moping on a Saturday night because some boy did not ask me for a date—nevertheless my relationship with boys had its share of anguish and delight as my diary will attest to. The institution of dating as our counterparts in the U.S. experienced it seemed ridiculous and artificial to us, and certainly to me. Even those who had paired off remained an integral part of the group and our activities. Sexual behavior—kissing and so on—was restrained and certainly not on public display.

To be asked by a boy to be his girlfriend (*chavera*) was a serious request. "Falling in love" in the way we used it in our conversations with friends meant a serious

commitment of time, lots and lots of talking and no
wish or expectation of any kind of sexual intimacy.
I would not call this Puritan, because the concept
of sexuality as a sin was absolutely foreign to us. In
fact our relationship with boys was exceptionally
wholesome—no alcohol, drugs, or make-up. The
culture of the Palmach and the general value
system embodied in it filtered down to our youth
movement. There was a lot of swagger, but casual
sex as touted by the contemporary media and as we
know it today was unheard of.

Singing in unison was an integral and
indispensable part of our youth movement's sabra
culture. Singing together in public (*shirah betsibur*)
was often a spontaneous group activity. Unlike a
choir, we required no rehearsals. Songs about love
of country, Palmach songs, love songs—we all knew
the words and melodies, and wherever we found
ourselves, with whatever group, we could easily join
in with these familiar songs. The singing in our
Scout group and all the other youth movements was
binding, exhilarating, fun, and at times nostalgic. It
offered spontaneous closeness, caring, and solidarity.
Singing was a particular part of our long excursions
on crowded buses and open trucks.

Fun at summer scout work camp.

*Scout gathering on Saturday night. Dancing the hora
in the schoolyard.*

Folk dancing, too, played an indispensable role in our social life. The hora
involves a circle of dancers all moving to the same rhythm. The lively music from
only a harmonica, or an accordion, or our own voices, and the joy, the freedom
we felt to break into the circle—any circle, at any point—and lock arms with the
person to your left and right gave you a feeling of profound connection, belonging,
and deep joy. The enthusiasm and vitality was infectious, and the circle of dancers
moved like one body.

Long cross-country hikes, the summer work camps in the kibbutzim, the
strong attraction between teenage boys and girls always under the surface, the
singing and folk dancing—all these were part of the glue that held us together and

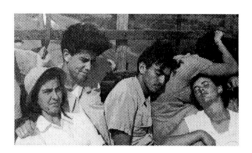

Hitchhiking in an open-air truck.
From left to right: Dalia, Yossi, Yoel, and Raya.

Rafi Freund

contributed to the success of our youth movement and our strong sense of identity and purpose. All of this was then splashed onto the broad canvas of events in the country, which were always a catalyst for important discussions. Our conversations came easily out of the major issues of the day, especially those confronting the larger community—cultivating the brown parched land, absorbing immigrants, realizing independence. Much time was also devoted to running the internal affairs of our group: electing committees, deciding on activities, and general discussions about the quality of life of our group. All this was done through noisy, serious debates and unsparing self-criticism before arriving at some general consensus. Scout activities were inseparable from my school experiences. They all melded together, especially since so many of our teachers were also instrumental in leading our Scout groups.

A special end-of-camp gift from the kibbutz—a trip in the Galilee in an open truck.
Second row left to right: Peter, me, Ora and our counselor Sonia.

Shoah and horror.
Defiance, struggle and redemption.

73

THE OUTER WORLD CERTAINLY IMPINGED on my personal life, especially during World War II. At some point during the war, indications of what was happening to the Jews throughout Europe came through to us. The Holocaust was like the beat of a distant, muffled drum—like an ongoing, dolorous Greek chorus. My first memories relating to the horrors date back to elementary school in the early 1940s. Our school badge, which was sewn onto our uniform, was surrounded by a yellow border as a sign of solidarity and pride with the European Jews who were being forced to wear yellow stars of David in order to separate and humiliate them before carting them off to the trains. I also remember writing childish notes to my Jewish peers in Europe, telling them I hoped they could get out quickly and come and join us in the Land of Israel.

Outside my apartment building complex in Haifa, 1950.

As the war wore on, the conversations at home and at tea time between my parents and with their friends was about the eastward drive of the fabled German general Rommel and his Afrika Korps, who were marching along the coast of North Africa towards Egypt. The Jews of Palestine understood what was in store for them if Rommel, who was sending the British reeling out of Libya, succeeded in knocking out the British Eighth Army then under the command of General Montgomery. Rommel's victorious army seemed unstoppable, the general himself seemed larger than life, and our morale was at a low point. I therefore sensed the immense relief that my parents felt hearing the wonderful news of Rommel's defeat in the battle of El Alamein in Egypt and the Allies' ultimate success in pushing the Germans out of North Africa.

The next stories to numb us were the tales of terror told all night long by refugees who had just landed on the shores of the Land of Israel, some of them survivors of the Warsaw Ghetto uprising, and also had been smuggled through the British blockade and dispersed in the dark of night among the kibbutzim. Everywhere, beginning right after the war, these people had the visible dark-blue numbers tattooed on their arms, the effect of which was to reduce them to the level of cattle being readied for the slaughter. I'd be standing in the aisle of a moving Haifa bus, swaying from side to side, when my eye would land on an anonymous arm, hanging onto a hand-strap of the bus, with a dark blue number tattooed on it. An instant wave of horror and compassion would sweep over me. Or I'd be lucky enough to find a seat on the bus going from Herzl Street downtown all the way up to Mount Carmel. Noticing that the woman sitting next to me was elegantly put together, I'd glance at her again and then see that on her forearm, between her gold watch and cotton pique short sleeves, was the telltale tattoo. It seemed that every second person in the country had a personal story of brutality and survival. We did not have to study the Holocaust in school; it was all around us. I knew full well—and never forgot—that it could just as easily have been me.

Two fairly peripheral people in my life stand out from this time: a dressmaker and a hairdresser. I remember them vividly. The dressmaker's name was Margit, and I was terribly fond of her. She lived in one small room on the first floor of a building on Tel Hai Street. The room was divided into two parts by a flowered cloth curtain. She slept and ate in the front part and sewed behind the curtain. She was a refugee from Hitler's Austria. Her mother, father, grandparents, sisters, and brothers had been hauled off to the gas chambers, and she had come to Palestine all alone with Youth Aliyah, a group organized to bring young people to the Land of Israel and educate them there—mostly orphans from the Shoah. She was thin, with a long face and large protruding teeth. Mummy treated her with great respect and always paid homage to her sewing capabilities, commenting on the side to me on Margit's teeth and what a neglected childhood she must have had. Margit worked incredibly hard, lived alone, and to me she seemed always sad and down. I owe her a great deal, since she was the one who sewed many of the good and most memorable clothes of my youth. I sometimes sought refuge in her little room and spent the morning with her, especially when feeling insufficiently prepared for my Arabic or math class, and terrified that I would be found wanting when called to the blackboard to recite or do long division. When I could not face it, I played hooky at Margit's. When the clock on the cupboard struck the hour school finished, I'd gather my school bag and go home. Margit never betrayed my confidence. While a customer was being fitted, I would crouch behind the cloth curtain and listen in on the conversation. Peeping through a tiny opening in the curtain, I'd see the ladies tucking their ample flesh into long bras and corsets. Over those interior fortifications, they'd put on immaculate white slips. They had lots of talcum powder sprinkled under their armpits and in their white summer shoes, too. While hiding behind the curtain, I was careful not to sneeze or cough and be found out. I felt that Margit, and the undressed customer and I were sharing huge feminine secrets—secrets discreetly hidden under their dresses, girdles and slips.

One day, Margit confided to Mother that she might be immigrating to Canada. She had a cousin she thought of joining. For Mother, this was a blow and a dilemma. On one hand, she pitied this lonely orphan who had so little in life other than ghastly tragic memories and this one Canadian relative. On the other hand, the Youth Aliyah and the Jewish community in the Land of Israel that had saved her, protected her, and given her a new home. Mother wondered aloud who else in the world would have ever given a damn about Margit.

The hairdresser to whom I headed for haircuts was Tania. My head would be tilted back in an uncomfortable position while she washed my hair. Rubbing my scalp and gently but thoroughly rinsing it from all angles with wonderfully soothing warm water, she'd tell me how she lost her parents, brothers, and sisters when the Germans appeared one day, rounded them up, and shot the family one by one, her mother and father last. She had honey-colored skin and hair, one silver tooth in the front of her pretty mouth, and was a little heavyset. She would repeat again and again, in Hebrew softened by a Hungarian accent, that after all of that, nothing could ever frighten her again. Of course, her life was not easy—Tania and her husband worked very hard in her makeshift hairdressing "salon" in a part of their modest apartment—but she did not want her children to grow up anywhere but in Israel. She was clear that this was where they belonged. At that point, the shampoo would be over. I'd raise my head from the washbasin, ready to stand up but also emotionally drained from having heard her story so clearly and completely. After leaving Tania I felt more mature, more seasoned. And I felt incredibly grateful to the very depths of my soul for having been born and forged under the brilliant blue skies of the Land of Israel. Just being alive, just dodging the busy traffic pouring down Mount Carmel with a fresh new haircut felt so very sweet!

From those days on, I saw life through a different prism. The Holocaust became my measuring rod for evaluating difficulties, setbacks, and tragedy. Mother and I were often invited for an afternoon coffee and rich chocolate torte at one of our German-born neighbors'. Usually it was around five on a winter day. It got dark early and because of rationing we used little electricity. Mother would get a bit down and urge me to join her for a walk around our neighborhood, and innocently wangled an invitation for a visit. She was immensely popular with our neighbors. I listened and absorbed into my soul their stories of escape, heart-wrenching losses, and ultimate survival. I so well recall then that the sayings on the walls of our classrooms, which I stared at every school day, reinforced the strong commitment both to moving toward the new reality of our longed-for country and to affirming the importance of "never again." One especially—Theodor Herzl's "If you wish it, it is no fairy tale," a Zionist motto referring to the force behind reestablishing the Jewish people in their historic homeland—seemed to speak directly to me. The meaning was clear: if you wish something strongly enough, it will become reality. I no longer remember the exact wording of another saying on those classroom walls, but its meaning is with me still: We are the last generation of slavery and the first to be redeemed. It resonated with all of us, the first generation to live free in our historical land.

Thousands of years of history, starting with the Biblical period, claimed me and helped forge my sense of identity. The text of the Hebrew Bible was ours. It was an important part of who we were. I identified wholeheartedly with the history and characters and stories of the Hebrew Bible. Yes, it was a delicious feeling to be born a sabra, a native Israeli, and I was proud to be part of the Jewish people, part of the sabra culture, with our deep roots in the land. And, yes, I was part of a privileged class, but did I do anything original or special to earn that status? No—it came through a sheer fluke of history. As these Holocaust stories washed over me I acquired a philosophical sense of humility about life. Had I been conceived in Paris, Amsterdam, or Berlin, my parents and I would probably have perished in the gas chambers. Many a night, I'd lie in bed before falling asleep and wonder if my parents would have known how to get out in time. Would they have read the writing on the wall? I felt that, though my mother may not have been physically strong, she was a quick improviser. If necessary, she would have bribed the Frenchman, the Dutchman, even the German, and maybe saved us. My father, on the other hand, was physically strong, never sick a day in his life, but rigidly honest and straightforward. He would never have resorted to bribery, and thus he would have been the first to be hauled off. Hot tears would flow onto my pillow, and I'd fall asleep quietly sobbing. These feelings and thoughts I never shared with Mummy and Daddy. What was the point of upsetting them?

All of the activities of the Scouts for the young, and the Palmach for those a bit older, intensified as it became more and more clear after World War II that a homeland for the Jews was imperative. Although the war ended in 1945, the tension in our land grew more evident, heightened and made poignant by the rage we felt about what the Germans had wrought, the compassion for their victims and the responsibility we accepted for saving the remnant of our people from Europe's descent into madness.

The mood of the Jewish community toward the British changed drastically with the end of World War II. It was no accident that I was moved to start my diary commemorating the Night of the Bridges that took place in June 1946. The atmosphere became tense and hostile and fraternization ended between the British and the Jews. Nothing upset the previous more balanced state of affairs between the two communities more than the British stand on immigration—immigration of any kind was completely cut off in 1945. The British set up a blockade that the Jewish community—the Yishuv—was determined to circumvent by means of "illegal" immigration. While some ships and boats carrying unfortunate refugees reached their destination, many were sunk or seized by the British. Though it was only one of the heart-wrenching stories around, in 1947, the ship *Exodus* became a symbol of defiance against British insistence on sending ships full of wretched, traumatized Holocaust survivors back to the European ports from which they had departed or to Cyprus to live behind barbed wire yet again. With the perspective of many years, and the knowledge of other colonial powers, I have realized that if one must come under colonial rule it had best be that of an established democracy with a free press back home such as that of Britain.

MY COUSIN DANNY had worked to bring to the Land of Israel many hopeful immigrants, fresh from the death camps of Europe. At one point he got romantically involved with a pale, fragile-looking young woman on a refugee ship. When he said he wanted to marry her, our family was not too happy about it. Danny had grown up as a sabra, with no inkling of what it was like to be wary of one's own shadow. She, poor thing, had lost both her mother and father in the Bergen-Belsen concentration camp. We never knew how she actually managed to survive, nor did she volunteer any details. She seemed hundreds of years older than Danny—he was not yet 21 when they met. They were worlds apart and never did marry.

Life for Danny had become more and more intense. Quite early, he had joined the Palmach, and by 1944 he enlisted in the British Army's Jewish Brigade, which was recruited in Palestine and deployed to Italy and along the Western front. When the Jewish Brigade was disbanded after the war, Danny came home and rejoined the Palmach. His application to study marine engineering in England was accepted and he asked the Palmach for permission to leave for the course. The Palmach said that they needed him in the country, and that was that. He rejoined the Palmach right away and settled in Poria, a lovely kibbutz overlooking the Sea of Galilee (*Kinneret* in Hebrew). The community was new, and the average age of its members was 21. He was in charge of its defense and did not suffer fools lightly when it came to security.

The closer we came to independence, the more petrified I became for Danny. I felt all along that he carried a lead bullet deep in his heart, and that one day that bullet would explode and claim his life. I never dared share that fear with anyone and felt it mostly at night.

A spontaneous picnic in the classroom celebrating the day of the U.N. General Assembly's partition resolution, November 29, 1947.

THROUGHOUT 1947, THE UNREST IN MY HOMETOWN of Haifa and throughout the Land of Israel continued. Certain days in particular stand out in my memory, only a few of which are recorded in my diary. One of those remarkable days occurred in late November 1947, when the United Nations voted in favor of the partition of Palestine, which would replace the British Mandate. I clearly recall us Reali students standing for a long time in the heat of the day in orderly rows in the large schoolyard. We hardly moved. Our whole attention focused on Dr. Biram, our school principal. I could feel the perspiration trickling down my back and neck under my carefully ironed and starched school uniform with its white collar and cuffs to match. Dr. Biram, in his deep German accent, solemnly told us we must be ready to be called on at any time for any amount of sacrifice—physical, psychological, and financial. In the not-too-distant future, the fate of the young state would be on our shoulders. Jewish people all over the world would be focused on us and trusting us to rise to the challenge. He underlined what a tremendous historical privilege we had before us and stressed the great responsibilities and duties that went along with it. Almost as if it were yesterday, I remember him calling for more of us to settle on and reclaim our dry, barren land. Dr. Biram spoke with a strong sense of vision and repeated again and again the importance to each of us of inner discipline, responsibility and duty. I felt I belonged to a special generation, a special history, a very special place. You could hear a pin drop; nobody moved till he finished. I felt as if I personally had been waiting two millennia for this to happen. I was exhausted but euphoric. Looking around when he finished, I saw my fellow students appear dazed, delirious and emotional. Typically, though, for Reali, where classes never got cancelled, the word went out that we would return to class immediately, consistent with the idea that inner discipline must conquer all. I was amazed that the administration would stick with this decision even in light of an event of such historical magnitude, and wondered what would happen if the Messiah came, thinking he might be asked to wait until the Reali School students were let out of class. Our mood was actually out of control, though, and eventually classes were liberated and school was at an end. The boys pushed their way out of the doors first and dancing began immediately. We went on dancing with new circles of dancers growing and multiplying, stomping our feet, arms interlocked and perspiration dripping. Our voices became hoarse from so much singing.

The city was full of people, too, all dancing and moving excitedly through the streets, circles upon circles undulating in locked rings of spontaneous hora dancing—all of it creating a sense that we were all in this together.

When I got home, I told my mother about all that had happened. Mother was transfixed by my descriptions. My father kept hovering in the background. He, like his father before him, detested any show of uncontrolled emotion or public demonstration. He made fun of the idea of our neighbors, the good, stout Dr. Matzdorf and his wife, dancing in the streets, and he personally refused to join the so-called masses in their exuberance. So be it, I thought. I ignored his comments and concentrated on my mother. I couldn't believe that I, Naomi Harris, was a living part of all of this. I did indeed feel privileged—as Dr. Biram had suggested we should feel. I felt chosen.

AMONG THE WATCHWORDS pounded into us at school and in the Scouts was *tsav ha-shaa*—the call of the hour, or that which was expected of us at that moment. In my day, that call was twofold: to rescue the ragged remnant of European Jews after World War II, and to settle on the land, cultivating it and protecting it. Settling on the land also meant building a brand-new community based on a shared vision of social and economic justice and equality. By the time we finished school, we would have created a community nucleus ready to settle wherever the country needed us. We would be ready to start a new kibbutz from scratch. Not everybody rallied to the call or stayed on to become a lifelong kibbutznik. It was an idealistic way of life that required self-discipline, commitment, and responsibility to the welfare of the group. However, the values of that time and place—ingrained in our psyche whether we acted upon them or not—gave direction, a sense of purpose, and a clear understanding of belonging and responsibility to all of our activities, social and otherwise. I've never come across

A group of us visiting our counselor at Kibbutz Sarid.

finer values and ideals than those cultivated in the kibbutz culture. I've often wondered if I, who so admired this way of life, could have been self-disciplined enough to be fully committed to it and to stay with it over the long haul.

For the pioneers in the kibbutz movement, the ideals demanded that the good of the community always come before the concerns of the individual. The kibbutzim were responsible for making the desert bloom, and when "illegal" refugees landed on our shores, they were hurriedly absorbed and hidden among the kibbutzim, as were the war orphans who were quickly adopted by them. The kibbutz members occupied leadership roles in the ranks of the Palmach, and, after Independence, in the military. Hand in hand with the emphasis on group and community culture, individual leadership was always encouraged. Especially early on, the rules of communal life were rigid, but the kibbutz was always a free community and one was free to leave it at will.

Among the most vivid memories of my youth are the times I spent on several kibbutzim. My first experience was in the summer of 1947, when a few friends from the Scouts and I went to visit our old counselor Sonia at her kibbutz, Sarid,

Group shot at Kibbutz Sarid. Lower left is Arza next to me, above are Ora and Sara, and our beloved counselor Sonia above.

in the Jezreel Valley. She was delighted to have us there and we could feel how proud she was of us as she introduced us to members of her group. We arrived on a Friday evening, Sabbath eve, and people were wearing spanking clean white shirts and blouses. Despite being dead tired after full, rich days of work, everyone from Sonia's group gathered in the communal dining room and joined in the singing. When patriotic songs were sung, I heard the voices become deeper and grave—it was a serious time, and the atmosphere was laden with heavy hearts. I listened carefully to all of the conversations around the tables the whole time I was there. I recall only positive and hopeful thoughts being expressed. There was a lot of talk about the British, but the kibbutzniks to my amazement seemed to understand the British mentality and didn't speak out of blind hatred. They even talked about the average British soldier with a certain amount of sympathy. All the while they exuded a quiet and reserved self-confidence. I felt totally secure, safe, and so content in their midst.

In October of that same year Danny picked me up and we went to Poria, the kibbutz where he had been living for some months and intended to stay forever. My memories remain as clear as if I were seeing them exactly as they happened those six and a half decades ago. I was captivated.

We had stopped at Kibbutz Mishmar HaSharon along the way. I loved watching the older settlers as they greeted Danny with such warmth and respect. He had trained there with the Palmach and many of them knew him. I remember, too, that when we came upon the Sea of Galilee it looked to me like a highly polished silver platter. Everyone at the kibbutz seemed to be in their late teens or early 20s, all from different backgrounds, schools, and youth movements. To a person they appeared to be so adult and aware of the heavy load of responsibility heaped on their shoulders. In the evening, peace and quiet descended on the young people of the kibbutz, and also seemingly on the whole area of the Sea of Galilee. I was attentive to the fact that Danny, a leader at the kibbutz, was working every minute of the day. He had an easy style of leadership. With one hand he built, and with the other he defended the land, giving orders, lending a hand, encouraging, prodding, and even joking. Not exactly a light-hearted boy himself, Danny had a lively, sweet, very cute girlfriend at the time by the name of Yardena. Her eyes were green with yellow flakes, and she had a perfectly round face framed by dark, soft curly hair. Her teeth were perfect and shone in their whiteness. She was completely secure in her femininity and fully aware of her strong impact on Danny, who never failed to respond to her kidding and gentle teasing of him. He laughed a lot when near her.

When I left Poria, I felt so good and so fulfilled, carrying with me strong, positive impressions of an incredible group of youths, a dedicated community of men and women—boys and girls, really—and a unique way of life. I so wished I were older.

Uncle Tommy sitting in front of his son Danny's residence in Poria which Danny named "Jane Eyre" after his mother's favorite book.

Me with my friend Dalia in Haifa.

THE UNREST THROUGHOUT THE LAND INTENSIFIED on the day Israel declared her independence: May 14, 1948, the last day of the British Mandate. During the years 1947/1948 there had been severe fighting, and in Haifa, under the relentless goading of the irresponsible leadership of the Arabs of Palestine, the people were told to run away and were promised that they would return victorious. The Arabs were defeated by the Haganah and the Palmach, few in number and poorly armed and trained though they were, and contrary to the dire predictions of U.S. Secretary of State George C. Marshall and other foreign experts. A Jewish state was reestablished on this ancient land where the Kingdoms of Israel and Judea had been, and from which the Jews had been exiled three times; first by the Assyrians, then by the Babylonians and in 79 A.D. by the Romans. Yet the spiritual and historical bond had never been severed.

While the fighting raged across the land, two episodes in particular stand out in my memory. One was the day on which my father called me to join him on the balcony of our apartment. He pointed to Haifa Bay, literally covered with small boats carrying much of Haifa's Arab population fleeing northwards towards the town of Acre, obedient to their leaders' instructions. The other is expressed simply in excerpts from a penciled letter written on July 11, 1948, at 4:45pm, by my 15-year-old friend Dalia Salamon from an air-raid shelter in Jerusalem, then under a protracted siege:

Dalia's letter written during the siege of Jerusalem.

"...With us, it's already very lively and the war has started up again. Today we were bombed from the air, but the airplane was knocked down. I am writing to you while at the same time I hear the whistles of the shells and the explosions. We have managed beautifully and our air-raid shelter is secure on the first floor. We have been stuffing the windows of the apartment with heavy sacks of sand that we filled with our own hands...Our neighbors from the third floor and above us have joined us in the air-raid shelter and it is comforting having us all together. The actual work of filling up the bags was lively with singing and joking and at the same time we were dripping with sweat. I'm sitting here on pins and needles, and with every opportunity I run out to the garden for fresh air and to read because the air-raid shelter is dark...Our youth group was furious to hear that your group is going out to a summer work camp, and we are staying back in Jerusalem. However, there is a lot of work waiting for us to do and we will fulfill our roles and responsibilities...Dear Naomi—even though we have not spent much time together I have become very attached to you. You cannot imagine how happy I'll be to receive a letter from you. I hope we shall meet soon in our new Jewish state and Hebrew Haifa. Yours with love, Dalia."

My cousin Danny.
War and victory.
Pain and pride.

WHAT SHOULD HAVE BEEN cause for great and lengthy rejoicing turned quickly to intense pain—both for the new country as a whole and for my family and me personally. The excitement and joy of a 2,000-year-old hope materializing was dampened and restrained because with the declaration of the new state, no less than five Arab countries attacked us and our family paid a very high price indeed. While the members of Danny's kibbutz—whose average age was 20—were dancing the hora in celebration of the declaration of independence and the creation of the new state, Danny had gone off early to bed. His friends had called to him to come out and join them, but he had responded that he had to go to sleep because "the trouble would only start tomorrow." He must have sensed the storm that was brewing and the price that would have to be paid.

The situation in Galilee had become even more tense as an invasion by the Syrian army became increasingly certain when the British Mandate came to an end. The Syrian army was well armed and trained. The kibbutzim that lay in their path in the Jordan Valley south of the Kinneret—Alumot, Kinneret, and Degania—were undefended and vulnerable. Danny was ordered by the Haganah to gather volunteers from these kibbutzim to block the Syrian advance. He went from one to another to gather them and bring them down to the abandoned Arab village of Tzemach on the Kinneret's southern shore.

Eight young men from his kibbutz, Poria, answered Danny's call. The members, men and women all in their twenties, stood together on the hill in Poria to bid the nine farewell. Amongst them was Danny's girlfriend, Yardena, who silently stood on the steps of the communal dining room seeing his small group off. Danny promised them that he'd bring them all back alive.

The nine from Poria and the other volunteers under Danny's command occupied the buildings of Tzemach's small railroad station on the Haifa-Damascus route facing the approaching Syrian army. They were vastly outnumbered and very poorly equipped. On May 15, the day of Israel's independence, the Syrians came pouring down from the Golan Heights, as Lord Byron wrote in a poem describing an Assyrian king's attack on Jerusalem, "like the wolf on the fold." The boys rushed from window to window firing from the abandoned buildings to make it seem they were many more in number and well equipped.

They fought day and night through May 15, 16 and into the 17th. The promised relief failed to appear, yet the volunteers under Danny's command held

A view of Kibbutz Degania and the Lake of Galilee, 1951.

off the Syrians. Danny was an excellent sharpshooter, and the Syrians eventually identified a window from which he was firing. The Syrians targeted him and the bullet that I had long feared would claim my cousin found its mark on May 17, 1948, when Danny was just 21 years old.

With his death and no relief in sight, the exhausted and famished defenders pulled back towards Degania, but fortunately the Syrian advance halted.

The nine brave boys from Poria all came back—eight survivors carrying Danny's body. They buried him at midnight at a spot overlooking his beloved Kinneret. His was the first and only grave in that young community. We later learned that he had told his parents that if he died he wanted to be buried overlooking the Kinneret.

They lost the battle and Danny lost his life, but he and his boys had held off the Syrian westward advance long enough to allow the Haganah to shore up Degania's defenses, and a few days later, to win the decisive and strategic "Battle of Degania" that pushed the Syrians back across their border. If Danny and his small group had not been able to delay the Syrian advance, Degania would have fallen and Galilee and the road west to Haifa would have been next. They were so few in number, but their achievement was beyond measure.

It was noontime on May 18, 1948. I remember as if it were yesterday. Three men were walking up the hill toward where I was standing on the sidewalk in front of my home, having just come from school. They were in kibbutz working clothes, their young faces drawn and ashen white, and their eyes dark and deep. As they got closer and closer, I thought, my God, all of them are from Poria. One of them was looking directly at me. He was grave, pale, and his eyes were fixed on mine. He said nothing, but I knew right away—I knew, I knew. I let out a loud yell, a horrible scream; the immediate pain was unbearable. I left them on the sidewalk and ran up three flights of stairs to my friend Esther Marcus' flat, rang the bell, dropped my schoolbag on the floor, and fell upon her weeping uncontrollably. My cousin, my cousin Danny…

While shaking with sobs, I somehow collected my school bag, ran down the three flights of stairs, and got home. What a scene. My father was pacing up and down the hall. Mother was sobbing in one armchair, and her best friend, Sara Salamon, was red-eyed in another. The three young men were in the room, sitting silently, their faces exquisite with suffering. The air was heavy with pain, tragedy, and heroism. The boys kept adding pieces of how it happened until the jigsaw was complete.

I REMEMBER SAYING to my devastated parents that Danny's life up until his very last breath was fuller, happier, and more meaningful than any other youth in the entire world. I meant that with all my being.

Profound, exuberant joy and gnawing deep aches went hand in hand throughout Israel from the beginning of the new nation. For a country with such a small population, casualties numbered in the thousands in the Arab-Israeli war that followed independence. Each casualty was a searing a loss. Reality came knocking at the door loud and clear. There was no time to wallow in contentment. David had achieved another miraculous victory over Goliath, but at a great cost.

For a long time, I experienced a dull heavy pain inside me, firmly lodged between my chest and my stomach. My reactions on a daily basis for weeks on end were varied and unpredictable, but the ongoing chronic ache remained. I never dared stay alone in our living room, where Danny, stared down at me from his photograph. His face was grave and handsome, his forehead square and strong, his gaze intelligent and intense. He looked so alive, with eyes that seemed to look straight into mine, somehow communicating with me, asking "why?" I had no answer for him. From there on, the atmosphere in my Aunt Esther and Uncle Tommy's home was somber, heavy, and so, so sad.

Danny wearing the uniform of the Jewish Brigade. His official photo.

Opposite: Danny and his mother, my aunt Esther, in Jerusalem.
Above: Danny's tombstone in Poria. "Danny...Daniel Reuven—A member of Kibbutz Poria, the son of
Tuvia and Esther Coussin, born in Jerusalem...Died a hero's death in the Battle of the Jordan Valley, 1948."

DADDY WAS PROUD OF THE YOUNG STATE OF ISRAEL and expressed his pride in his own understated way. After the 1948 War of Independence, especially with the torrents of new waves of immigrants, there was strict food rationing, and my mother, who never touched the black market, allowed herself, though rarely, to comment: "I wish Naomi could have another egg." Daddy would jump at her and say, "You wanted a State and now you've got it. If it's going to stand on its own feet, it'll have to be difficult for at least the first 100 years!" He admired David Ben-Gurion, the first prime minister of Israel, for having the foresight and wisdom to disband the two rival undergrounds, the Haganah and the Etzel, and unite them into one army at the very inception of the new State. Thus, he believed Ben-Gurion had averted the possibility of a bloody civil war. My father brought that point up over and over again.

Mother raved about the youth in the country—their resoluteness and strength of character, their unflinching grasp of reality. For her these young people were a new type of Jew, one who wasn't looking over his shoulder to see what others thought of him. He was what he was, for better or worse, and had an awful lot to show for it. She was touched and amused by the characteristic responses, in Hebrew of course, of these young Jews to all difficulties or problems, especially in the life of the country and even of the most overwhelming kind. "It's not a problem," they'd say, even when there was a huge problem. "It'll be good..." or "it will be OK" were typical responses. No one was denying reality; rather, they were expressing the belief that if there was a problem, they felt resilient and strong enough to deal with it. By dealing with it, they would also overcome. "It'll be good" was a shortcut for expressing faith and hope, rather than wishful thinking on their part. Another expression often heard was "there is no choice" or "we have no choice"—acknowledging that reality was often difficult and unpredictable. First one must be realistic, acknowledging the difficulty. Then one must deal with it, coping, and ultimately prevailing. This youthful philosophy was a potent cocktail of resilience, self-reliance, optimism, and a strong dash of faith. The concept of having "no choice" remains firmly rooted in the Israeli psyche and in the expressions and language used widely today. It is the mark of recognizing reality while at the same time staunchly reaffirming a commitment to move forward into the future; it is never to be interpreted as pessimistic, cynical, or fatalistic.

*The mood of the
Jewish community
toward the British
changed drastically
with the end of
World War II.
It was no accident…*

On the Day of Independence, May 14, 1948, everyone gathered at the Reali School.

Danny's mother, Aunt Esther, and me waiting for a bus to return from the annual pilgrimage to Danny's grave in Poria, July 1952.

Me, Father and Mother on holiday in Prodromos, Cyprus, 1947.

Above: Me, carrying groceries from Schwartzapfel's grocery store.
Opposite: We played Chinese checkers, a gift from Peter's former governess
Eleonore von Schaumburg, on the old battered balcony sofa all summer.

Above: My best friend Ora Yarkoni at Kibbutz Yad Mordechai, July 1952.
Opposite: With Mother on the beloved sofa.

Falling in love. The navy.
A ship called Aleph Sheshesrei.

FROM THIS POINT IN 1948, a purposeful but tense atmosphere permeated every aspect of my life. Reading provided great distractions. Immersing myself in books was one of the best imaginable escapes into an easier life, one where one's personal troubles were the most crucial, without having to be concerned about the country as a whole and one's responsibility to it. I avidly and emotionally read through some classics that were also among my mother's favorites, including *Pride and Prejudice* and *Jane Eyre*. My lifelong crushes on Mr. Darcy and Rochester stem from this time. How I longed for what came across to me as the peace and quiet of those people's lives. I, too, wanted from time to time to agonize over which path I should take a walk on, or what color ribbons I should use to refresh an old muslin dress. I remember that Boswell's *Life of Johnson* was being serialized in the London *Times*. I loved reading it and found that it, too, provided a marvelous escape from the ever-present feeling of that heavy sense of responsibility to the Land of Israel and to the Jewish people. Our new state seemed like a young child in need of constant protection and attention. Both my father and Dr. Biram at Reali emphasized patience, saying that it would take another hundred years before Israel could stand on its own feet. When Dr. Biram reminded us students that "Rome was not built in a day," it didn't sound like a cliché but quite real and applicable to our new state.

Changes were everywhere. Gone, of course, was any contact with the British; by then there had long been a general and pervasive feeling among the Jews of Haifa that the British were actively pro-Arab, and we began to have facts and evidence to substantiate it.

Curfews, shootings, and casualties took the place of our previous Scout meetings. Yet at the same time, despite the tensions and continuing assaults and agitation, my life as a 15-year-old was full and teeming with activities: I balanced schoolwork, always a preoccupation of mine and my parents (I had to have a private tutor for arithmetic as well as Arabic) with a full social life in my youth movement. I spent a great deal of time wondering which boy liked me or might actually be in love with me, assessing how serious and committed his intentions were. How I should behave and respond were weighty issues analyzed and talked over for hours with my girlfriends.

This ruminating over boys took quite a turn on June 29, 1949, when I met a 15-year-old American named Peter Rosenblatt. Peter had been invited to visit Israel by Chilik Weizman, an old family friend and brother of Israel's first president. Peter's father—his mother had died the previous year—felt comfortable accepting the invitation, as his brother, Judge Bernard Rosenblatt, one of America's earliest Zionists, and his Texas-born wife, Gertrude, a founder of Hadassah, lived half of each year in Haifa and promised to keep an eye on him. Gertrude let my mother know that Peter was interested in meeting some girls, but I learned later that it was really she who believed it was about time Peter meet a girl, so she actively introduced him around.

He appeared at our door one day with a gift of canned of peaches under his arm, sent all the way from Bloomingdale's in New York City in one of his aunt's weekly packages. My wise mother, nonchalantly and seemingly spontaneously, suggested that Peter and I go out for ice cream. From that June day we took our first walk downtown to the Snir Café on Herzl Street, and then on the walk back up the hill on Mountain Road to my house, I felt totally happy in Peter's company. Any time we crossed a Haifa street, I would go on talking without paying attention to the traffic because his hand was always at my elbow ushering me safely across. From that day on, little did I know that my future was being decided on.

Peter and I just back from the beach on our second date, 1949.

That first summer was especially magical. We talked all the time, simply and effortlessly, and laughed happily and easily. Our conversations ranged across a wide spectrum, from comparing 16-year-olds in Israel with those in America to discussing whether American capitalism was destined for failure. He told me all about American "dating," and I told him I found it all so artificial. Probably the most memorable of our talks took place one evening when we were sitting high up on Mount Carmel under a full moon and looking out over Haifa's harbor below us. The harbor was filled with ships and boats and more were out at sea, all sparkling like a diamond necklace. It was there that I told him in great detail the whole story of my cousin Danny. He never once interrupted. Then, Peter shared with me about his mother. That evening made us much closer.

We spent nearly every day together during those summer weeks, going to the beach, to the movies, and having supper with my parents at home. Peter would

Peter, age 15, on the beach in Haifa.

Me on the same beach on the same date in Haifa in 1949. Bathing suit compliments of a South African care package.

stay late, and when it got very late, we would hear my father calling out from the depths of the darkened bedroom in a sleepy, cranky voice, *"hasn't that boy left yet?"* Then my mother would come out in her dressing gown and slippers and gently say she thought it a good idea that Peter leave because it was late, and "Naomi will be too tired tomorrow." Peter listened to them good-naturedly, but left reluctantly. Since he stayed past the time that the last bus left, it meant that he'd have to walk up the steep hill to the Lev HaCarmel hotel where he stayed with his aunt. It was 45 minutes to an hour, all the way uphill! I knew he never walked that much in New York City.

Sometimes I would go to his hotel, either to meet Peter before we were going out or to pick up something, usually his camera. We would rush in from the street and skip two steps at a time going straight to his room. I loved to look at and touch all of his leather accessories, his slippers, camera, toilet bag; they exuded comfort and a sense of plenty, which neither I nor my peers were used to. We'd lean over the balcony and gaze at the Carmel woods, the cars and the people. I loved simply being there.

Peter had—and has—a clear, uncluttered mind and strong sense of self. He was then and remains perfectly natural, with no affectation and relaxed about how he feels about himself. He quickly gained the affection and respect of my friends, especially the boys. Despite his upbringing, which I only learned more about as we got to know each other, he was not spoiled and never pretentious. From the beginning, he seemed to be self-assured and self-possessed. In short, he charmed me. Happily, he charmed my mother, and thank goodness, my father too.

Me and Peter on a walk around Jerusalem, July 1952.

My friends and I at a summer working camp.

1949 Ein Zeitim—Peter and his tentmates during his first summer work camp in Israel. (He's back row, first on the left.)

Above: Summer work camp in the kibbutzim, Ora on the far left, me on the far right.
Opposite: Babysitting the kibbutz "littles."

*Among the most
vivid memories of
my youth are the
times I spent on
several kibbutzim…*

1947 in Kibbutz Alonim for summer camp, on the water tower.

The boys of our group during the summer of 1950 at Kibbutz Beeri. Peter is back row, second from right; Yossi is middle row, second from right.

Group photo at Ein Zeitim. Peter first row, fourth from right. I am second row third from left.

A hike in Galilee.

A hike in Galilee.

I had been planning a trip with my Scout group to Kibbutz Ein Zeitim in what was the barren landscape of northern Galilee, and Peter decided to join us at the suggestion of several of the boys. On the appointed day, when we were to leave Haifa, Peter appeared, rucksack and all, ready for the trip to what I imagined would be a very far cry from his own upbringing in the Plaza Hotel in New York City where his family had an apartment. After a dry and dusty journey, we tumbled out of the back of the open truck and found ourselves in what looked to me like a brand-new kibbutz. It had actually been settled earlier but its population had dwindled over the years since its original settlement. The kibbutz had been twice overrun during the 1948 war. We did not have running water for showers in the first few days. There was no shade and much sweating as we labored to put up the tents in which we were going to live and sleep. We girls washed up as best we could after the day's work and relaxed outside our tents. Peter actually strode over to my tent and sat down beside me, absolutely relaxed despite the bevy of girls surrounding us. From that first day on, we spent all of our free time together. Even at the time, I thought what new and delicious feelings I was experiencing. I remember thinking that I wished I could keep them in a locked box for the far-off future.

My father and Peter in Galilee.

The communal room, where we had our meals and often gathered, was a large one with rectangular tables and benches. Each table had a big bowl—a *kolboinik*—in the middle where the members would empty the scraps. People sat down or got up as they pleased. The girls wore sandals or ankle-high laced brown boots and short shorts, with aprons hanging down to their knees or tucked into the gathered elastic of their shorts. They passed by the tables with the trolleys carrying the food in large bowls filled with fresh vegetables such as tomatoes, cucumbers, and green peppers.

There was no pretense or formality or any sense of conventional manners. People came in straight from the fields with their *kova tembel*—a hat commonly worn by Israelis throughout the land—perched on top of their heads, dusty boots, tanned faces, arms and legs. I loved seeing the whiteness of their foreheads once they removed their hats.

The evenings were memorable, too, particularly one spent with Peter in which we sat and talked for what must have been hours. Under a clear, moonlit night sky, he described exactly where he would take me on my first trip to Europe and what he'd show me there. As usual, Peter was in earnest, but I somehow took it all in as a fantasy and didn't allow myself to put much store in it.

He and I took a long walk one night, heading to the ancient town of Safed, five kilometers away. We went to visit a war memorial (which I mention in the diary) that I considered sacred and was especially moved thinking of Danny. I distinctly recall thinking that Peter must feel himself to be a stranger there, out of place, alien to the war and to the fallen.

Peter and me during our first summer camp at Kibbutz Ein Zeitim.

We went to an old established restaurant, and I was sure Peter wasn't very impressed with the meal. Because of the severe rationing, there was no variety and few choices. I personally thought the food was great, so much so that I even remember what we had—some sort of thin soup, schnitzel, and a side dish of cucumber salad. Throughout the dinner, the waiter looked at us suspiciously and probably rightly so. We were an odd couple: both under 17; one very American, rather sophisticated and paying the bill; the other very Israeli, outwardly unsophisticated; both speaking in English, and obviously immersed in each other. Other diners, few as they were, were mostly middle-aged or older, so we presented quite a sight and a kind of mystery.

We walked back to the kibbutz along the winding hill road. It was a moonless evening, pitch black, and no traffic. The war was well over, but I was rather tense passing empty houses, thinking who knows who might leap out of them. We were very quiet the whole way back.

For the whole of that first summer's visit we remained inseparable, except during work and at night. I had had an emotional farewell with him—with lots of embracing (despite my objections) and a little chaste kissing, which I allowed only on the outer corner of my mouth—when he left the kibbutz to head back to Haifa and then to Europe to meet his father. However, I only had a day for my own thoughts when he burst back on the scene, saying he had missed his plane and gotten permission from his father to stay longer.

My whole scout group outside our truck at Solomon's Mines in the Negev on the way from Beeri to what would become Eilat.

After he did leave that summer, my friends and I were back at work, sitting on the haystack and chatting, when a postcard arrived from Peter from Gstaad, Switzerland, with a picture on it of the very fancy hotel where he was staying with his father, adorned with the royal name "The Palace." The kids all looked at the photo and Riva said, "Poor Peter, stuck in some hole in Europe!" Given that none of us had the faintest idea of what Gstaad was like or represented, we all nodded in agreement and in great sympathy for "poor Peter." We were quite sure he would have preferred to be with us on the haystack in Galilee.

Returning to Haifa, I did not leave the house for a few weeks. Nothing was of interest to me except, of course, imagining Peter's next visit in great detail; how he would be elated to be back in the country, how polite he would be when greeting my parents, and that we would then immediately retreat to my room for a few moments alone. He would want to kiss me and I would be shy after not seeing him for so many months. Once he left, I spent the rest of the summer waiting for the start of school.

The following summer, in 1950, Peter returned for a two-month stay. I didn't write much about that summer in my diary because I was so occupied being with him. But it, too, was memorable. At some point I recorded a few of the many highlights of our time together, especially the languid, lazy afternoons we spent together at my apartment, talking and talking even as it got dark, never seeming to notice the time slipping by and the day fading into night.

In July of that memorable summer, Peter joined me and my scout group at a work camp in Kibbutz Beeri in the Negev, close to the Gaza border. We'd climb up the bales of hay behind the kibbutz dining room and spend hours playing checkers and talking. We'd go for long walks and then, drowsy from the lateness of the hour, drop into the communal dining room—which served as a great gathering place—for the always-available masses of thick slices of dark bread, jars of jam, and pots of hot tea. We'd sit on one of the benches and ravenously devour this wonderful midnight snack.

Most days after work, supper and a shower, we'd rush up the narrow ladder to the very top of the watchtower/water storage tank, which, given its position, was the only place we knew we'd be away from other people. We began to regard that as "our" place. It was there that we had our first full real kiss. It was also there that he asked me to marry him. I answered him with the enigmatic and truthful: "I don't know what will be... ." I was being flirtatious, realistic and also coy, not wanting to give everything away at once but wanting to keep up his interest in me for some time to come. Peter never received a straight answer all that summer. I did, however, ask him repeatedly to say "I love you" in a Southern, drawn-out accent, which, although absolutely unfamiliar to my ears, always delighted and amused me.

At Hamachtesh Hagadol in the Negev with (from left to right) Reuven, Ruth B., Ruth N., Arza, Ora and Yossi.

At the end of our work camp, the kibbutz gave us the use of a truck and we all went down through the Negev to the vacant beach at the northern tip of the Gulf of Aqaba which would become the city of Eilat, now a teeming resort. It is a landscape of whites and pale yellows. At the place where our truck pulled up, there was only one tap of dripping water set up by the Army for that whole vast area. It came out only in a small drizzle, but our truck full of people waited patiently in line. We all had a

The water tower in Beeri where Peter and I sought some privacy.

wonderful time splashing in the Gulf. Peter had a moment of showing off a special talent when he would bend his leg in such a way as to prove that he could put his big toe in his mouth. Much giggling ensued, all while trying to balance ourselves in the water. The big-toe business, for all its insanity, was endearing to me because it was a

Playing in 1950 at the northern tip of the Gulf of Aqaba which would become the city of Eilat, now a resort.

Peter and I sitting on my apartment's parapet, summer 1951.

reflection of the fact that, despite his worldly travels and cosmopolitan air, he still retained some of the innocence and flexibility of a young child.

During many of our conversations that summer I nagged him for more and more stories and details about his family, his brothers, sister-in-law and governess, to whom he referred as "Fraulein Eleonore von Schaumburg." It was she who had given him the leather travelling box, made by Mark Cross, with little compartments for checkers, chess, cards, and tiddlywinks—all of which we played that summer, but especially checkers. I found the leather-bound box, with its neat compartments, to be the epitome of luxury and aesthetic design.

Some of our conversations toward the end of our time together that summer were tinged with sadness, especially when we discussed Peter's future plans and dreams. The sadness came in part because of the feeling that it wasn't possible for me to have a part in them. We never discussed, promised, or asked each other for fidelity. We lived so far apart, and felt we couldn't make demands of one another, but for my part at least, the idea of infidelity by the other was horribly painful. In short, though, that summer was simply a perfect holiday for a 17-year-old girl.

Peter did indeed return in the summer of 1951. At 18, I had just graduated from Reali and Peter had finished his first year at Yale. Together again, we spent our carefree days, with much laughter, hitchhiking around the country and visiting my aunts in Tel Aviv and Jerusalem.

For me, the immediate years after Independence consisted of agonizing over national obligations and personal life decisions, all of which made for a life full of meaning and purpose, as well as intense, painful and unavoidable conflict. The biggest conflict centered on my youth movement's decision that we would perform our national duty by going out on the land to a brand-new kibbutz called Tel Katzir at the southern end of the Sea of Galilee. As my diary will attest, I had grown so close to Peter that I was at sixes and sevens about what to do. My concern for my relationship with him took precedence over the expectation that I would go out for two years to Tel Katzir. Although I was deeply conflicted, I decided instead of the kibbutz to fulfill my national service by joining the navy. I knew I would be stationed in Haifa, where seeing Peter when he came to visit on college breaks and holidays would be much easier. Even at this point in our relationship, I clearly did not want to risk losing him.

In Bat Galim in my naval uniform.

My scout group did go on to kibbutz Tel Katzir as part of Nahal, a program that combined military service with establishing new agricultural settlements. Ora and Rafi, by then her boyfriend, went, as did most of my close friends. Of course I felt torn and thought I should have joined them, and I spent hours brooding about what to do. The decision I made was solely my choice. Neither Peter nor my parents were consulted nor did they have any input. Despite my strong sense of loyalty to my group and duty to my country, I picked what felt right for me. Was it a selfish, self-serving decision? To a few of my friends it was absolutely so, for others not. At some point, I realized that my feelings pointed clearly toward Peter. I was continuously focused on his next visit. Peter was my true north. I decided on the navy so I could stay in Haifa and make it easier for us to be together.

Off I went, first through basic training in Sarafand, which had previously been a British military camp situated on the road to Jerusalem, near Ramle. I was not crazy about this camp—not because I found it strenuous, but because it was a different type of discipline from the one I was used to in school or in the Scouts. It was a lot more arbitrary and impersonal. Our sergeant was a small, roly-poly woman with a snub nose who took herself very seriously. The uniform given to me was a few sizes too large, and I felt I looked like Charlie Chaplin, which, because we were all girls, didn't matter except to me. However, we soon discovered that across from our camp a paratrooper course was in full swing. We'd see the young men through the fence, training and learning how to safely fall to the ground when parachuting. One of them took a fancy to me. We'd talk after supper with the fence between us as dusk fell. He said he'd grown up in England, and in fact, we talked in English because he hardly spoke any Hebrew. His English sounded peculiar to me. For all I know, it might have been a strong regional English accent. He'd try to get in touch with me during the day, too, all through the fence that separated us, and to the great amusement of the rest of the girls, but I made myself inaccessible. I did not want him to see me too clearly in my Chaplinesque outfit, under the scrutiny of the brilliant sun.

He was striking in the paratrooper uniform. We managed to sneak out of camp a few times. It was cool and dark, and he would show me into one of the airplanes from which he jumped. I trembled the whole time because I knew we were breaking military rules. His conversation was simple, his behavior gentle and reserved.

At our farewell party from the training camp, we made up poems for each other about our life in camp. For me, the girls paraphrased paragraphs from the Bible, out of the "Song of Songs," some of which went: "I raise my eyes to the heavens, from where my Paratrooper will descend" and "Here he comes, skipping over hills and dales, barbed wires and fences." Once I got home, he visited me a few times, we went to the movies, and the relationship slowly faded away, much to the relief of my parents.

For the rest of my service, I was assigned to work at the naval cadet training camp at Bat Galim in Haifa, right at the foot of Mount Carmel on the Mediterranean coast, so close to home that I actually slept there. I'd leave my house every morning at 6:00 a.m. Mother stood on the balcony watching me until I disappeared down the hill. I walked down all those hundreds of steps to the German Colony and waited for the bus to take me to Bat Galim. My uniform was wonderfully washed, ironed and starched, thanks to the ever-available Harris laundry (my mother), and my shoes were polished. I knew I looked good in the naval uniform—all the girls did—but I was self-conscious about the required

sailor hat, with its ribbon at the back. The hat was supposed to be worn low on the forehead. Because I felt it made me look ugly and hard and emphasized the frown line between my eyes, I would tilt the hat until it settled at the back of my head, which I took to be a lot more attractive. No sooner would I pass the threshold of the naval camp when I'd be stopped by the military police, pointing to my hat. This infraction of military rules was a running sore throughout my national service for which I was punished many times, often being grounded during precious weekends. However, vanity transcended my sense of obedience.

Wearing my naval uniform in Bat Galim, Haifa, 1951.

Shaul Avni, the major or captain (I can't remember which) in charge of me, always wore a pleasant expression. He was a very decent, mild-mannered man who treated me with respect and reserve. His forehead was slightly lined, and I felt there were burdens in his personal life to which I was not privy. He must have been in his late 20s or early 30s, but to me he seemed older. He'd call his wife during the day and before he went home. He did not relegate any heavy tasks to me but took care of all of those himself.

In due time, I was sent to a typing course, where I learned very little. Once I had supposedly mastered the art of typing—I was hopeless at it—I was sent to work as a secretary on the training ship *Aleph 16* (A-16) anchored in the Port of Haifa. Rumor had it that the ship was originally an ice cutter donated by generous American Jews. During my time in the navy, the ship never left port. I'd leave the house before dawn as usual, but instead of going to Bat Galim, I'd take the bus to the port. The port was bustling, full of sailors, both Israeli and foreign. Many ships flew foreign flags. It was all new, intriguing and adventurous.

Once I walked through the gates of the port, past all those foreign ships, I felt as if I had entered the lion's den. The walk to my own ship seemed endless alongside those foreign ships with their sailors everywhere, constantly washing and repainting the sides of their ship while suspended on ropes. Whistles and cheerful comments came from all sides as I passed by. I never dared look up or

make eye contact but kept my eyes straight ahead, my sailor's hat firmly at the back of my head regardless of the disciplinary consequences. Relieved, I'd finally get to my ship, with its familiar Israeli sailors and cadets. I served on a ship full of men, the only woman among them, reminding me of the phrase in the Talmud that likened the children of Israel to "a lamb amongst seventy wolves," which I applied to myself in this quite different situation.

I worked in a tiny cubbyhole and would have been bored to death had there not been a constant flow of visitors in and out of my very small office. One of the cadets who'd pop in unexpectedly for short conversations had been a few classes ahead of me in school. Dark hair, dark eyes, a handsome pale brow, and loads of self- confidence, he would make his visit known by unexpectedly picking up my chair—with me in it—and cheerfully asking how I was. Before responding, I'd make it clear that I wanted the chair put down immediately. He'd put me down and then hoist himself onto my desk and we'd talk and laugh. Then he'd disappear until the next time. People felt free to pop into my cabin for short or long chats, some of which were mere teasing back and forth while others were serious and even quite personal.

My head was all the while full of Peter. He wrote me nearly every day. I was not as diligent, and found it difficult to write a letter in fluent English without doing a draft first, which meant some self-conscious writing with bits of input from my mother. Although I didn't permit myself to get attached to anybody else, to be in the navy without one or two admirers seemed out of the question. One was a naval cadet, a sabra, stocky, wholesome, direct, and awfully nice. He took the cadet course seriously and did well in it. He knew about Peter right from the start but never gave up. He once gave me an embroidered Yemenite blouse for a present. I brought it home and my father was furious. He was sure I had sold my soul to the devil in exchange for that blouse. I knew I should feel guilty but wasn't altogether sure about what, but it's telling that when Peter visited my naval camp, I did not introduce them.

The other boy was in an electronics course. I think he was Swiss or French and had come to Israel not long before I met him. I remember only that there was something sad and vulnerable about him, possibly because of a difficult childhood during the war in Europe. There were so many like him, uprooted, orphaned, and young. He was tall and very thin, with deep-set blue-green eyes, and a noticeable French accent. Jean and I ate our meals side by side in the large dining hall. He was marvelous company, well-educated and worldly. Our conversations covered a large array of subjects with lots of teasing and laughter. He knew about Peter's place in my life. I knew all along that Jean was not the man I could commit myself to for the rest of my life.

Once when I was confined to the barracks as a result of another dress code disobedience relating to my sailor hat, Jean asked me to go for a walk within the base. We did. He suddenly blurted out that he loved me—I had carefully avoided ever getting close to that subject—and wanted to kiss me. I knew that what he wanted was not out of place, and I also knew, only then and there that I should have made an excuse and not gone for the walk in the first place. I knew full well it would be wrong for me to comply with his request. After all, I was not in love with him and never would be. Furthermore, and above all, things were very serious with Peter and me. How could I kiss anybody other than Peter? Especially as I never had up to that point? When I moved away, ever so slowly, he lost his patience with me and became furious. He caught my wrist with his hands and it felt as if by a pair of pliers. I felt a sharp pain but also felt I deserved it. He let go of my wrist with what I felt was disdain and never talked to me again. He was right, and I still feel guilty about the whole episode and misleading him.

He appeared at our door one day with a gift of canned peaches under his arm, sent all the way from Bloomingdale's in New York City in one of his aunt's weekly packages…

Peter and I walking in Haifa on Herzl Street in 1951 before my navy service. Peter is carrying his ever-present newspaper.

Peter and I near Crusader Fort in Athlit on our second date, June 1949.

Peter and I outside of the Persian Gardens across from the apartment.

Eating "sabras," the fruit of the cactus, in Kibbutz Harel, near Jerusalem. L–R: Peter, me, Neri, and her brother Yerri.

My mother's sister Aunt Mary in Tel Aviv with Peter and me, summer 1951.

Colonel Hammel took me aside and asked: "Why do you have to marry an American? Aren't there enough nice Israeli boys?"

Opposite: The first "selfie"—Peter (in the popular Russian shirt) and I taking a photo of ourselves.

Friends in the navy base in Bat Galim.

Navy cadets and me.

A disastrous facial on the way to the wedding canopy.

At the end of 1951. Peter saved up the maximum number of cuts he could take from classes at Yale and returned to Israel in advance of his Christmastime vacation. I was up every morning at 5:30 a.m. to get ready to go to work. Peter, on the other hand, slept later and would come to the naval camp at lunchtime each day and we'd meet outside the gate. We'd walk to a small restaurant next to the sea in the neighborhood of Bat Galim. Because of *tzena*, the continuing austerity measures, his special tourist coupons were very welcome. We were usually the only people in the restaurant. The proprietor fixed us a table in the garden and I knew he wondered about us, especially about me and what kind of girl I was. The weather that December was clear, crisp, and lovely. We could see the Mediterranean from where we sat. Peter insisted on holding my hand for all to see on top of the table, and being unabashedly affectionate and demonstrative. The menu was exactly the same every single day. Hot delicious meat broth with a couple of noodles floating around, a salad of cut-up tomatoes, parsley, and cucumbers, and cold, dark pink plum soup for desert. After the lunch, which I thoroughly enjoyed, we'd stroll a little by the sea, hand in hand, and then hurry back to the camp for me to be on time. I must say, I felt a little uncomfortable about leaving my navy friends to go off with Peter for a private lunch. I never discussed with anybody where or what I had done during lunch. They knew I was with Peter, whom they knew by then was my boyfriend, and that we were planning to get married. Peter wanted me to wear the engagement ring he gave me, and he described himself as my fiancé. Even at the time and despite being very much in love, I was mortified when he used the fancy term "fiancé," and I chose not to wear the engagement ring while I was serving in the navy. One officer, Colonel Hammel, took me aside one day and asked, "Why do you have to marry an American? Aren't there enough nice Israeli boys?"

Eating a sumptuous lunch in the midst of rationing at our table in a restaurant near the navy base in Bat Galim, Haifa, 1951.

Peter and I took a few days off and went to Tel Aviv. As a joke, he bought me a cheap copper wedding band, which I wore on the trip. On the way back to Haifa, just as we were stepping out of the *sherut* shared taxi, the driver shouted to me in Hebrew, "You better take off that ring before your mother catches you and spanks you!" I loved that!

Peter and his mother Therese Steinhardt Rosenblatt in the Villa d'Este in northern Italy in 1947, some months before her death.

Peter and I on our wedding day, July 1, 1952.

As we grew even closer and the prospect of marriage became more of a reality, I had so many thoughts about Peter. Our upbringings were so very different. Until the age of eight, he had grown up on Park Avenue; then because his mother, Therese, fell ill, his father moved the family to the Plaza Hotel. He attended Riverdale Country School, and later went on to Yale. He complained a lot about New York's materialism, the Junior League, and the spoiled, indulgent, rich New York City girls of his age and he rebelled against the exclusive dancing classes he took with the renowned Viola Wolf.

Peter was well brought up, a proud American from a family deeply involved for generations in politics, public service, law and business. Though his parents were entirely committed Jews, acknowledging major Jewish holidays much in the manner of other secular New York Jews, they gave Peter no religious education.

Little did anyone imagine that that first innocent trip by a 15-year-old visitor would lead to a love affair and a lifelong relationship—certainly this was beyond what my mother and father were thinking, as my diary reveals. But I very quickly came to know the essence of Peter and to know what a fundamentally decent person he was—and is. I remember even thinking to myself that if he ever "wandered off the reservation" or found himself attracted to another woman, he would handle it discreetly and not blame me and leave the family, but rather see it as his responsibility and deal with it. I knew at 15 that he was the type of man who, if my face became disfigured in an accident or by acid thrown at me, he would not walk away.

Marrying Peter was a natural. There was nobody else either before or after I would have preferred. One of his outstanding qualities was clarity of thinking. Another was tact, also a characteristic that had been extolled by Mother. Never did he mention to me or to my friends anything about his own standard of living, which turned out to be such a contrast to mine, especially when compared to the austerity and rationing of the war years that we were living through. The only telltale signs of his life in New York were his leather accessories from Mark Cross and his total sense of comfort in looking into a café's glass case and ordering without a moment's hesitation what to me were extravagant choices—delicious rich chocolate cakes and marzipans, iced coffee with lots of whipped cream swirling on top. He always paid for our treats. I never had any cash on me except change for the bus. Because Peter was a foreign visitor, he was not subjected to the rationing that we endured in Palestine under the British Mandate, during World War II and in Israel after the War of Independence. He lived in the Lev HaCarmel hotel when he visited Israel and he would bring my parents and me chocolates and tea, leather shoe laces and soles. Once he even brought us frozen steaks.

So many factors were in Peter's favor. First and foremost, he was Jewish, which implied a broad, shared common denominator of loyalties, concerns, culture, history, and values. My parents respected his character, conduct, and tenacity and therefore trusted him. Peter was always and still is affectionate—I treasure that. Many years later, when my father was quite old and I had gone to visit him, I asked him what he thought about my marriage to Peter. He answered without hesitation, "Peter brought everything to the marriage."

"And what did I bring?" I asked.

"Identity," he replied.

I went away feeling bewildered and do not know till today what to make of his reply, wishing he would have been more explicit.

I'm sure my devoted parents must have suffered some anxiety when they realized I would be going thousands of miles away, especially at a time when air travel was prohibitively expensive and they were not, as my mother often commented, "moneyed people." Email had not been dreamed of and we had not yet acquired a telephone. They must have decided to take the risk and support our decision to marry; never did they reveal to me a shadow of doubt. I don't know what Peter's father William thought.

Very early in the morning of the day before our wedding, I dressed to the nines to meet Peter's father, his brother Rob, who was 11 years older than Peter, and Rob's wife, Helene. His brother Dick, seven years older, who was serving as a pilot in the U.S. Air Force in Germany, could not come. I put on my spanking white navy uniform, sailor's hat and all, but as we left Haifa on our way to the airport in Chilik Weizman's jeep, it sputtered and came to a sudden stop. We jumped off the jeep, leaving Chilik waiting for help on the hot and windy road, to hitchhike a ride to the airport. A rattling old cement truck stopped for us and we hopped on. By the time we appeared before Peter's family at the airport, my white uniform was dark grey spattered with cement dust and I was windblown and worse for the wear, to say the least. What a way to meet one's future father-in-law for the first time, as well as my glamorous future sister-in-law and her husband fresh from their holiday on the French Riviera. Due to our youth we took it all in stride and have been chuckling about it ever since.

I was never privy to Peter's discussions with his father about his proposed marriage, and Peter did not share them with me. I did not probe, nor was I particularly curious or concerned. At the time, Peter didn't seem to be perturbed, so why should I be? I discovered much later that he had written long and logical arguments to his father in favor of the marriage, but I remain amazed that he was not stopped from getting married at such a young age. He had a relationship of trust and respect with his father, and for his father's enduring love for his mother, Therese, who had died in 1948, when Peter was 14. Possibly, Peter's dad felt that she would have been in favor of her son's choice.

Somehow it never once occurred to me that marriage might mean leaving Israel for good. Never. It never struck me that I was going so far away and for so long. I simply did not think it through. All I knew was that I was going with Peter—safe, secure, and loved—and we were heading into our future together. At a certain point I turned to my mother and said, "Mummy, you don't have to worry about me anymore. I'll be okay." I felt I was giving her a gift.

Peter and I were married in Haifa on July 1, 1952. Because I was so preoccupied with my duties in the navy, for the most part I was oblivious to the wedding plans. Women were permitted to be discharged from their military duty when they married. It was only later that I was told that my mother was concerned I would not have enough time for personal matters between my discharge from the navy and the wedding. Out of the blue very early one morning, she called the wife of the head of the Israeli Navy, Commander Mordechai Limon, affectionately known as Mokah. After having commanded several ships that had helped to smuggle stateless Jews into the Land of Israel, at only 26 years old, Mokah had been named Commander of the Navy. It's incredible to think that he was only seven years older than I was.

In any case, Mother had once met his wife, Rachel, at a friend's house and had no compunction phoning her. Mother told her that her daughter was getting married in two weeks and that she herself, as mother of the bride, would very much appreciate it if I could be discharged a week early because she was afraid that otherwise "Naomi would be too tired and look exhausted" at the wedding. Mrs. Limon got back to my mother to say that her husband, the Commander, had granted our request and wished the family *mazal tov*. All this was transacted between the two women on Dr. Matzdorf's telephone, unbeknownst to me or to Peter. Of course, this transaction took place in 1952, when the state was very young; I'm not sure that the possibility of looking droopy at one's nuptials would be sufficient today for an early discharge from the Israeli Navy.

Because austerity was still in effect, with shortages everywhere and little to buy in the shops —and with my parents maintaining their vow not to touch the black market—Peter had gone to Best & Company department store in New York with his sister-in-law, Helene, and bought my wedding dress, veil, shoes, and stockings. He added a blue Yale garter, and—to my great amusement—he showed me what to do with it. He brought everything with him to Haifa.

A couple of days before the wedding, I was dispatched to the apartment of a Romanian lady living a few doors away to get a facial. Romanian and Hungarian ladies were supposed to possess the secrets of feminine beauty. Both Peter and I giggled at the very idea, but my mother and Aunt Esther insisted. The woman first dunked my face in a tiny sink with boiling hot water and then massaged it with freezing cubes of ice. When my face was as red as a beetroot, it was patted dry and the Romanian cosmetician, bending over me with her whole bulk, covered my

My mother (L) and her very best friend Sara Salomon.

Wearing my wedding dress and veil, brought to Israel by Peter from New York, with my parents.

face with white talcum powder. From a flaming red face, I turned chalk white. After what seemed like ages, I was let go. Freed from captivity, I remember jumping down two steps at a time from her third floor flat and rushing home to Peter and my mother and father. My 18-year-old soon-to-be husband was speechless at my appearance, clearly thinking I looked better before the facial than after. My father said nothing, and my mother was tactful and reassuring at the same time.

In order to get the essential marriage certificate signed by the Rabbinate, I was supposed to have written proof that I had been to the *mikveh*, or ritual bath. Had I been consulted, I would have gone voluntarily. My mother, however, felt differently—and strongly so, although I never bothered to find out why. Without my knowledge she marched up to the Haifa Rabbi and told him that only over her dead body would her daughter go to the *mikveh*. An argument ensued. At that point, with me in tow, my mother, glaring at the Rabbi, asked him how long he had been in the country. When he said five years, she retorted that she had settled in the country in the 1920s, way before him, and he was therefore in no position to dictate to her what to do. Being a wise Rabbi, he must have realized what a force of passion he was dealing with. He signed the necessary document without further ado.

Peter and I got married as the sun was setting, in a lush garden at the home of my mother's best friend, Sara Salamon, at 87 Sea Road on the Western Carmel. The house was an excellent example of the Bauhaus architectural style. Dark red bougainvillea, in full bloom, seemed to be everywhere. It was a simple and lovely ceremony. The rabbi, of Czech origin, was a dignified-looking man with a grey beard and a high forehead. Ezer Weizman, a future Air Force commander and President of Israel, my cousin's husband, Haim, and two friends from school and the navy held the *chuppah*, our wedding canopy. I walked around Peter seven times for each of the seven blessings, and he broke the glass with great gusto. My navy friends, school friends, and our families were all there, as was Sara Salamon's daughter Ronnie, and Tamara Levin, who to this day remain among my very closest friends whom I love. Few people traveled to Israel in those days, and so no one from Peter's more extended family came, nor friends of his family.

Right after the wedding, we were put into a taxi and dispatched to House Cohen, a very quiet, elegant German Jewish pension in the pretty seaside town of Nahariya, in Western Galilee north of Haifa. We really would rather have stayed with everybody in Haifa and did not yearn for the privacy and tranquility of a highly regimented German type of pension. However, we did what we were told. I, the bride, crouched the whole way to Nahariya at the bottom of the taxi. I was so embarrassed, lest anybody see me riding in an "extravagant" private taxi. The next day we cancelled our reservations and hurried home to my parents to view the wedding gifts. It was two in the afternoon, and we were inconsiderate enough to wake my mother from her afternoon nap. Mummy, Daddy, Peter, and I settled down on the balcony with tea and the ubiquitous chocolate cake to look over the wedding gifts.

We stayed on in Israel for another month, visiting Tel Aviv and Jerusalem and enjoying a carefree time together. In Jerusalem we stayed at the Salvia Hotel where the proprietor refused to give us a room until we called my Uncle Tommy, resplendent in the uniform of a senior police officer, to vouch for the fact that we were indeed legally married and not living in sin.

When, at age 19 and newly married, I moved to the United States, I took with me my favorite Yemenite blouse with its delicate red embroidery, a flowered cotton skirt, a pretty white cotton blouse with a scooped neckline, two paperbacks of poetry (one by Ibn Gevirol, an 11th-century Jewish poet and philosopher living in Spain, and another by Chaim Bialik, who came to be recognized as Israel's national poet), my songbook, and my Bible. These few items were hugely significant to me. My school Bible, with its pages upon pages of interpretations, was first in importance. Second was my *shiron*, or songbook, where I had meticulously written out by hand (over more than 60 pages) all of the songs of my youth. As for the poetry books, although I hardly ever reread them, somehow they were a comfort to me. These few items were the only tangible evidence of my first 19 years, of my family and of Israel. And they were all essentially without significance to my new relatives and friends to whom Israel, its people and lifestyle—an integral part of my being—were largely unknown. These belongings, mainly my books, along with the values ingrained in me by my parents and Reali, seemed to sum up who I was.

They accompanied me as I went forward into my new life in a new and unknown land—new family, friends, and customs—all the way to the waiting Rosenblatt clan at the family apartment in the Plaza Hotel in New York City, and then on to New Haven and life with Peter at Yale in the early fifties. These few belongings stayed with me in my new life and are with me still.

I was confident and ready to follow my 18-year-old husband anywhere in the world. Had he said we're off to Ghana rather than America, I would have followed him without a second thought and started teaching Hebrew and the Bible in Ghana. I trusted Peter and I trusted myself, and I was confident about the two of us together.

Little did anyone imagine that the first innocent trip by a 15–year–old visitor would lead to a love affair & a life–long relationship…marrying Peter was a natural.

Opposite: Wedding day.

156

L-R: My boss Lt. Col. Shaul Avni, a senior officer, me, and base commander Captain Harel.

Part of the wedding party. Front: My cousin Ruthi and her husband Chaim to the left. Second row, L–R: Peter's father, my father, me, my mother, Peter, Aunt Esther, Uncle Tommy, and my cousin David to the back.

Above: The one outfit I took to the USA—standing outside the entrance to my apartment building with my mother.
I wonder what she was feeling. Opposite: One of the last "snapshots" before leaving Israel.

6.6.47.

THE DIARIES

Part II

עץ עם עצמי.

יער חיים של נער יאיר בינו.

(סיפורים על ד"ר אליעזר פרוינד
"אלוף").

6.6.47   חיפה.

אלוף – ישראל.

With Myself

A year since the death of the 14 on the A-Ziv Bridge

June 6, 1947

Our Scout group met. The meeting was dedicated to the memory of those who
fell at the A-Ziv Bridge. They read to us of the lives of the fallen. Ahuva, our
petite, hazel-eyed counselor, told it to us in such a way that none of us felt like
playing afterward.

She also recounted to us that she and her group in the Scouts were riding a bus
by the A-Ziv Bridge a month after the tragedy. A young man rode the bus with
them. He was lively and talkative the whole way. As they approached the bridge, he
quieted down until he seemed paralyzed. A member of the group asked if he was
all right. The young man then told them that he too was at the bridge that night.
His duty was to guard the area, and that his best friend fell that night.

I was so struck by the story that I felt I had to write it down and not let the
memory fade away. My mother had bought the newspaper with the account, and
we both wept over it during supper.

That afternoon when I returned from the Scout meeting, I sat in the bus
in the front of fat Miriam Kempner. Miriam and her friend were on their way
home from their English High School. (She's as English as I am Hottentot!)
Both girls were laughing and giggling in English. I was still very sad. When she
turned around and asked me why I was so sad, I ignored her. I wished that one
of the brave fallen young men would get up and take his revenge of her, for her
arrogance at laughing and giggling so loudly in English on such a tragic day!

Opposite: Original title page of my first diary in Hebrew, entitled "With Myself."

JUNE 10, 1947

We had a Scout meeting in which a short story by the author Bar-Yosef was read to us. The story is about a woman, a clerk, who was named "Sara the telephone operator." She was abandoned by her husband in her sixth month of pregnancy. The boy that was born to her was named Uri. The author's description of Uri rings so true that I savored every word.

Bar-Yosef describes Uri as an honest-to-goodness *tzabar*[1] and focuses on the mother's admiration for her son—his strong body, his strength of character, and his suntan.[2] The story ends with Uri getting killed while helping on a refugee boat. I was shaken by the ending and especially as the mother could not reach her son, so as not to awaken the suspicion of the British authorities. He was thus buried as an unknown soldier.

After the story we were tested in Morse code. A young boy by the name of Yehezkel tested us. I giggled throughout the test, dying to irritate him. (By the way, the same writer also wrote *A Meeting in Spring*, to my mind a wonderful book.)

JUNE 11, 1947

I'm in the middle of an arithmetic class and my mind is wandering. I feel like writing. Since the arrival of the new boy on the block, many things have changed. Daniel is a nice boy, and good-hearted. He also is far from being ugly. I have noticed that since his arrival I've been going out in the yard much more. All of us congregate on Friday night after the Sabbath dinner on the sidewalk, sitting on the low stone wall under the street lamp. Because of Friday night, we are better dressed and groomed than the rest of the week. We play, talk, and sometimes use bad language. Each one of us thinks Daniel is in love with her because he compliments and flatters one a great deal. (Maybe he is used to this kind of relationship between boys and girls on Mount

[1] A term for a prickly pear cactus—which is spiny on the outside but has sweet pulp on the inside—from which the word *sabra* derived. After the 1948 War of Independence, sabras appeared as cultural heroes in song, poetry, and theater. Sabra remains today a generic term for the native-born Israeli.
[2] His suntan is referring to his work in the fields.

Carmel—his previous neighborhood.) Anyway, that is the impression he gives. After much thinking I've decided that is simply his nature, and not to take it seriously.

Once Miriam told me that she told Daniel that she had something confidential to tell him. So his answer was "what is it?" "Is it something about my being in love with Naomi?" I did not know whether to take that information seriously, if I should be happy or not. However, I have noticed and think that he's in love with Esther. He behaves that way, and furthermore they correspond. This disappoints me very much and also hurts me. It always works out that people fall in love with Esther. However, I cannot be jealous, because after all I am not in love with him.

Esther is my best friend in the neighborhood. She is a class ahead of me, therefore we don't socialize at school and only acknowledge each other furtively at the bus stop on our way home. We spend time together nearly every afternoon after we have finished our homework. We talk and talk and talk.

Esther is immensely attractive, and if I were a boy I'd fall in love with her too. She is petite and graceful in her movements. She is the most graceful of dancers and learns the new steps right away. She laughs a lot, which is contagious, and all of us in the neighborhood recognize the sound of her laugh. Her skin is flawless, and she has long reddish-brown loosely braided hair that reaches down to her waist. She tosses her braids around as she talks. The braids dart back and forth over her shoulders, like two lively fawns. We tell each other our most personal secrets. We bought our first bras together. She was so afraid of telling her mother, that she didn't take it off for a whole month, till it became green in color. The size we got was 0 plus, on Pevzner Street. My mother found out (there is no privacy in my life) and wondered if I was fast becoming a tart.

Esther got a letter from Ora L. In it, she invites both of us to go to Tel Aviv. Esther has gotten permission to go, and I'm allowed to go, on condition that I stay at my Aunt Mary's.

I am so happy and so excited. My mother is having a dress sewn for me especially for the trip. That evening, unexpectedly, Daniel appears and asks Esther and me when we are leaving on the trip to Tel Aviv. He and his friend are planning the same trip and would like to go with us. I could hardly believe it. I was not able to sleep one wink that whole night. I spent the entire night planning. I decided in the middle of the night that in the bus between Haifa and Tel Aviv they would sit in front of us, so that they would have to keep turning their heads back when we talked, and maybe get a crook in their neck, and not us. Daniel also said that his friend Ehud was coming on the trip and wanted to meet Esther and me. Seeing that the next day would be the special day of *malkosh*[3] and we all had a day off from school, we decided to go to the beach together.

Both Esther and I giggled that our first meeting with Ehud would be in bathing suits—very partially clad. I was not very happy about that prospect because of the poor condition my bathing suit was in—it was all out of shape. The bones shaping the bra went in all directions except the right ones. However, Esther fixed the bones of the bra, more or less, by reshaping them. She's very handy.

Today I got my swimmer's license. I swam the length of the Bat Galim pool nine times, and at the end I had no more strength.

JUNE 12, 1947

Esther and I got to the bus station and waited for Daniel and Ehud. When they arrived, I had to blush and laugh quietly to myself. Why, I don't know.

At last the two of them appeared. The first impression was definitely bad! Ehud appeared as a *yekke*.[4] He wore sunglasses and rubber-soled shoes. We met each other by shaking hands. The next impression was far better. Ehud was really nice and so polite. When we climbed the steep steps onto the bus, I could not help feeling how grown up we'd become because the two boys stood back to let us on first. The whole way I was smiling inwardly. As we were nearing our stop we were constantly planning trips on the *Yarkon*,[5] going to the sea and to the cinema.

Ehud is very rich and was given two pounds to spend on himself. Daniel, poor boy, saves every penny.

Esther and I wore our towels around our neck, all because of my shapeless bathing suit. Ehud really amazed Esther and me when he asked if he could bring along another girl on the trip!! Esther and I hoped that Ora, our hostess

---

3   From Deuteronomy 11:13–14, this essentially refers to the rain that falls just before the harvest time.

4   *Yekke*—a German Jew, a new immigrant. The German Jews were known as *yekkes*. They dressed more formally than the sabras. Even in the heat of summer they wore jackets— *jacken* in German, from which the term *yekkes* derived.

5   Yarkon—a river that forms a long coastal waterway, running from the port of Tel Aviv through the town to the sea.

in Tel Aviv, would not be getting her period while we were there, so that we would not be stopped from carrying out all our strenuous plans.

I'm embarrassed to write this down, but I think Gideon Schwartz is in love with me. On the bus trip to Bat-Galim the other day, he chose to sit on the seat in front of me when there was plenty of room next to the boys. Our eyes kept meeting all the time.

In the evening, when I was terribly tired after having spent one day after the other on the hot, exposed beach, there was a sudden knock on the door and Arza appeared. My heart sank like a stone. My mother was not at home. My father and I were supposed to have supper together and I knew that Arza's spontaneous visit at supper time would not sit well with my father and that he would not handle his irritation with her gracefully.

It was seven in the evening. We had not eaten yet. I knew that Arza would be shocked if we did not ask her to join us, and there simply was not enough prepared food for the three of us.

The following scene took place: My father, Arza, and I were in the dining room. I, trying desperately to sound nonchalant, told my father that Arza would join us for supper. He, instead of being good-natured (as her father would have been) and inviting her to join us, muttered in a very cranky voice, "but not the other one, too?" [The reference was to her brother Uri who was supposed to join her.] At that moment I wished the earth would have swallowed me. Arza understood what was going on and declined to eat with us. Nevertheless, I fixed her a sandwich. Uri joined us later. The rest of the evening was heavy and I felt so awful.

JUNE 13, 1947

I feel that I am writing in my diary too consistently. But I feel that every day is of immense importance! I try to be grown up about it, and only record the important happenings. But the real happenings have not happened as yet.[6]

I'm also anxious about the upcoming report card. I'm going to get mediocre marks in Arabic and English—and that won't do. In English, I don't care. I hate the teacher. He never addresses a single question toward me.

---

[6] What I'm really referring to is that as yet I had not heard a boy's confession of love.

Last night I couldn't help it. I blurted out to Mummy what happened when Arza visited me last night, and Daddy's rude behavior. I'm afraid it hurt her, but it leaped out of me.

JUNE 14, 1947

This morning we were deep into reading "The Male & Female" and "Human Sexuality." We giggled quite a bit and there were sections that made me want to throw up. On the other hand, there were sections that touched me—the fact that the man must treat the woman tenderly, and what an important, serious occasion is the loss of virginity.

At dusk as I was walking up the hill on my way home with Nitza, we bumped into Esther, Danny, and Ehud on their way to the Hadar.[7] I felt a little hurt that they had not invited me, too, but after all I had been at the Scouts' meeting.

In the house opposite us, the British installed a projector-radar. It lights up the whole neighborhood and the woods near our house. It has a beautiful effect, but their intent is evil.[8]

JUNE 16, 1947

Dr. Horvitz, my history teacher, called me today to the blackboard to answer questions. I could not answer all of them. He said, "Harris, a girl who does not study consistently deserves to have her mark lowered!" I was dying to answer this ass back, but tears were choking me. I ran to my desk and started to cry, at which point he says "…had you studied, there would be no need for this comedy!!!" I thought I would disintegrate. He hated me so. I remember him calling me a liar during an exam and insulting me. At that moment I hated the Reali School and all its teachers—those monsters. I wanted to break away, run to a wide-open field and scream "shame on you!"

---

[7] Haifa's downtown.
[8] The intent was to catch the refugees, survivors of the Holocaust, desperately trying to get to the Land of Israel.

I came home from school in a horrible mood. In the bus, Esther told me that we would go to the Urion Cinema to see *It Happened in the Month of May*. I said it was a wonderful idea because we had little homework. I came home, it was washday and my mother, too, was in a bad mood.[9] I had not uttered a word when she started shouting. She pointed at the ink stains on my blouse—because Putti in the nature study class asked Gideon how quadruplets get born; he went into great detail and I began to laugh and turned around, so Putti got embarrassed and hit my back with her pen, and with that the drops of ink from her pen sprinkled on my shirt. Mother shouted that I never help her, that I don't eat enough, that I'm too thin, and therefore my skirt keeps falling. I knew there and then that nothing would change the situation. I was also afraid that if my report card was not going to be good, my mother would say it's because I went to the cinema instead of having studied. So I climbed up three flights of stairs, two steps at a time, to Esther and told her I could not go. At this point, I feel like running away from school, from everybody, to a kibbutz. I feel like rolling in the fields and being free, free, free!

Later that day, as I was returning from the dressmaker's, I heard the newspaper hawkers shouting that the three men[10] who attacked the Acre jail were sentenced to death. What a terrible, mysterious word death is!

---

[9] Interestingly, my mother was almost always exhausted and in a bad mood on wash day. The whole apartment seemed to be taken over by the laundry. A very nice little Arab lady helped her. She sat on her haunches with her skirts rolled up over her knees, exposing her thin thighs, a large basin filled with hot sudsy water in front of her. My mother lugged the dirty laundry to her and then would carry the washed laundry onto the kitchen balcony to dry. The kitchen was always steamy, and lunch on laundry day was never very tasty. My father and I would keep to the farthest point in the flat, away from the busy kitchen. We knew that my mother was totally consumed by her relationship with the wash lady and unavailable to us.

The Arab lady had been coming to us for years, and my mother was caught up with the washerwoman's personal problems. Her small hands were covered with silver rings and delicate dark bluish-green tattoos. Both women communicated in a grammarless language, with bits of both Hebrew and Arabic only they could understand. When she would leave the flat, my father got up from the depths of his armchair, insisting on seeing her to the door.

One day Mother spotted bruises on her arms and asked where they had come from. The woman giggled good-naturedly and brushed the question aside. This happened a few times before she admitted that when her husband got into a foul mood, he hit her. The next time the stocky husband came to pick up his wife, my mother took him aside and politely and quietly told him that if she ever saw any more bruises on his wife's arms, she'd call the police. There were no more bruises from then on.

[10] These men belonged to the Stern Group or Gang, a militant, extremist Zionist group founded by Avraham Stern during the British Mandate in Palestine in 1940.

I personally am a little afraid that if the Irgun[11] will go on bombing, there will be a curfew and we won't be able to go on our trip to Tel Aviv as planned. Well, so be it, these events belong to history and are so much more important than our trip to Tel Aviv!!!

This evening, my parents heard we had gotten accommodation in Cyprus for a holiday. I am more or less looking forward to going, my parents very much!

My friend and neighbor Judita [Marcus] is leaving for a holiday in Italy on Shabbat.

JUNE 17, 1947

I went to see a movie, and I left with my handkerchief soaked. The movie starts with a family sitting in front of the wireless when all of a sudden the music is interrupted with the announcement that Pearl Harbor has been bombed and each person must be on guard. Those words fell on me like heavy stones. The scenes of men saying good-bye reminded me of the war[12], when the British soldiers would visit us and then invariably say good-bye before they were shipped off to the front. I was sobbing the whole way home.

The scenes in the movie reminded me of the day an English officer (Dryland, I think his name was), who used to come a great deal to our house and who drank endless cups of tea, accompanied by ginger snaps, came late in the afternoon to say good-bye. He was being shipped to the front. We all laughed a lot and joked together till the door closed behind him. I could not contain myself and ran into my room sobbing. My mother followed me and quietly sat next to me in the darkening room. I know the British were brave during the war. Two types of feelings were warring within me. One was of love for them when I remembered the war they were involved in in Burma, the desert and other places, their bravery courage and their fearlessness. The other side of me was hating them because they were the masters of our land. I quickly comforted myself that our boys, Palmachniks, are endangering their lives for our country. I reminded myself of

---

[11] Irgun—a right-wing faction, but more moderate than the Stern Gang. In 1948, Ben-Gurion integrated the Haganah, the Jewish paramilitary organization that operated in the British Mandate of Palestine from about 1920 until the state of Israel was declared, and the armed faction of the Irgun into the Israeli Defense Forces.

[12] Here I'm referring to World War II, of course, which had only ended two years before this entry.

Nissan, Danny, and Pini. Their memory brought about a fresh new stream of hot tears running down my cheeks.

JUNE 18, 1947

During my geography class, Dr. Braver, this ass, caught me chatting. So he says to me... "Shut up there, you who are like Rabbi Zadok's Adam's apple." Obviously, he was referring to the fact that I was thin, and it hurt me a little. But, Braver has a sad life and is so pathetic that I cannot really blame him or stay angry with him for long. What I am really afraid of is that the name will stick to me for perpetuity! It is interesting that he himself has a huge Adam's apple that keeps bobbing up and down when he holds forth.

Walking home toward evening, I noticed that many of our small neighborhood children were standing around two Kalaniots[13] who were explaining to them the parts of the rifle. The Poppies were fair-skinned, blue-eyed, wearing khaki shorts, part of their uniform.

As I came close to the scene, I smiled to myself. But as I approached the children, I said, "Don't you have anybody else to talk to?" The children did not answer, but one of the soldiers muttered something under his breath, while looking at me. I said, looking at him, "You there, shut your mouth!" He thereupon took out his revolver. I felt my heart beating fast, but I did not stir, and he returned it to its holder.

I had not noticed that as all this was going on, Danny [my cousin] was walking up the hill toward us. He must have noticed from afar off that this was no laughing matter and shouted, "Naomi!" It stopped me right then and there from responding further to the British paratrooper. I was brimming with pride as I looked over to my cousin.

All the rest of the evening, Danny was great fun. I don't understand what has happened, but he began to laugh with me and began to be a lot more sensitive toward me. I don't understand and I'm not sure if he was merely showing off in front of the girl he had brought with him. Or maybe, having seen my behavior with the British soldiers,

---

[13] Soldiers of a British Airborne Division who were stationed in Palestine. They were called Kalaniots—poppies in Hebrew—because the paratroopers wore red berets that were the color of the flowers.

he thinks I'll join the Palmach one day. I hope I won't disappoint him. That evening, I was delighted to hear that he was planning to move to [Kibbutz] Poria.[14] I had been afraid my Brigade boy[15] might be turning into a pale city dweller. But I see that he has found his right place in the kibbutz. I had thoughts that after he had started studying for his matriculation, he would be stuck in an office in Jerusalem. (What a joke!)

JUNE 19, 1947

In the evening, we were sitting with some guests in the living room, and we heard loud shots and shouts of soldiers out of control. I got so frightened that I felt pins and needles pricking my hands. I went outside and the light from the projector was beautiful but you couldn't see the street because of the intensity of the light. The street was brilliantly illuminated. I have no idea what happened and probably will never know. What a laugh, when we are told that the British are here in the name of "law and order."

JUNE 21, 1947

In the morning we left for Tel Aviv. I did not sleep all night out of sheer excitement. We met Ehud at the train station and left Haifa. At last we arrived in Tel Aviv where my aunt and Ora Legum were waiting. Overcome with excitement we forgot all about Ehud and left the station without a proper good-bye.

I was dying to chat with Ora, but my Aunt Mary insisted on butting into the conversation and taking over completely. It irritated me very much. When we got home, she fixed me a delicious meal, and we sat and chatted.

In the evening, I went with Ora and Esther to Ora's school to see a production of *A Midsummer Night's Dream*. On the way my sandal tore and we wasted precious time looking for a shoemaker. The play was marvelous and the actors and actresses very attractive. They seemed so self-confident and much more sophisticated than us in Haifa. Esther and Ora walked me home. I got home at 10:30 p.m. Nobody was home.

---

[14]   A kibbutz perched on a hill overlooking the Sea of Galilee.
[15]   Referring to the fact that Danny had been a member of the Jewish Brigade that fought in Europe.

JUNE 22, 1947

On the second day, Ora and Esther came over at 10:00 a.m. and together we went off to Holon [a suburb of Tel Aviv] to the swimming pool. It was fantastic! The pool looked like it was out of *One Thousand and One Nights*.[16] There were very few people. At 1:00 we went to get dressed. Ora took pictures of us on the lawn. Ora then went home. Esther and I took the bus to our aunts. Ora had told us that we should get off the bus at Dizengoff Square.[17] Tel Aviv is vast! We are all alone on the bus, strange to the city, and apart from that there are countless squares in Tel Aviv. As we approached one square, Esther tells me that her instinct tells her that that's Dizengoff. Of course once we got off the bus, we found it was not so. So we got onto yet another bus.[18] At last I got home.

At 5:00, Esther came and together we went to Ora. Ehud appeared. We rode bicycles, and in the evening we went to Li La Lo,[19] and for the first time I saw Shoshana Damari[20] face-to-face. I got home in a taxi at 12 p.m.

JUNE 23, 1947

In the morning we got to [the swimming pool] Galei-gal and there we met Ehud and it was wonderful. We went to get dressed. What a hilarious scene that was. According to the clock, it took us a full hour to get dressed. Esther of course is bashful in front of the other women, and I was infected by it. First we slipped on our undershirts. Then somehow we managed to wriggle into our bras that went on under the undershirts that were already on us, the whole time cracking up and dying of giggles. When we went

---

16   The pool itself was vast with lovely green lawns surrounding it. Haifa had nothing like it, so it was all new to me. The pool's name in Hebrew translated to "waves of joy," and it was.

17   Dizengoff Square is one of Tel Aviv's landmark public squares, built in 1934.

18   All of this is still a vivid picture in my mind: two young girls lost in Tel Aviv. We eventually climbed onto another packed bus, both of us swaying from side to side, hanging onto the straps, the middle of Esther's back still wet from her dripping long braids, with me determined not to rely anymore on her instincts.

19   A well-known nightclub in Tel Aviv.

20   Damari was a Yemenite-Israeli singer who became known as the "queen of Israeli song." She sang "Kalaniyot" and "Hatender Nosea," whose lyrics I loved. It was hard to keep the audience from humming the song with her.

out, Ehud was fuming because he had been waiting for us for over an hour! The main point, however, is that we got thousands of photographs.

We went to Ora's to eat. Even though we were dead tired we dragged ourselves to the Carmel market to look for hand-embroidered "navy" belts. We could not continue because Esther got terrible cramps so we went back to rest at Ora's. In the evening we went to the cinema with Ehud, went back to Ora's, and listened to records. They walked me home.

JUNE 24, 1947

This morning I was subjected to a long sermon from my aunt [Mary] about what wonderful parents I have, till I nearly missed the bus to Jerusalem and I had to sit on the last bench. At the bus station I met Danny and together we went to get a pass for me. Otherwise the British would not have permitted me to enter the "zone."[21]

Danny and I reached the Government office for my pass just as it was about to close. After all, the government is *very* punctual. The main thing is that Danny talked his way into seeing the British officer in charge. He happened to be a cute Scotsman who explained to Danny with much politeness that the authorities had to be careful because all kinds of strange and dangerous characters might wander in. He looked me over carefully and decided that I should be allowed to enter the zone and get a pass. They fixed for me a piece of paper and wrote my name on it with many mistakes and we left. We had thanked them, they had thanked us, and it all made a great impression.

That evening Danny gave me a lecture on Rembrandt and others. We laughed a great deal. Before he went to sleep, he saw what I was reading,[22] bent down, smiled and kissed me on my forehead goodnight. I love him so much.

We had laughed at supper at [Danny's] father's expense, that he is still so terribly English, and Danny calls him "Sir Thomas." I found among his books

---

21 Zone—Jerusalem was divided into sections, which were sealed off one from another, and you had to have a pass to go into them.
22 When at my Aunt Esther's I slept on the Persian carpet in the living room. That night I was reading Hannah Senesh's diary. Hannah Senesh (Szenes in Hungarian) was a well-known poet living in the Land of Israel who was trained to join the underground partisans in Europe during World War II. She was caught by the Germans at the Hungarian border, tortured in prison, and eventually executed.

Between the Walls about a Hebrew prisoner. The book is good and gives a clear picture of the atmosphere in the prisons.

June 29, 1947

I returned with Mummy from Jerusalem to Haifa. I looked at the pass and I saw how they wrote my name with lots of unnecessary letters. The trip back to Haifa was very pleasant, but when my bus approached Haifa, I felt that I was returning to my home, my place. The same fields, same houses, same British soldiers carrying guns, half-hidden behind bushes, and the same jeeps speeding up and down the steep mountain road toward their camp on the French Carmel.

July 11, 1947

Since I returned from Jerusalem, nothing special has happened. I spent the time nicely. We went walking on the Carmel, and we went to movies and the sea. Ora came to Haifa and stayed with Esther. I began embroidering a belt. Ora and Daniel introduced themselves. It interests me what impression she made on him. But, anyway, he made a great impression on her…

We went off to visit Ehud to surprise him—his home is an absolute castle—but he was not at home. It was cool, so we went on foot till the Merkaz.[23] We had another evening where we went up to the Carmel where we did meet with Ehud and Daniel. They arrived, and Daniel always loves to wrap himself up in mystery, and declared that both of them had to go off somewhere, but couldn't tell us where. We had a little money so we went off to the movies. We met with Daniel afterward and we walked and were arguing the whole way if it was nice for girls to wear short pants. Ora gave me all the pictures that we took in Tel Aviv and they came out well.

In the last few days I have a heavy weight on my heart. I feel that as the head of the culture committee I am not doing enough. I'm lucky that yesterday we prepared a program. Arza, Ora, and I made up cute sketches. We were supposed to show

---

[23] The Merkaz was an attractive shopping area on Mount Carmel, full of cafes and restaurants.

them to the group yesterday, but, instead, Youda Butler came and told us about the Negev.[24] I guess we will present the sketches tomorrow.

Daniel is nagging me, he wants a passport picture of me. I have to go and be photographed.

They announced to us in the Scout meeting that we'll have a Scout camp in [Kibbutz] Hefzibah near Hadera, with the rest of the Haifa Scouts. For me, it will be wonderful. I'll be coming back from Cyprus on the 7th of August, the day we leave for the camp. At camp, we'll be saying good-bye to our two counselors, Sonia and Ahuva. When I think about it, I get a funny feeling in the stomach.

Yesterday I had a very unpleasant thing happen. Because there is a plague, we were afraid we would not be let into Cyprus. So Mummy and I went to get injections and a certificate that certifies [the shots]. We went down to the German Colony, got the shots and entered a large room for the certificate. There were a few young Arab clerks sitting around. We came to the very same clerk in charge of the certificates, a young Arab clerk between 19 and 22. We told him what we wanted and Mummy asked him a few questions, and he didn't bother to respond. I began giggling and then decided to stop, because that wasn't nice because maybe he was mute and unable to speak. But I saw him talking to the clerk sitting next to him. Mother went on talking and he still did not answer. I began laughing but not aloud, so he addressed me in English and told me to please leave the room. I was furious, but left. What asses! With what authority do they order me out of the room. They think they can rule over us Jews! After I left the room, my mother gave him a piece of her mind.

JULY 12, 1947

Today, Shabbat morning, Drora invited me to her place for her birthday. We were just two girls as guests, Tutti and I. As I was walking along, I was surprised that none of the British soldiers were around, because only today, two were kidnapped out of revenge. At noon when I went down to a Scout meeting, a jeep with British soldiers swerved right by me as if it was about to run me over. The

---

[24] The Negev, the southern part of what is now Israel, was totally new then, all desert. No one had built anything or settled there yet. At that time it was completely empty and we had never hiked there. Later on we hiked there many times.

jeep was a few centimeters away from me, even though the rest of the street was empty. I stared into their faces on purpose, with narrowing eyes.

At our Scout meeting, we are beginning to prepare ourselves for the oath. They explained to us what it meant and we had a discussion about it. I am getting very excited because I know that from the time I make the promise, I am taking upon myself a burden that will turn me into a *ben Adam*,[25] and that from that day on my duty will be to help my people and my fellow man—an undertaking that nowadays is quite dangerous. This is, anyway, how I felt on this matter.

We came home on foot. I'm ordered by my parents to shorten our usual walk through the fields. It was dark and the British soldiers were hiding behind the bushes. Only their red berets and shiny insignia warned us they were there. We spoke quickly and, in order to irritate them, quickened our pace, and I purposely spoke in a loud voice in Hebrew and kept mentioning the word "ambush" many times, knowing that it had the same meaning in English as in Hebrew. It's a wonder we got through the fields without an incident. All night I was unable to sleep because the projectors kept lighting up my room. The lights blinded me.

JULY 13, 1947

I lay in bed this morning, thinking. These days we feel pressure from all sides. At that time [referring to the battles of 70 A.D. against the Roman armies], the blood of the brave in Jerusalem was spilled on the outskirts of the town and on the walls of Jerusalem. The last fortifications are falling... and in our time, we are fighting the British conqueror. In our days, the brave of the Palmach and Irgun are training in all the pathways of our country against the oppressor.

On my way to the committee meeting, I met Daniel and was happy that he trusted me so. He proceeded to tell me that Esther is angry with him, and he went on to say that he is not in love with her anymore and, therefore, cannot just be with her and her alone. I gave him my advice and when I left I felt that he told me something that was personal to him. I was happy about the trust that he put in me and I was happy to be a helpful friend. I always like Daniel and his good qualities. He's a little bit light-headed at times. It is true that for two years now, he has not really been in love with anybody,

---

[25] A mature, responsible human being who does the right thing.

even though I must admit that he and Esther behaved as if they were a real couple. They held hands, exchanged glances and secrets with each other. But still, I am sure that Esther is misleading herself because I think that he's the first boy that she really loves.

What a wonderful feeling when a human being puts trust in one. It is the first time I've responded to a boy in this manner. I find that being truly helpful to a friend is the best and most pleasant feeling.

178

August 6, 1947

Today I've returned to Haifa from Cyprus after three weeks. I will never ever forget the trip.[26] The boat's name was *Fuadia*, and it belongs to an Egyptian ship company. She is the worst of ships. We embarked on the ship at 5:00 and went down for tea. The dining room was in the belly of the boat, hot and stuffy. I stuffed myself in order to please my mother and show her that I had already started getting fatter! And of course all night, we vomited. Only Daddy went down to the insufferable, small, hot, stuffy cabin and slept like a baby. Mummy and I vomited our guts out all night long. We got off the ship looking greenish-whitish.

In the hotel, they put us into a small, yellow, hot stuffy room. I, from exhaustion, fell asleep right away. Mummy decided that this is not how we want to spend our time. We got in touch with Mr. Karizes, our hotel owner, and we got another new nice room. The windows were open, it was cool because we were in a small village at least 1000 meters high.[27] In the afternoon, we went for a walk. The scenery is magnificent. Everything is green and covered with forests. The mountain air is so pure that I got a slight headache. Daddy showed off the whole time wearing his army boots that are wonderful for hiking.

In the mornings we'd sit in a small café in the village, Prodromos. The whole village sits there, the women sit in clusters knitting, and the men play a game similar to dominos. From age 3 to age 70, they play the game.

---

[26] Indeed, I never have forgotten the trip. Just thinking of it makes me seasick.
[27] What I really remember is that someone led us to a lovely room whose windows were flung open, allowing cool, clean mountain air to stream in. The mountains themselves were completely covered with trees of a dark green shade. It was all so new to me. At home, the colors were always yellows and browns, with very little green. The trees that had been planted at home were trying to grow on arid terrain and were not yet tall. To be surrounded by so much dark green was alien to me, but very welcome.

I got friendly with three Greek girls. Their names were: Levki—she had a beautiful figure and always looked elegant. For the morning, for the afternoon and evening, she had a special dress. Dimitra, the girl who was staying in our hotel: She was very nice, lively and full of spunk. She came from Cairo, also rich and has fifty dresses. Lula: a girl of 17. She has braids, but not like village braids. Instead, she turns each braid into a large loop pinned behind each ear, to which she adds a large ribbon. Bela and her sister Vaso also, both are very conservative. Woe unto him who says a word in favor of the Greek partisans. The poor things are quite homely, but seem to be very rich.

All these girls were such new types for me—the way they dressed, their polite behavior. Once I was walking through the rooms and whistling quietly to myself. Dimitra then motioned to me to stop, because she felt it was not very lady-like. They are very nice girls and invited me on all their walks and I enjoyed their company thoroughly, though I could never take part in their conversations, because I don't speak Greek and they don't speak Hebrew...[28]

On the morning of the second day, we got the newspaper and read about the terrible situation in which our country finds itself. The situation is grim and terrible.[29] Three terrorists[30] were taken out to be hanged, and as revenge they then hanged three British soldiers that were being held hostage until then. After the murder the whole Yishuv[31]

[28] Levki was my favorite of these girls, but they were all interesting to me. Their behavior was cultured and decorous, kind of rarified from my point of view. I doubted if any of them had ever been on a hike, or carried a rucksack on their back, boys and girls together. Not only were our upbringings and values so different, but we did not even have a language in common. Yet we spent all our time together and somehow we communicated, despite (or maybe because of) the fact that they seemed so foreign and exotic. I felt they all could have come from another planet.

[29] The situation in the country was indeed grim. The roads were all dangerous, with constant sniping from Arab villages along the highways, and casualties were mounting on all sides. You took your life in your hands to travel around the country. When I use the term "situation" in the diary, I'm referring to the whole set of political and military conditions in the country. In Hebrew, it was a common term to characterize this state of affairs.

[30] These people, labeled as terrorists, were part of the Etzel movement, a right-wing organization. My personal experience with the Etzel was that I was asked by a classmate to go with her to a youth meeting of the group. My conscience bothered me whether I should or should not go. What swayed me against going was the fact that I believed then that one of the group's core values was that the end justified the means, and I knew that I did not want to go in that direction. That realization brought me peace. I imagine the fact that my family was not in favor of the Etzel must have played an unconscious role in my decision also, but I never discussed it with them. The nature of my struggle was my admiration for the zealots that fought the Roman Empire, so I was wondering if the Etzel were walking in their footsteps. Therefore, why would I not admire the Etzel, modern-day zealots fighting the British Empire?

[31] The Yishuv refers to the Jewish community in pre-state Israel.

was shaken to their core and we were sure there would be martial law. Then we got the news: 4,000 refugees that were brought to the shores of our country were turned back to France! That was horrible. The events spoiled my mood completely. The next day, we were sitting in a café, and we read that the Haganah blew up a British warship. I shrieked with joy. My father, of course, walked away from the table, disgusted at my behavior. At lunch I cried from joy…

A few days later, we went to visit Platres, a very posh resort. There Mummy and I went to have afternoon tea at the Park Hotel, the most aristocratic. It's the place where King Farouk spends time. The place is really beautiful but didn't make any impression on me. I shouted in Hebrew and drew attention to myself because of my simple clothes and Biblical sandals. After a cup of tea we went to see a Greek play that made a strong impression on me.

I must add that I have finished knitting one side of the sweater.

After a few days there was a ball in a close-by hotel. All day I ran around dressing Dimitra and helping her curl her hair. She told me the next day that they danced till one in the morning!

We all went off to Nikosia, the capital, which looks like our Ramallah… From there we went on to Kyrenia to see the antiquities. We went to a church, Bellapais Abbey. The church is old and beautiful. We took photographs with the priest. We were taken for a visit to a couple, the man of which was British, a sort of actor, living with a Jewish woman, even though they were not married. They lived in a charming house with a tiny swimming pool, in which I swam.[32]

In the evening we left for Famagusta from which we'd sail in the morning. The hotel had dancing in the evening. I sat and stared at some crazy woman in long tight pants, a very tight red blouse, and long yellow hair reaching her hips…

The voyage home was not bad. Mummy and I ate nothing, so we were not seasick. There were young men from Kibbutz Degania who told stories and we all cracked up. In the morning, a few of us were on the deck, and so we were the first

[32] Oddly, although I didn't write about these people in my diary, I remember them well. The priest had gray hair pulled back in a bun, and under his long black robe he carried a large protruding stomach. The couple seemed glamorous to me, especially the woman. She had dark red hair cascading to her shoulders. She was wearing a strapless cotton bra and a cotton shirt with her tanned midriff showing. Naturally I thought her particularly fascinating. After we left, I heard my parents talking about them, wondering about their backgrounds and what they could have in common. We all certainly found them interesting and above all intriguing—for me, it was especially worthy of note that they lived together under one roof even though they were not married.

to spot the shores of our country through the morning fog. I took my mother's hand and we joined dancing the hora! Returning to my neighborhood, I told them about the island, miracles and wonders—all were splitting their sides laughing. In the evening we got together for dancing. I learned to tango, rumba, English waltz and Viennese waltz. My upstairs neighbor Vicky dances well... .

AUGUST 8, 1947

On Friday I went down to our Scout shed because I so missed my group. Those who were there were happy to see me. And again I was in my own atmosphere. The same children, the same blue shirts, the same jeeps and the same barbed wire. When I was among the group I felt that they belonged to me, and I to them. On Shabbat I wanted to go to a Scout meeting, but Nitza came back and said that she's afraid to go because the English soldiers pulled at her hair. In the evening we went to the cinema because Ora wanted to see *The Sign of Zorro*, with Linda Darnell and Tyrone Power. It's a wonderful movie. They are both so handsome, and he simply conquers hearts. Daniel did not join us because he is busy courting Tzipora Salik. He only met her a day before. But anyway he's a type unto himself...

On Sunday I went to Shavei Zion, and from there to Nahariah to go swimming. It was lovely. On Monday, I was told that Esther had joined the work camp. She had not been permitted to go because of the "situation," but a week after her whole group had gone to Tel Yosef, her friend Hasia arrived, suntanned and healthy, and influenced her mother so that they allowed her to join the camp. (Lucky her!) I wrote a letter to Sonia who has already left us (what a pity!!!). And she's in Kibbutz Sarid. How much I love her, even though I never felt that I was that attached to her. A sweet girl.

On Monday I invited Ora to the May [Theater] to see *Tarzan and the Kingdom of the Lions*. Wonderful. I spent twenty-five piasters. [Known in Hebrew as "grush."]

AUGUST 12, 1947

When I came home yesterday, I saw an Englishman sitting there. It was extremely unpleasant. What do we have in common with the English? He was a soldier during the war and now is in the commercial navy. He doesn't seem to be aware that the army is not supposed to fraternize with civilians. It was good that we got rid of him very quickly.

In the morning Daniel told me how he finagled an introduction to Putti[33] and all that it entailed. Anyway, he's such a caricature. He says he wants to meet as many people as possible, so when he walks in the street he can say shalom to as many people as possible. At this point, he does not know whether to belong to the Carmel Scout group [uptown] or Bilu [downtown] Scout group. He dances at all weddings at once.

On the 17th, we'll be going to a work camp in Kibbutz Tel-Yosef. Wow! I am so excited and just hope I'm permitted. Yesterday, Arabs attacked a Jewish café and killed five people. Of course, the British are egging them on. My mother is worried, and that's going to make it more difficult for her to make a decision.

AUGUST 14, 1947

My mother went yesterday to talk to Ahuva [my Scout counselor] about the work camp. Ahuva convinced her to let me go. Only my father is at this point a stumbling block. Boy, does he irritate me!!! Sonia [my old counselor] appeared yesterday from her *hachshara*.[34] I hugged her until she could breathe no more. I made up my mind that if she goes, so do I. I came home and realized that with my father, it is impossible to even talk. He simply says that it's the principle that matters, and that he does not permit me to go. One cannot even discuss the matter with him. I keep nagging them all day long.

The situation is getting worse and worse, I must admit. But the trouble is still far from Tel Yosef and the other Hebrew settlements.

I don't know what Arza's mother is made of. She always permits her to go. Boy, do I envy my future children! I would have gladly given up the holiday in Cyprus in order to go to the work camp and be with Sonia.

Those British! I am only waiting to take revenge on them and the Arabs, whom they provoke and egg on. It was a pleasure yesterday to see Sonia and Leizer [our

---

33 Putti was a very popular girl with the boys.
34 Her first year on the kibbutz, a preparatory time to settling on the land.

old counselors]. These are happy people who feel that there is a purpose to their life. They are suntanned and full of energy and spirit! And I have to rot in the city, while my group will be having a great time in the country.

AUGUST 17, 1947

Until yesterday, they did not permit me to go to the camp, and, boy, was it lively at home. Because more and more Jews are being murdered, the Haganah responded. However, after a few days we found out that we will go to Kibbutz Yagur [close to Haifa], so then I too was permitted. The place is not great, but better than rotting in the city. I'm packing, washing and ironing. Wow! I am so excited. Arza brought me a letter that Sonia had given her, together with this picture. I feel exactly as I look in this picture, but let's see if I will overcome.[35]

AUGUST 18, 1947

We spent the morning and afternoon in the Scout shed. We got further details about our camp. By early evening all was ready and packed. I was about to go to sleep at 9:30, when the telephone rang for me. Ahuva phoned to say there is no camp! I nearly fainted on the spot. I burst out crying! I cursed the dogs in power who are responsible for us not going to the camp. (Everybody knows they [the British] are constantly provoking.)

[35] Sonia had attached a charming cartoon-like figure, depicting me sweating under piles of papers representing the burden of my responsibilities for the Culture Committee. In the bottom corner, she had written: "It is a little difficult but nevertheless... ." At the very top of the cartoon, she wrote, "To Naomi, a memento from Sonia."

AUGUST 19, 1947

A day beforehand Sonia kept urging us and asked that we come to visit her in Sarid.[36] At last I was permitted to go. I fixed my things and on Friday afternoon at 2 o'clock we traveled.

We started out with great success. Already in the bus it was very nice. We sat next to two young cute guys (one had blue eyes) and laughed the whole time. They asked how come we were traveling without our mothers and so on and so forth. We reached the place and got to the camp. Sonia was so happy to see us.

We entered the showers…! So primitive! A divider made of sacks separated the boys from the girls. We were persuaded from the start that there was no peeping, but I was not totally convinced as long as I was stark naked.

I am standing with the water pouring down on me when I suddenly see an ankle and toes intrude under the divide into my section. I thought I'd die! I will never forget that moment. I got so frightened.

In general, the people are very nice and are typical sabras. We were in the showers and we heard young men coming in after work. Despite their fatigue, they were happy and they were singing. Our hearts dropped when we heard them sing a song that went "when she takes off her sweater…" That was all we had to hear. We were already giggling. The song continued and was in no way crude. They heard us laughing and asked us who we were and how old we were. Ora fibbed and said we were 15–16. One of them then said, "If so, then it's worth it." We laughed to ourselves. We went outside, immaculate, and we introduced ourselves to all of them, and learned each one's nickname. After supper, we returned to camp. We got into one of the tents where the gang was talking. The relationship between the boys and girls is lovely. It was getting too warm and Sonia suggested that we go out into the wood. Those moments I shall never forget. It was dark and

[36] A kibbutz where her group was spending a year of preparation, before settling on the land and starting their own kibbutz from scratch. The word *sarid* means remnant, mentioned in the Bible in the book of Isaiah, referring to those Jews returning from Assyrian exile. In this case, *sarid* refers to the remnant of European Jewry in the 20th century. There will always be a remnant in the Promised Land.

cool, and the moon sent its rays amongst the tree branches. We sang, and we were also quiet… . An evening in the valley…[37]

After some time, a bell rang, and we went to the club [kibbutz cultural center]. There was no program but the atmosphere was festive. The members were dressed in holiday clothes and they were singing. The singing was wonderful. All sang together, with one rhythm. They were happy songs, and I felt that these were young people with vitality, happy and content, singing in unison. There were patriotic Palmach songs, and then they sang in deeper voices, and from those songs I felt that here were sitting 40 Hebrew people, with a definite purpose to their life, ready for any obstacle or setback, ready to prevail and fight together. After the singing and the music, one of them with an accordion played and they danced. Lovely folk songs. Horas full of energy and also lovely couples' dances. After about three hours of dancing, the *Shmuznikim* [the "dirty" ones] came in—with work shirts hanging out, hair messy—as if they didn't know at all that today is the Sabbath!

Slowly, slowly, the *chaverim*[38] left the hall, in a spontaneous way, a sign that this was a healthy community, and we went to the woods. We sat in a circle around the campfire, one leaning on the other, and drinking from the *finjan*.[39] The singing went on till 2:30 a.m. Only then did we go to sleep. We [Ora and I] got a tent to ourselves and we slept on straw mattresses. It was soft and lovely. In the morning we got up at 6:00 and I found I had gotten my period. I took care of it as best I could. The rest of the *chaverim* got up at 8:30 because it was Shabbat and the members were tired. We spent the morning in the kibbutz. Sarid happens to be a lovely place… .

---

[37] This was reminiscent to me of a well-known song, referring to the Jezreel Valley. This was the song that I used to sing to my mother in the kitchen. She always begged me to sing it, and we would inevitably get weepy and emotional over its references to the completely fatigued people coming from their fields, meaning the new type of Jew we were all so proud of, and to the idea of going to "sleep in the valley, you beautiful valley, we will be here to protect you… ."

[38] The *chaverim* refers to the kibbutz members here. The word literally means friends, comrades, and refers to both men and women. It's used especially in the Palmach and kibbutz culture, but has seeped into the rest of Israeli culture. The impact of that term evokes a sense of unity, solidarity, and caring for each other.

[39] *Finjan* is a sabra term for the pot used to make Turkish or Arab coffee over an open fire, which is in itself a kind of Palmach ritual. There's a famous song, the refrain for which is something like: "here the coffee is ready, we will drink it and praise—there is taste, there is smell, and the finjan goes round and round." The song tells a tale of gatherings over time, groups of friends around the finjan after a battle, with references to "one will not come back here anymore" and "for tears there is no end."

That evening, Pini [the nickname of an older counselor named Phineas] came in from Ein Gev.[40] We congregated in Sonia's tent and the *chaverim* were talking. They're all in the know. They know everything and they speak about the "situation" rationally. They don't get excited as the city people do. Their manner of talking left a powerful impression on me. Their quiet exuded that sense of self-confidence. No excitement but an understanding of the British mentality. When they talked about the British soldier, they talked with understanding as if they really pitied him. These are sons to be proud of. Next morning, we got up and bade good-bye to all of them. I got home by 3:00. I later heard from Tirza that we made not such a bad impression.

AUGUST 21, 1947

I've spent the last few days buying books, the thing that is most hateful for me.[41] This morning I went to check the curriculum. I'm in the Humanities section, in section three, where all the better students are. What came over my teachers to place me there, I do not know…

SEPTEMBER 2, 1947

The classroom teacher is Dr. Shapira. I must admit that the classes are difficult, but quiet and interesting. We captured the best places. Behind our bench are the "best" boys in the class, Rafi, Yosef A., Rindenau. It's wonderful. The French lessons are lovely. That Kalugai woman [the teacher] with her bowed legs and her quiet and exacting voice!… I sit near Raiah. Only Arabic is very hard, and at times I feel I won't be able to keep up.

[40] A kibbutz on the Kinneret, the sea of Galilee.
[41] I always felt this way when school time came around, with some trepidation about what the challenges of the school year might bring—there was a certain amount of fear, getting ready for a demanding academic schedule. Would I meet the challenge of a demanding schedule?

September 6, 1947

Time crawls by lazily. All is on track, lessons and so forth. I must point out that some of my classes are lovely.

Today Danny suddenly appeared—suntanned and cute. Mummy congratulated him on passing his matriculation so well. He is happy in Poria, and is thinking of staying there forever. I want to visit him during Sukkot but I am bashful.

September 14, 1947

Today is a holiday, the eve of Rosh Hashanah, and I have time to write. The last two weeks have been taken up with the overcrowded *Exodus* refugee ship.[42] After they were left to drift on the sea for three weeks, they were then "returned" to Hamburg, the hell from which they had come. Many among them are Jewish young men from the Land of Israel. They worked as sea captains and sailors. (Just like in the song, "he stood upright without ribbons or rank…") There were also young American Jews that are taking part; some are Christians. One of them is a relative of Mrs. Solomon. He was with the refugees and he stayed last on the empty ship that anchored in the port [Haifa]. He climbed the mast and stood by the Hebrew flag.[43] The [British] soldiers came and demanded he climb down. He refused. He said he would not leave the flag in their hands. They ordered him again to come down with the flag; he refused. The officer appeared and said that if he didn't come down, he'd be shot. He shouted in English: "I will not hand over the Hebrew flag into your hands!" They fired at him and he of course fell down. He was not badly wounded. When he lay on the pier, a young English soldier, humble, bent down and whispered in English "Forgive me, friend, that I have wounded you." The American waved him away out of pity. These are brave people who are ready to lay down their lives for these refugees. I knew four of them, one a Christian. One stuttered because he was shot in the mouth. They were not arrested because they were American citizens. The stories make one's hair stand on end.

---

[42] Those on the boat were physically—and, worse than that, psychologically—in terrible shape.
[43] This is what I called it in my diary and it must have been a precursor to the Israeli flag of today. I recall it being blue and white and having the Star of David on it.

Yesterday Ronnie[44] [Salomon] had a birthday. Only two girls were invited. We sailed in and around the harbor. We ate lunch on a raft in the middle of the sea. It was wonderful. We swam and took part in a regatta. After that, we got back to land at 6:00. I did not go home, but went straight to a Scout meeting. The whole group was meeting. Our guest was a man who told us of his memories of the [Jewish Brigade]. While listening, I felt as if something was stuck in my throat. After that we went out dancing to the schoolyard that was lit up, and others joined us and there was much merriment.

SEPTEMBER 19, 1947

What is there to write? There isn't much, except that, thank God, we've already had two exams. Or, that we've been corresponding with boys by carving names of couples on our school desks. Actually, there have been lots of thoughts, many of them strange, that were woven into my mind, but it's hard for me to put them on paper. They are strange, and I am ashamed. But I'll get over it because after all this is my diary, and no human being will read it except me. I don't know, at night when I'm alone, suddenly it jumps into my head that I am Yoel's girlfriend. That means that he has suggested it to me. And I am thinking in my head what will be, what will happen, and how will I respond? I don't know but I have a feeling only at night, when nothing is realistic that it is as if somebody will come to me tomorrow and suggest that he wants to be my boyfriend, and I'm fearful. On the one hand I don't want to be attached, because I'm not in love with anybody from my group. On the other hand, it would be pleasant if someone wants to walk me to the bus. Or, when I sit in the late afternoon, as the day closes, that there will be a knock at the door and one will appear. And anyway, how pleasant to feel loved and worshiped by somebody!! And that I will be able to say with a light heart, with a little pride and self-confidence, "What does this nudnik want from me? Why does he hang around me all day?!" (This sounds mean, but to say it nevertheless is pleasant.) At the same time I feel a silly worry (I mean this with all seriousness!): what if I will love somebody and he me, and we'll be boyfriend and girlfriend. After all, we're not

[44] Ronnie remains one of my best friends. She lives in Tel Aviv and was the daughter of my mother's best friend, Sara Salomon. Perhaps because our mothers were such good friends, we, too, developed a close friendship that has deepened through the years.

going to get married, and how will we ever break up? Let's say that he goes out to settle on the land and I want to go somewhere else? (Oy, I'm afraid that somebody will take the diary by mistake and open it!!!!)[45]

Today is Monday, and we had a group meeting in the Scout shed. We had a visitor, a Scout in his past, who had just come back from an International Youth Meeting in Prague. (He's not a Communist.) After that, he volunteered on the *Exodus* ship. The scout meeting was terrific and I must point out that it had a strong impact on me. He described it all with terrific colors and also about the exodus from Europe. The propaganda in Prague was good. The performances were successful but for those Jewish communists who kept interrupting all the time. After all, they profess that they believe in the fellowship of all people. The stories of the refugees were full of bravery and spectacular, the same courage that distinguishes Israel and helped her survive, the same faith and hope!!! While he was talking, we heard the sound of a machine gun.... Our hearts guessed, but he didn't say anything. At the end of the meeting, two people came in and whispered something. Amos [our counselor] stopped and told us that we must scatter because the [British] soldiers were out of control and it's best to take off. We should not go home in large groups in order to not bring attention to ourselves. Nitza and I with the help of God came home healthy and in one piece.[46]

October 1, 1947

In the morning Danny calls and declares that within an hour he'll be at our place to take me to Poria [his kibbutz]. Mummy, of course, resisted. When

---

[45] When I reread this passage, I was touched by the gravity of my thoughts and also by the yearning and the longing to get attached to someone and yet at the same time wanting to stay rational and keep these feelings under control.

[46] I must confess that when I heard about the response of the Communist Jews I wondered to myself when will they learn that it is a wonderful luxury to care about the world. I recall even thinking at the time that our prophets preached it in the 8th century B.C., that swords will be turned into plowshares and that one day the lamb will live with the lion. But first, we must take care of our own; nobody else will. His tales of courage and tenacity reminded me that day—yet again—of an important quality of the people of Israel, our bottomless capacity to believe and to hope.

Danny arrived, I was all ready. He appeared with another cute boy, dressed in dirty kibbutz work clothes. They made a great impression on all our neighbors, especially the *yekkes*. I was beside myself with joy and pride… . While Danny was fighting my case, his friend stood by him and didn't say a word. His name was Shmulik, very shy and reserved, but a wonderful young man, strong, blond, blue eyes, and a very pleasant face. While my mother was telephoning my father to find out how he felt about my going, Danny winked at me behind her back to get my suitcase ready. He hurried me on and said all I needed for the trip was a towel and a toothbrush, and the rest would be given me in Poria. After that, I was happy that "his honor" had to wait another five minutes while I took with me the toothbrush because who is crazy enough to borrow a toothbrush! At last we climbed into the truck, left Haifa at 9:00 and reached Poria at 7:00 in the evening, a half hour after the start of curfew, because on the way, we stopped at [Kibbutz] Mishmar Hasharon for lunch. Poria herself is perched on a hill opposite Kibbutz Alumot.[47] As we were driving up the hill, we could see the Kinneret [the Sea of Galilee] and the twisting River Jordan. My, a view like this I shall never forget. It was cool, the moon shone, and the Kinneret shone!!!

We entered the kibbutz [Poria]. In the place, there are some buildings that Kibbutz Alumot built and some buildings, broken down, that were already there, a large communal dining room with white oilcloths covering the tables.

Danny's room is in a dilapidated, charming old structure, named "Jane Eyre."[48] On one wall hangs a long sword with gold filigree. On a second wall hangs a Shabaria.[49] A week beforehand, a group of Bedouins attacked the kibbutz. The boys scattered them off, and Danny, who's in charge of security affairs, was asked to deal with the sheik. The sheik gave Danny the Shabaria. The Shabaria is impressive. The blade is bent into the shape of a half-crescent. The scabbard is dotted with small glass stones in green and red and little bells. The room is charmingly gotten up, but very dusty and untidy.

Next morning, we rode a cart to bring back ice to the kibbutz. Shmulik held the reins, and Esterke and I sat behind him. I felt so good. The cart swayed from side to side, and all I saw of Shmulik was the back of his neck, tanned from working in

---

[47]   A famous member of Kibbutz Alumot, which was just to the south of the Sea of Galilee, was Shimon Peres, currently president of Israel (and twice the country's prime minister).

[48]   *Jane Eyre* was his mother's favorite book.

[49]   A Shabaria is a short knife, often used by Arabs.

the fields. The scenery was wonderful. We girls were in short khaki pants and red kerchiefs on our heads. I felt that here we are, Jewish farmers on our own land.

The group as a whole is awfully nice. Danny is very popular and knows how to flirt with the girls. The *muchtar*[50] is Danny Trifon, who is a very decent person. In the evening, after dinner, one gathers to sit on the steps in front of the communal dining hall and gazes onto the Kinneret. One of the people plays a mouth organ, another tells of memories of the Palmach days. On Thursday, the situation in the country got tense, serious, and we waited for the Arabs to cause trouble. All of Galilee is on alert. Danny [my cousin] is preoccupied and grave. During the day he does his normal work. At night, he's up at midnight and works till 4:00 in the morning building fortifications and receiving arms. At this point, he is the most important person in the group. His stature rose in my eyes. I did not see the Danny anymore that didn't finish school or the Danny who is restless. Instead, I saw a workingman, an important individual, a man of labor and of the Haganah.

The arms that arrived were concealed in our room. In the evening, I sat with two more members of the kibbutz, and I helped with the loading of bullets. The mood was foreboding. Nobody left the place, and reinforcement arrived to help. Danny was responsible for all these matters, and he gave orders and was running around all day because he was in charge. To our relief and luck, nothing happened. Our neighbors [referring to the Arabs], seeing the cautionary steps taken by the Jews, did nothing.

The evening before I left there was much dancing and merriment. I returned to Haifa with two more young men from the kibbutz. I sat like a lady, while they ran around to get tickets and good seats in the bus. I came back to Haifa with a great impression of Poria—a wonderful youth, happy people, and wonderful lives. I want to spend my Hanukkah holidays there. I also feel like traveling during Hanukkah.

(Once, after everybody went to sleep, it was about midnight and it turned out that I and another young guy were left. I got ready to leave too. I started descending the steps of the dining hall, when he suddenly said to me, "Hey, *chaverah*,[51] why don't we go walking a little?" I thought I'd wet my pants right then and there! I answered him that I was too tired. He said: "It doesn't matter!"

---

[50]   The head of the kibbutz.
[51]   Meaning "friend" or "female friend."

All my blood at that moment rushed to my face and I blurted out, "I am falling asleep while walking!" and I ran away as if I was being pursued.)[52]

SEPTEMBER 26, 1947

There isn't much to write about. I've been sick the last six days with strep throat and have been in bed.[53] We have recently received a letter from Aunt Esther from England,[54] saying that my aunt told her that if the situation gets very bad I can come and stay with them. (It's very generous of them, but what would it say about me if I took them up on it?)

I have changed my hair parting from the middle to the side. I'm ugly both ways and I don't know which to decide on. I am skinny, like a stick, and my forehead has a deep frown in the middle, and red pimples—in other words, ugly!!!

Soon there will be a Scout meeting of the whole Haifa group, and I might take part in the dance performance. What's the use? I'll have to return with the 9:00 p.m. bus, because Mummy will not permit me to stay late because the day after is school. I always have to rush back home. What's the point of going if I always have to run home with Nitza before everybody else instead of walking home slowly around 11:00 p.m., boys and girls together? I don't call that living!!!!!!! That at

---

52   I added this in my diary parenthetically as if it were a footnote to this entry.

53   Like many children who endure a childhood illness, even something that lasts only a short time (although a strep throat without antibiotics could easily last well over ten days), my memories of these days remain vivid. Mummy propped me up on three pillows and piled blankets on me. I remember the top one had been hand-knitted by my grandmother in Glasgow. It was blue, fuzzy angora wool and soft to the touch. Mummy's close friend Sara Salomon would pop in each morning around 11:00 for tea and ginger snaps and conversation. They would sit together in my room for at least some of the time, and I was always fascinated by their conversations, which ranged from analysis of current issues to books to the cinema to human relationships. A stove had been set up in the middle of the room to try to keep the damp cold out, and a full teakettle was perched on top of it, always on the point of singing. My bedroom windows were constantly covered with steam during those days. The room itself was an island of warmth and coziness, and I was well cared for. I dreaded going down the long hall to the bathroom, which, like the rest of the flat, was freezing. Only my room had the stove going. Mummy, sure that if I ventured out of my room I'd catch pneumonia, spoiled me even more by bringing in a portable potty. I well recall sitting on the potty with a large blanket covering my legs so that nobody could tell. It was my secret.

54   Aunt Esther, of course, lived in Jerusalem but must have been visiting England and had seen there a woman named Teema, whom I called aunt as an honorific.

least one should love me or want to accompany me home, that I should have some contentment. I don't need a boyfriend or something similar, but not that I'll have to rush home with Nitza and that that's all!!! That at least I should go home with the group or that I should be accompanied or that there should be buses[55] and that I should be able to remain a little bit longer with all my friends.

Arza and Ora have been chosen to head the Culture Committee for the whole group! Only I have to be part of a dance performance for our local group. That's how luck will always have it. They're at least working on a broader horizon and the work is much more interesting. For me, to work just for these petty girls, where nobody pays attention or cares. Of course, I'm not right. Because the girls sense what I feel and know that I want to work also with the boys. But what can one do. This is how I feel. But only when I'm at home. When I'm with friends, I don't feel it and I'm happy, but when alone, reality appears to me in very dark colors, and especially when one doesn't know on what hairdo to decide!!!!!!!!!!!?

DECEMBER 1, 1947

It is over a month since I last wrote in my diary. Many things have happened in the life of my group, but not with me personally. I don't remember what the date was, maybe about three weeks ago, when all the Scout groups in the Haifa area convened. The people from Mount Carmel and Kiryat Motzkin were not able to come because all the main roads were under a new curfew after British soldiers had killed a number of Jews.[56]

Because of that only the Bilu and Geula groups and we appeared. It was quite successful. Our group made a good impression with the dance our girls prepared for the occasion. The dance was very much admired. The Geula girls presented a play and the Bilu people a jazz concert. Also Yosef read aloud a witty short story. Then we all poured out into the schoolyard and broke into folk dancing. Most of our boys did not dance but stood on the side watching. They felt as if it wasn't good enough to take part in the dancing.

---

[55]   The buses stopped at 9:00 p.m. because of the danger on the roads and this was obviously always a nagging issue with me.

[56]   Every single day we looked in the paper to find out who were the latest casualties.

There was one blond boy from the Geula group who stood out. Imagine, even though he is only 13! He flirted most of the time with Putti and Batia. Daniel was the only one who came from the Carmel group. Nitza didn't come because the curfew was announced at 5:30 in the afternoon. I was not at home because I was in a rehearsal, but she was at home, and it was clear that we would have to walk home at 10:00 at night and her mother was afraid. At 10:00 at night I had to leave all by myself, and Daniel asked me if I was walking home. I said yes. I don't think he knew that my mother was waiting for me at the Krips Café.[57] I must admit that he did ask me to wait another ten minutes for him. But I knew that he would find it impossible to leave as long as there was anybody still in sight. That's why I left alone, and I felt a little hurt inside me. I met my mother, and we walked up the steep hill together to the house and got home by 10:30. The evening as a whole was a success, but nothing of a personal experience happened to me.

I forgot to say that about a week before, our Scout group met with the Geula Scout group alone. We visited them, and they received us very well. Even though they had not put a program together, they succeeded more or less. The mood was good; there was a lot of communal singing. Yosef told a funny story about a bathing suit!!! Michael A. told a very boring story to the group. We then went out to the yard to folk dance with great gusto. The boys from Geula you can't look at them, they are unattractive and crude, but they sure know how to dance. We all danced the hora, and they, while dancing, sang the song "we will sweat." And one of them, near me, kept banging his foot shouting, "We will sweat, we won't sweat...," till I thought I would dissolve in laughter. I began pinching Arza and we left the circle laughing wildly. I think he was a little hurt, but it was dark and he would not have been able to recognize our faces.

Friday, the 28th, we put on a group meeting that went off well. On the 29th, all the groups in Haifa met again and Kroch [the leader, the head of the Scouts] lectured us on the ideals and values of our Scout movement. I was sure we would not have the time left for a social evening and really we didn't, but still we did go out to the schoolyard and folk danced and danced. The people from Motzkin all left and so did the people from Geula and Bilu, so that we from the Carmel were left alone. We danced and we danced from 6:00 until

---

[57] My good mother, ever loyal and caring, always looked out for me. She was waiting in this case, as often she did, so that I would not have to walk home all the way by myself because it was so dangerous. My father was waiting anxiously at the gate for Mother and me.

8:50. We went up the hill, Nitza, Daniel, and I, on the 9:00 p.m. bus—it was lots and lots of fun, and I got to know many new faces.

I went quickly to bed so that I could get up before dawn to go on a difficult hike. I was glad to have found an appropriate water canteen and puttees. Oh, I nearly forgot to say that on Friday we all were shaking and very tense as we waited for the results of the vote having to do with our Independence.[58] During the morning, the entire school took part in a *misdar*.[59] And Dr. Biram gave a speech that we must be ready for everything, to sacrifice the body, the soul, and money. (At that moment, I thought maybe he's referring to taxes, which my father is always very nervous about.) He said that 20 pioneering kibbutzim just left to pioneer in the Negev. He said that the Negev continues to call and yearn for us. The speech was excellent, and the assembly great. (In the evening, to everyone's anger and irritation, the vote was postponed.

About 2 o'clock in the middle of the night (after the close of the Sabbath), I was awoken by a knock at the front door. Dr. Matzdorf and Hanna, with their faces gleaming, said that the news has arrived that we were given our independence, and that **A FREE HEBREW STATE** was declared![60] I thought I'd go crazy but by 3:00 I fell asleep again, I was so exhausted. At 6:30 the next morning I got up and, looking out the bathroom window, I saw Hanna, who had gone downtown to the Hadar at 2 a.m. that night. She told me that the whole Hadar burst into a frenzied hora and everybody was simply going crazy. At 7:00, I began to weep from all the emotional turmoil, and at 7:30 I stopped.

I didn't think that CHAGAM[61] would be postponed, so I went to school that morning laden with puttees, rucksack, my water canteen, and in uniform. The streets were packed with life, and Hebrew flags were flying everywhere. At school, we were told our hike was postponed, because the situation was very tense

---

[58] I realize how matter-of-fact I sound here. We were oblivious to the machinations of U.N. politics and, furthermore, we teenage sabras always felt independent and actually took our independence for granted. After all, we had never personally suffered the traumas and effects of life in Europe, as did those Jews who had made their way to the Land of Israel as refugees. Also, there was so much going on on the ground that the U.N. vote seemed to us if not irrelevant then certainly remote. I didn't give a damn what the U.N. decided. I had never felt like a second-class citizen and did not need affirmation from some faraway institution.

[59] Misdar—an outdoor assembly.

[60] This was the U.N. resolution referred to above.

[61] Our paramilitary training.

and that the Arabs and our counselors were very "busy." When the bell rang, Dr. Shapira told us that because no announcement had arrived from the Department of Education we should go back to our studies.

We burst out with anger, but we went back to our classes. Of course we didn't study and instead went a little crazy. Our Nature Studies teacher could not keep any discipline in the class. Suddenly, in the middle of class, we heard a loud bugle. We flew to the windows. The trade school boys, those "bandits,"[62] were marching by. We waved to them and cheered. During recess, spontaneously, all the classes burst into a huge emotional hora. The teachers could not drag us to go back to class. We danced very well. It was very hot. We began to sweat. After about an hour of dancing in the schoolyard, Dr. Biram delivered a short speech and told us that classes were dismissed. All the others went on dancing, but our class went into one of the empty classrooms and we prepared the food (because we had brought a lot of food for the hike) and organized a *kumzitz*.[63] Many left, so that there were 12 people left. We pushed the desks together to the middle of the room, and we sang for a long time. We then divided the food. After a half hour of singing and eating, we rearranged everything and it was quiet. Then we played the winking game and took lots of photographs of each other.

We all went back to the schoolyard and we took pictures and we folk danced. It was about half past one and we were the only ones in the schoolyard. I went home at 2 o'clock and at 3:15 went back to school for an assembly, and then to continue to a town meeting. At school we stood at attention for the raising of the flag. We then marched the length of Nordau Street, all of Herzl Street, singing in unison and marched with a nice rhythm, full of energy. We were dispersed to sell ribbons—the money to go into a national emergency fund—near the Beit Hakranot. There were hundreds of people and we had to push our way. The streets were packed, and there were emotional speeches and singing groups everywhere. By 5:30 we stopped and we returned the money that we had raised. To our amazement, it was dark. We saw the schoolyard floodlit and there were wild horas, and we quickly joined the circles. And again we danced with the groups from the Carmel, Bilu, Geula. We danced beautifully. I taught Yoel the "taish"[64] dance. We danced

---

[62] I meant this affectionately.
[63] A picnic or gathering around a campfire, part of a Palmach tradition and which became a popular term.
[64] A kind of folk dance with couples, rather than in a circle as was more usual. It reminds me more of American folk dancing.

until 7:30. At 8:00, I walked up the hill home with Daniel. The next day my legs did not obey me.

Arza told me that our friends went on going crazy and dancing till 9:15, and she even said that on the Eve of Independence she actually danced in the streets. Now, however, we must harness our energies for serious work. Already on the news we've been told about seven who've been murdered by the Arabs and now we have a neighborhood watch—never mind, this happens only once every 2000 years!!!

LONG LIVE THE HEBREW STATE!!! (By the way, all the school reprimands and punishments have been cancelled. This, however, does not affect me.)

DECEMBER 10, 1947

The Hebrew state costs us dearly. Sacrifices, sacrifices, sacrifices, sacrifices, sacrifices, blood, blood, blood, blood, blood...... attacks, battles, and again casualties. It's really terrible. All the time one hears shots and explosions. People are being killed left and right. The two senior classes at school do not study three days a week. They are "busy."[65] This last week, the kibbutzim were not touched. To our horror we just heard that six of the young people from the Negev were attacked and murdered, and the eldest of them was 20 years old!!! All our counselors are deeply involved. I came home crying. Amos and Amirav were arrested. Dear, dear Amos! They were spotted on watch and that was during the time the Arabs of Rushmia[66] were on the attack. The Arabs started throwing bombs, and of course the English were nowhere to be found. Then they started throwing hand grenades and after that the bastards went away, then the government appeared and of course arrested them.

I am sitting alone at home...bombs blowing up. God knows who has been murdered, wounded, or has fallen. I'm in an awful mood that I could die from.

Today I was waiting for my father near Café Snir; a taxi drove by full of young men, two from the Negev unit. Maybe they are being sent out of Haifa. God knows where. Oh, how awful!!! I wish I were of an age that I, too, could get out to the fight and

---

[65] This means they were caught up in the fighting that resulted from the six Arab countries attacking Israel after the UN acceptance of the idea of independence, these 17- and 18-year-olds were already participating in the effort.

[66] An Arab town near Haifa.

pour my anger, my rage, across our land, in the open spaces of my homeland, our tiny country. I wonder what is going on at this time in Poria??? There is fear of martial law.

December 13, 1947

On the 12th of December, I went in the afternoon from 2:30 to 4:30 to the cinema with Daniel. The film was *Tarass Boulba*[67]—a cute movie with lots of Cossacks. Danielle Darrieux was the heroine; she is so feminine. There was a Cossack there [in the movie] that when he smiled, he looked just like my cousin Danny, like two drops of water. The cinema was nearly empty. People were afraid to go on Friday because of the Arabs. What is this! Any place I enter with Daniel, all the girls stare at him!!!! I must admit that I felt very special, as if a knight is walking with me. But I knew that this doesn't amount to anything and I had the feeling as if he had nobody else to go with. All in all, however, it was very nice.

This evening, my parents and I took the bus up to the Chissicks'[68] .... a nice young English Jew joined us. I noticed him looking at me a lot. And really my mother told me that he thought me "very okay"! The old ladies decided that I had a nice figure. I never get compliments from the people that really count!!

Today is Shabbat. We had a Scout meeting this morning, and in the evening a Hanukkah party was planned. I came home at 12:00 p.m. and Joshua Ginsberg had a Bar Mitzvah. I went and it was very nice. The cakes were great and we square-danced to the music of a mouth organ. In the afternoon at 2:00, a curfew was declared for 36 hours! We were furious—only in the Jewish sections! At the time that the Arabs are making all the trouble. I'm sure there will be searches. Because a) during a curfew they don't tell you how long it will last; and b) in Tel Aviv it lasted four days and so our Hanukkah party was canceled.

[67] This was an Austrian film that was later remade in 1962 as *Taras Bulba*.
[68] We had dressed for dinner. My father was perspiring in his tie and jacket on a warm night. The bus was packed, and I felt a little ridiculous being so dressed up in the midst of a crowded public bus. I distinctly remember feeling embarrassed and wishing that the earth had opened and swallowed me up.

Everybody in my neighborhood rushed to Schwartzapfels'[69] and we stood in line. There were lots of people and little food. I walked up the hill[70] and at five o'clock all the neighborhood kids climbed up to Esther's third-floor flat. All of us girls were wearing long khaki pants. At first it was fun. After a time, Esther and Daniel broke away from the group and were creating a new dance together. At first, it was interesting, but afterwards to keep watching them all the time became boring. The rest didn't feel that, but I got into a bad mood. If I were a boy I'd fall in love with Esther. She is similar in her face and behavior to Ruth in *A Spring Meeting* with her two unraveling braids jumping on her back. Afterward, I did not take part in the games and felt very sorry for myself, and it hurt me. And anyway it's no wonder that the boy has fallen in love with her again. But that is not what hurt. There and then I decided to stop giving Daniel advice and to always be virtuous and "a good Christian," even though I like him and her just as much. And then, of course, I began thinking of Poria, a patriotic life—as if these kinds of things don't happen there too.

This gave me such an awful mood that right after supper I put it all in my diary. My father started nagging me about the homework. I thought I'd go crazy. I had finished my French, and Mummy was brushing my braids.[71] I told him

---

[69] Schwartzapfels—the name of our local grocery store, owned by Mr. and Mrs. Schwartzapfel, who worked side by side from early morning until late at night. He had escaped the Holocaust and was a bundle of nerves, with silver teeth lining his mouth and a deeply lined face. Mrs. S. had a lovely Madonna-like look to her, with smooth skin and a high round forehead. She was always smiling, at least outwardly the epitome of calmness. That night, Mrs. Schwartzapfel looked more harassed and tense than usual. Mr. Schwartzapfel's cheeks and mouth were sunken, his silver front tooth so prominent. His Hebrew was poor and laced with Yiddish. His little round wife helped him, calming him down, always at his side. Her hair was white, pulled back in a bun, light-blue eyes and fine clear skin lined in the finest of lines. She was always patient, making peace between her husband and the customers. They both seemed ageless. The shop was slightly dark, with big sacks of lentils and dry beans lining the walls. I hated being sent to their shop, because I then had to carry the heavy bags of groceries up the steep hill to our house. My mother felt sorry for Mr. and Mrs. Schwartzapfel, and felt that he must have escaped an awful past in Poland. My mother didn't buy a loaf of bread or half a stick of margarine without inquiring after Mr. Schwartzapfel's health and complimenting Mrs. S. on her fine porcelain-like complexion.

[70] I failed to mention here that I was carrying heavy bags of groceries up the steep hill to our apartment.

[71] For the life of me, I have no idea why I wrote the word braids, except that it might have been wishful thinking. I always had short, curly hair.

to wait, but he went on and on. I felt every nerve in my body tensing up, till I exploded and said to him: "You're going to turn me into a bundle of nerves, and I don't want to be like you." At that very moment my mother then began to tell me that my ears were dirty. I don't know what I said that my mother started to shout about the approaching end of the semester, that I blurted out: "I hope you die." At that moment, I wanted to bite hard into something to get over the shock. My mother adds oil to the fire and begins to say: "this is the generation that we're now bringing up in the Land of Israel," etc., etc., etc. I want to go to bed and cry, cry, cry............ **I AM HORRIBLE!!!** I am ugly, mean-tempered, and nervous. I just think that I'm really not such a bad girl. But still I don't wish to remain this way. *To change, to change, to change.*

DECEMBER 30, 1947

I'm more or less at the end of the book *Ben Haaretz*[72]—an excellent book. I would like a boyfriend of this type, because he knows how to combine all of the qualities that I would want. He is wise, he is not empty. He's a *hevreman*,[73] and hand in hand with his education he also knows how to dance the *Kozachok*[74] and go for a walk with a girl. If he loves, his love is pure and complete.

JANUARY 12, 1948

On the 30th of December 1947, I wanted to write a lot, but I had to stop in the middle and I don't recall. A lot has happened in the last few weeks and I shall try to sum up.

[72] A title that translates to *Son of the Land.*
[73] Essentially this translates as a good sport—self-confident, open to people, and not afraid to take risks.
[74] A Russian or Ukrainian dance where you hit your thigh as you're making your moves, with lots of hand-clapping.

A) The troubles. The barbaric act in the refineries and so forth.[75]
B) And especially what happened in Kfar-Szold where 600 armed Arabs from Syria attacked the village.[76]

That reminds me that a week ago I came home and found Danny. He was dressed in old working clothes and had grown a ginger (reddish) beard. He was handsome and sweet. [Our neighbor] Mrs. Matzdorf decided that he looked like Jesus of Nazareth. But I thought that he looked like the picture of the [British] sailor on the cigarette box [Player's]. His truck had broken down and he came to stay with us until it would be fixed. He drove through Rushmia[77] during the shooting—idiot (hero?). Mummy hugged him the whole time. By and by he needed to call Poria to talk about security matters, because he's in charge of security. We didn't know what to say on the telephone until eventually we telephoned[78] and Danny identified himself to the operator in Alumot [the kibbutz] that he is "Danny, the driver from Poria." This pedigree shook something in me!!! "Danny, the driver from Poria"!!! He announced to them that the "working tools"[79] were in the shed. The young man understood.

The next morning he left us. In the afternoon he telephoned from the law court. He has been arrested! Because they [the British] found him carrying arms!!! I felt as if my breath flew away. In the afternoon, Mr. Salomon was in the law court and because of his influence Danny was freed. Mr. S. told us that that very same Danny, the hero, when he spotted somebody who knew him, got tears in his eyes![80]

[75] It took the British and the Mandate Police an hour to arrive at the British-owned refineries. As I recall, there were six Arab casualties and 46 Jewish casualties.
[76] The attack was eventually repulsed with the help of the British.
[77] Rushmia—a large Arab village in a valley located east of Haifa in which there was lots of fighting. When you drove by it, you took your life in your hands. It was particularly dangerous at this time because the tension between the Yishuv and the Arabs had risen to a pitched level and the British were trying to get out of the country as quickly as they could and favored the Arabs.
[78] Like most of the rest of the population, we didn't have a telephone so we always had to go across the hall to the Matzdorfs', who were given permission for a telephone because Mr. Matzdorf was a doctor. In this case, we had to be careful because this was dangerous and serious stuff. It was illegal to talk about arms and yet we needed it for defense because part of the troubles was all about fighting for our survival against armed Arabs. It was illegal to carry arms—the British didn't permit it—so it had to remain secretive. It was a very tense and dangerous period.
[79] Working tools—his code words for arms.
[80] Mr. Solomon was a prominent lawyer whose wife, Sara, was my mother's bosom pal, so he had known Danny since babyhood. It was by sheer coincidence but certainly serendipitous that they saw one another in the court that day.

Also, the sister of Yael Zuta (Bubba) was murdered.[81] It came as a ghastly shock to all of us. She was a wonderful girl.

Apart from that, I cannot go down at all after 6 p.m. in the dark, down to the Hadar where my group meets. And from this a lot of bitterness grew in me. Arza and Ora organized a little group and wanted me to join. I was terribly happy, but… . The tension in the country also caused tension amongst us because we are a border neighborhood and a lot of *Yeckes* live among us.[82] Our parents are out on patrols. Daddy went out once and right away got sick with sciatica. So that for him it stopped. But Mummy goes on patrol every two weeks from 7:30 to 1:00 at night. After this, when the situation got worse and worse, the issue of patrolling during the day came up. It was decided that the children over 14 would guard and act as messengers. A committee was created with Robert Prezente[83] chosen to be head of the neighborhood committee. He fulfilled the job with such fidelity and seriousness that sometimes it causes us to smile. We are very simply "a people under siege!"

Nothing special happened. There were some attacks on the Windsor House,[84] and the shots shook up the neighborhood. When my bus passes by the Hotel Carmelia (some passengers have already been killed on bus route #30), everybody bends their heads slightly [so as not to be exposed] and chats more so that the other passengers will not notice their fear. One crowds together when an Arab is seen running from one house to another.

I went to some Scout evenings in our shed and to the cinema, but less and less because of the situation. We had a Scout evening on a very rainy day. There was terrible rain and many storms, but even so I went down with Daniel. We ran the whole way. He raised the collar of his battle dress,[85] and I felt as if we were rushing away from the police. The evening was really nice. We saw a movie, and after that our counselors left us alone in the shed, and we went nuts. I danced a lot, especially

---

[81] She was murdered by the Arabs along the road from Haifa to Tel Aviv, going by Rushmia.

[82] The tension in the country also caused tension among us because we were a neighborhood on the porous border between the Arab community and the Jewish community in Haifa. I'm not sure why I even mentioned the German Jews in this context.

[83] I remember him as being Romanian, which is evidence of how mixed and international our neighborhood was. Each one was talking his own language, seemingly just a few minutes removed from Europe. These people were all educated, middle-class and up.

[84] The Windsor House was an upscale apartment house overlooking the road from downtown Haifa to the Carmel, right up the hill from our house, just beyond the Persian Gardens.

[85] This was a short jacket copied in the mode of the British army uniform, much in fashion at the time.

with Giora. The boys began imitating the girls' walk and talk, and we literally lay on the floor bursting with laughter. At 9:00 p.m., Daniel came to get me and we left. We were near the Armon Cinema[86] when a bus came by. We heard a loud shot right near us and I saw someone fall dead. I wanted to run toward the action, but Daniel's practical mind pulled me away and we left and walked home through dark back alleys, not uttering a single word to each other.

On Shabbat, Ora and Joel walked up to visit me and it was very nice. Daniel comes by a great deal. Mummy is already starting to hint that he must find me appealing. She does not understand that he hasn't got Ehud with him so that's why he talks to me. (Maybe, who knows!) After all, I am a good student and that's important to him. Apart from that, he would not acknowledge that I have not got the kind of standing among the boys that he would like in order to encourage him to love a girl, or that she could become his girlfriend.

I was delighted to receive a fat envelope from [Kibbutz] Dafna. I still keep up very close ties with my dear counselor [who had settled there].

JANUARY 25, 1948

Yesterday, on Motzei Shabbat,[87] the whole Haifa Scout group met for an evening. It was lots of fun. There were skits, a program, and dancing. I wore the blue pleated skirt with a white sweater. I cut my hair in a round shape with no need for pins or barrettes so that I think that I did not look ugly, and there were some that looked at me. I looked forward to a very nice evening. But, of course, as is my luck, I had to leave the group at 9:00 p.m., and I did not manage even one single dance!

On Saturday morning there was no Scout group meeting so I went for a walk with Miku and Robert and Ezra. It was very nice, and especially when you are one girl with three boys and you get all the attention. We walked up to Allenby Park and used the swings. Robert was all the time right next to me and got on my nerves. Ezra looked especially cute, tall and with unruly curls.

---

[86] The Armon had opened in 1935 in the area of Haifa that had lots of opportunities for entertainment. It was huge and could hold large audiences. My friends and I loved going there.

[87] A tradition marking the end of Shabbat.

A few days ago I went down on the bus with Vicky [Victor]. As we entered the stairwell he said to me, "Why are you so cute?" Of course, that gave me great satisfaction. But, I'm not used to compliments, so I picked up a stick and pretended laughingly to hit him. I don't know if he meant what he said seriously. Maybe because what I really want is for something to come out of this—that there should be some results. It's very nice to be cute, but what will come of it, of what use is it? I felt that in the last large group party, that if I had stayed something would have grown from it, if only I had been able to stay past 9:00 p.m. …but for the constant curfews…

In the afternoon, we had a school party for Tu B'Shevat.[88] It was very nice. What can I say? I think I looked very appealing. All the girls were impressed. But as usual, nothing came of it. I was told that in the large party on Motzei Shabbat, one boy, blond, "fell in love" with me. That gave me a lot of happiness, but I was afraid to ask for details lest I become arrogant and stop being natural. And I fear that. You would think from what I've said that I've had so much success. Not at all. It's simply a new feeling I have had the last few days. I am happy that I have something always to worry about, because I don't want to be in a situation where everything is OK, and of course, I mean it in a social context. I don't really have to fear that all will be OK. Because as long as the bus situation is not OK, nothing will "grow" out of this. They will look, they will talk, and nothing more.

FEBRUARY 15, 1948

On January 28th[89] I turned 15. It passed quietly, and anyway I had lots of homework for the next day. In fact, I received some very sweet presents. My parents gave me a Yemenite blouse, something really beautiful! I got a blue shoulder bag and a grey pleated skirt. Among the presents that I was most happy about, truly and honestly, was Daniel's. I don't know. The gift really brought us closer. It's a small album for

[88] Tu B'Shevat—a yearly ritual of planting trees by school groups and communities all over the country.
[89] This is totally odd to me: I have no idea why I would have written January 28th, when my birthday is and has always been the 27th. It's possible this hints at my fear of, or disinterest in, numbers.

pictures with a Bezalel[90] cover. On a note he inserted, he wrote, "To Nookie[91] (the mention of my nickname was enough to melt my heart already) with feelings of affection, admiration, and friendship." And I think thanks. (Those words played with me, and at that moment I thought that the single word that is missing is love.)

About two days afterward, we had a Tu B'Shevat assembly in the afternoon and in the evening a group party. I wore my Yemenite blouse and a blue skirt. I got so many compliments. The evening was very nice. Afterward, we went out dancing.[92] That same blond boy that they said had fallen in love with me—and I think they meant Joav—was near me, and when we danced, he came and stood next to me in the circle. As usual, I could not stay late and I didn't stay to dance the *taish*, in couples. Nitza, Judita, and I shared a taxi home and came home by 10:30 p.m.

After this we had another Scout evening that was very nice. Since then we had a Shabbat in which Joel was present but he did not enter the house and only came by for a few minutes.

Joel is a really nice boy. He has eyes—something fantastic! Anyway, he's the type of boy I admire, and he shows me feelings of affection. Many times I meet him in the Hadar and he walks with me a few blocks.

A few days ago, I was coming back from visiting Arza and was on my way to Yardena's.[93] Joel bumped into me and he told me that he was on his way to Arza. I told him that she was giving a lesson right now, so he accompanied me. We were walking on Nordau Street, and I wanted to walk toward Jerusalem Street. I didn't know how to interrupt him in the middle of his talking to tell him that. So we kept on walking toward the Scout shed, and he thinking that I'm my way to going down to Herzl Street. At that point, I decided to turn around and walk uptown instead of downtown, and then say shalom and leave. He then said he too wants to walk uptown. Again, I didn't know how to stop him in the middle of his story. At last we reached Yardena's house. Tensely, I waited for the end of the story. I blurted out shalom and bolted. After a moment I hear him saying calmly "shalom." I clearly see that I still have not

90 The Bezalel Academy of Arts and Design is Israel's national school of art, dating to the early 1900s. It was established by some early Zionists trying to create a national style that would combine Jewish, Middle Eastern, and European traditions and was named for Bezalel from the Bible, a man appointed by Moses to design and build the Tabernacle.
91 In Hebrew this has no sexual connotation. This was just a nickname for the Hebrew pronunciation of my name, Nomi.
92 Every time I mention dancing, it's always folk dancing. And we always had live music, usually the accordion, nothing electronic.
93 My modern-dance class teacher.

got enough self-confidence and the know-how of what to do on such occasions when weighty issues arise between "him" and "her," such as how to say good-bye.

Saturday night we went to Nitza's place. Vicky taught me ballroom dancing. It was the first time in my life that I waltzed without looking down at my feet. I simply forgot the whole world, the universe.

On Shabbat morning, Ora, Arza, Schmuel, and Joel walked up to my house. At first, we sat on our balcony and we talked. I learned what a Mauser was and what is better in a gun, a long or short stem. We then left my place, called on Daniel, and we walked up the hill. We picked huge bunches of cyclamens and red poppies. We went down the hill and they left, and it was very nice. Daniel and I are really good friends. I wonder if, under his friendship, love is lying hidden, but I have no reason to mislead myself.

Judita gave me the photos that I had asked her to develop from a Shabbat in which we had pictures taken. There is one photo of Daniel and me. I don't know how I had the guts, but it simply makes me nauseous. It looks as if I am leaning my head on his shoulder. His hand is on my shoulder and one of my hands is on his hip. I am ashamed to put it in my album. But in reality I don't have anything to be ashamed of. Because if he loved me, he would not have done that. But he seems as if he's one of my girlfriends.

MARCH 23, 1948

Yesterday we had the oath-taking![94] Yesterday, we "promised!" I feel as if I have committed myself to something. It left me with an incredible experience. But I must say that I was a little disappointed. I waited for more. However, in these tense times, we took an enormous risk.

Let me describe it in an orderly way. We were supposed to take the oath last year. However, Ahuva [our counselor] told us we were not really ready as a group to take on such a commitment. We looked good on paper but were not yet deserving. She really was right and at last we are now deserving of taking the oath.

At 4:30 p.m., an assembly was called for all the youth movements in Haifa

[94] This was the Scout oath, which we all took so seriously, part of our youth movement. In Hebrew, the term is *havtacha* and means promise.

of our age in Betainu[95] for the 11th of Adar.[96] I must admit that I looked nice enough. I wore the Chagam[97] hat, a green tie, and a good bra. (Ora looked well too.) She and I went to Betainu and we stood by the wall where we could see and be seen by everybody. We were stared at on the right and on the left. I felt great. The assembly proceeded nicely without stopping, except for two explosions that scared the audience. At 7:00 p.m., we proceeded to the Scout shed and there we got organized. Four boys from Esther's group carried the flags. I wanted to weep when I saw them. They had already taken the oath and they were known as good boys. And now they're coming with us, their younger brothers, to the ceremony.

We were supposed to take our oath in Migrash Hapoel.[98] And there, really, everything had been organized: a large Star of David made of fire and the Scouts' emblem. But, because we were anticipating more explosions, Gabi decided to move the ceremony up to Mount Carmel instead—a very huge risk because the Haganah does not allow large groups to go up the Carmel.[99] Nevertheless, we went up in buses. We sang the whole way and each one of us pretended that we had just come back from army training so that we sang "To the Negev O' You Young Ones" ["*La Negev Ya Shabab*"[100]]. We reached the Merkaz, and from there walked to the Love Forest.[101] It was an absolutely clear warm full moonlit night. The tall thick trees threw dark shadows, and the shrubbery made a noise under our shoes. Dr. Shapira [our headmaster of the upper school and in charge of the Scouts] appeared in a Chrysler, and we all proceeded to the forest and arranged ourselves in the shape of the letter *chet*. The girls were placed in the middle and two rows of boys on either side. In front of us were two torches, and the oath was written out on the ground. Dr. Shapira stood between the torches and our counselors on either side.

[95] This was the name of the big house in which we all met for the oath-taking. It was a huge meeting place.
[96] This refers to an incident that took place on 11 Adar (a day in the Israeli calendar), in this case March 1, 1920, when Arab Bedouins surrounded a small settlement called Tel Hai in the Galilee. The settlers there were led by Yosef Trumpeldor, who eventually lost his life in the ensuing battle. His last words were "it is good to die for our country." Tel Hai became a symbol of Jewish resistance, love, and, if necessary, sacrifice for one's country. On 11th of Adar, Trumpeldor's courage is commemorated.
[97] Chagam—one of the first pre-military groups organized in schools, predecessor of the Gadna.
[98] This was the soccer stadium in Haifa.
[99] This was, of course, for security reasons.
[100] Shabab is an Arabic word meaning youth.
[101] I assume that this area was called this because maybe couples enjoyed some privacy there, but I really have no idea. We just always called it the Love Forest.

We invited Amos and Ahuva [our Scout counselors] as honorary guests. After all, a lot of what we amounted to as a group was due to their efforts.

Dr. Shapira spoke to us. He's an excellent speaker. Short and to the point. He talked about our duties and the difficulties of being human beings searching for truth in this world of ours.... . (after America had changed her mind overnight regarding the Hebrew state) and then the actual ceremony started. One by one, we marched to Shapira and declared our oath. At first, we giggled quietly [a form of self-consciousness] because when one approached, one forgot the surroundings and felt alone: the person, the torches, the oath. There were some that one could hardly hear, but on the other hand, there were a few who said it all fully conscious and with a military cadence. Ora moved forward and said the oath as if she were reciting a poem. It was terrible. Nitza was right next to me. Slowly, our turn was coming up. I was getting more and more nervous. I moved from one foot to another. Ira [Kahn] finished, and then Nitza followed. I saw her coming back toward me and I knew my turn had arrived. Suddenly I felt that I had forgotten one of the words, but when I took the promise I said it slowly and correctly. Nobody heard me and I don't remember a thing. I only felt that I had finished and that I had to shake Dr. Shapira's hand. His strong handshake brought me back to reality. Many of the girls were weeping. Arza and Ahuva L. burst out hysterically. But everything went over well, with the singing and going back into the Scout house. The program was not so great and was dedicated to the 11th of Adar. What was missing was the feeling that this was to commemorate these past events. And also the group's diary was missing. Nevertheless the program finished and we went out dancing. The dancing was nice and full of energy. I danced so much till I couldn't dance any more and the dust in the Scout shed rose, and I couldn't do any more. Some nice games were played too. Rindenau and I exchanged looks, but of no great consequence. It turned out to be 11 p.m. and games were still being played, till Arza dragged Joel away, and he walked us home. (I spent the night at Arza's, because it was impossible for me to go home at that time alone.)

Today at noon, I went with Nitza to the cinema, and when I returned I met Daniel standing by the gate all smiles, and I felt that he had something very special to tell me. And he told me that I had promised him to go down to the Hadar to buy a gift for Ora. It was too late to get the gift, so we stayed at my place. I never have to be concerned about what we should talk about. Usually he is the main and sole topic of conversation—him, always him. But this time, I described for him the give-and-take between Miku and Begoiler, two boys in our group, and we both nearly fell to the floor laughing. Tears were running down my cheeks and Daniel was holding on to his stomach because he was laughing so hard. Once he left, I felt a sort of satisfaction. The friendship between us is really nice and we are good pals, even though I rarely, if ever, talk to him about my feelings or personal experiences. In the evening, we went up to Thea. The bullets were whizzing by the whole time. Her parents are cowards, so they insisted on keeping us in the hall of their flat all evening.

I don't know, but from time to time Daniel's gaze rested on me; I did not mislead myself into thinking he was in love with me because that is not possible. I do know that he highly approves of me and is truly very, very fond of me.

MARCH 24, 1948

Daniel and I went together to the Hadar to buy Ora a present. On the way we bumped into Arza and Joel. She does not bother asking us where we are going or if we are busy. Instead, she announces that she and Joel were on their way up to my place. Despite Daniel's gesticulations and protestations, we all went up the hill to my place including Rivah, Berale and Pesach. On the way, we also brought with us Matti, Joel, Arza, Daniel and I. We walked about the Persian Gardens. We went up a little and took three photographs. It was very nice. At 1:30, we walked down to the Hadar and Daniel fibbed that my mother was waiting for me near the chemist's shop. At last, so we said shalom and we ran off. He followed my advice and bought Ora a silver and red purse, and he was delighted with the choice. I want to visit Thea this evening.

APRIL 9, 1948

I have finished reading *Jane Eyre* for the third time. I finished it this evening. The book is simply marvelous. When I read about the pure love between Jane and Rochester, and especially Rochester's for Jane, my heart overflows. Sometimes when I'm all alone, I think what will be the future of the youth of my generation. We will never be given this land. If we have not been given this country in the last two thousand years, we will not be given her now and not in this manner. The Jews will receive their land only with redemption.[102] The land will not come after this or that battle with an Arab village, or the exchange of shootings with [Kibbutz] Mishmar HaEmek,[103] but instead in a much grander way.

However, I shall never leave this land. We might remain a community small in number and that is how I want to remain: a simple farmer, provincial, but a Hebrew.

A few days ago Danny came for a visit. We went walking in the evening and then driving around in his armored truck. I noticed his back, the broad shoulders, the blue shirt, and the green sweater carelessly slung around his shoulders. This is the kind of boyfriend I'd like for myself: strong and young, a Hebrew in all his sensibilities, who would know how to love like Rochester, who will love my smile, a curl on the nape of my neck and the way I stand.

Tomorrow, there's a Scout evening, a farewell party for Michael near a bonfire. There is no question even if I'll be able to go. After all, how will I get back? And that is why I'm not even asking for permission [from my parents]—why put them in a difficult situation? I don't see any change in the general situation. They [the British] are bringing more soldiers from Jerusalem to Haifa to the French Carmel, and Mountain Road [the road running by my house] will never be opened! If I felt that someone at the party would miss me during the evening, would feel my absence, it would make me feel better. If I were not bound to my youth movement, I'd be happy with my own neighborhood. But my best friends are in the Hadar and that's where my group is, and that's why I'm neither here nor there.

---

[102] I was in a deeply dark mood and it seemed to me that something as incredible as reestablishing our ancient country would only happen with divine intervention.

[103] On April 4, just days before this entry, this kibbutz had been attacked in the early evening by the Arabs, with heavy damage resulting. A Palmach battalion and three other Jewish Army brigades had come to the aid of the settlers there, and eventually the road between the kibbutz and Haifa and the North was opened and secured.

APRIL 16, 1948

Today I received my school report for the third semester and I'm in a horrible mood. Fritzi[104] will never let me get unstuck from a C+, no matter how much I try. I've been studying Arabic like a donkey. Twice I got Cs and once a B, and he gave me a D+.

I am walking home when I bump into Daniel and had to stand listening to the great qualities of Ora and how all the boys look at her. Daniel has arrived at the conclusion that she's the best-looking girl in the group with most of the good qualities. That doesn't bother me, but it gets on my nerves that I have to always listen and satisfy him that he is revealing to me what a wonderful holiday he will spend with Ora. Arza herself is a hard piece of stone that one cannot move. She will not go to the cinema with Joel. I find her stubborn, a little too tough, and she shares very little about herself. Half the things she doesn't tell me. I walk with her in the schoolyard and hold her hand, which she cannot stand. She doesn't know how to admire something. ~~Sometimes I've arrived at the conclusion that our group doesn't have good guys.~~[105] And sometimes I feel that from time to time I enjoy a bit of melancholy.

APRIL 18, 1948

Today, Shabbat morning, we had a Scout meeting. When we finished (near the Rothschild Hospital), we walked up the hill and decided to hitchhike to the Merkaz [Mount Carmel]. Each time a car passed us, we tried to stop it with Joel and Gideon at the head. At last, a small taxi stopped and we all piled in, Arza, Gideon, Yael, Joel and me. We reached the center of Mount Carmel and waited for the rest. They all appeared half an hour later on top of an open truck, laughing and shouting and singing, and they continued on to the Ahuza.[106] The five of us felt sad and abandoned, and we wanted to punish them. Again we tried to hitch a ride, till eventually a truck stopped and we all climbed on. We all stood up holding on to

104 The nickname for one of our teachers.
105 I actually drew a line through this sentence in my diary. I'm not sure why I deleted it, but likely was trying not to sound negative about the boys in the group.
106 Ahuza—a section of Haifa high up on Mount Carmel.

each other, keeping our balance, and we sang lustily till we too reached the Ahuza. This is the first time in my life that I hitched a ride on an open truck and found it to be super! We sang "Hatender Nosea" and reached the other group. I have never had such a pleasant trip. We got down from the truck and all settled down in the forest. Again we spoiled ourselves and did not want to walk downtown again, so we waited. After many trucks and taxis that did not want to stop for us, a truck appeared and we all rushed toward it. He had to stop because otherwise he would have run us over. In the meantime, the others climbed the truck from the back, and we went down the hill singing lively Palmach songs. What a marvelous morning it was!!!

In the meantime, I did not sleep all night. Shootings, bombs exploding basically shattered my nerves.

The Arabs (with British help, of course) have been setting fires to Jewish warehouses, and three huge fires were reported. Haifa reminded me of Rome on fire.

We received a letter from Jerusalem and my Aunt Esther says that there is actual hunger in the city. But since the Castel was taken (what courage that took!),[107] one hundred and fifty trucks appeared, laden with food, and Jerusalem went out in the streets, dancing. The boys accompanying the trucks simply did not know how to react in the midst of so much happiness, kisses, embraces with which they were received.

---

[107] During the late winter of 1948, Jerusalem had been under siege, with a severe shortage of food and the water supply cut off. The road from Tel Aviv to Jerusalem had been blocked at Sha'ar HaGai (in Hebrew, it means "gate to the valley"). The story of the armed convoys laden with food and medicine is a story unto itself. Many of the convoys were ambushed and burned. The skeletal remains of those armored lorries still dot the road. The village of Castel had been settled on the mountains overlooking the most strategic point on the way to Jerusalem. In April of that year (just before this entry in my diary), the Palmach and Israeli troops took the then-Arab village of Castel to stop ambushes along the road, and from then on the road to Jerusalem was kept open. Palmach soldiers lost their lives in the battle. It has become an iconic battle and symbolic of the importance of opening the road to Jerusalem. A national park in the Judean hills commemorates them.

At this point in the diary, we've reached May of 1948, a pivotal moment in history—the reestablishment of the Jewish state after 2,000 years of longing and wandering. It was a moment bursting with pride and joy, while at the same time a moment of searing pain and grief for my family and me, as my beloved cousin fell defending our country. That moment for us was both a great gain and a terrible loss.

I stopped writing in my diary for some months. The intense pain of his death was so bloody raw that I knew I could not reduce it to written words what I felt at the time. How could I possibly have written that Danny was gone forever, never to come back to us? With the wound so fresh, the slightest thought of him and his rich young life caused an outpouring of sobbing and, especially when I was alone, an uncontrolled shrieking at God. What more did He expect of us?

What's very telling is that I left a blank page in my diary, between entries where his death would have occurred, perhaps knowing that some time later I would record the day I heard what had happened.

Much later I did write down my memories of this time. I wrote it in English while living in the U.S., as a way of sharing those difficult days with my husband and my descendants—Danny's name, as I adamantly knew then and now, must never be forgotten.

Once I was able to write down my memories of the day I learned of his death, the actual writing assured me he would forever be remembered. It was a recognition and acknowledgement that Danny died for us, for the Yishuv, for the country and the Jewish people.

Life for me never felt entirely free after his death. The weight of memory and loss has stayed with me. Any scab that might have begun to grow over the wound always peeled off with the slightest mention of his name.

My diary continued several months later, reflecting a return to some level of normalcy in daily life, but still, this many years later, I deeply feel the loss of my dear cousin. An ancient Biblical verse expresses exactly what I feel. It's from 2 Samuel:

Your glory, O Israel,
Lies slain on your heights;
How have the mighty fallen!...
Ye mountains of Gilboa—
Let there be no dew or rain on you,…
They were swifter than eagles,
They were stronger than lions!...
How have the mighty fallen….

—2 Samuel 1:19–27

SEPTEMBER 6, 1948

Much, much time has passed since I last wrote. I see that I last described the terrible unending noise in Haifa. Thank God this is over and Haifa since then is in our hands. There is a ceasefire, and we have taken back many places, and I have advanced to sixth grade!!!

Other than that, Danny has managed to get killed, but his soul and image are with me constantly, in every place that I go. When I am traveling or I'm in a sad mood, he is always with me. This is the reason I have not written up till now. It is so difficult to write about him as if he only existed in the past—him whom I will never again see. The most difficult time has passed, and now he has become an integral part of me, and I respond differently in different situations. During my summer holiday, I spent a week in Alonim.[109]

This page I am writing two days after returning from a month's work camp in [Kibbutz] Matzuba. A month that, had I missed it, I would have been heartbroken. Our group grew stronger and closer during our time in Matzuba. We spent the month working with carobs.[110] The camp made us cohesive, the entire group, and helped make us into one strong group that in my mind I imagined to be like the Negev group.

MAY 21, 1949

Much, much time has passed since I last wrote. I did not feel the need to write. Not because I have a girlfriend to whom I confide everything, but a) my heart has not been so heavy that I had to empty it out a little, and b) maybe because nothing special happened. This does not mean that the year was boring—not at all! I did everything that I needed to do.

I spent Passover at my aunt's in Jerusalem. It was a very peculiar visit. On one hand, it was like a victory march. Never in my entire life did I receive so many compliments and admiration. Also with Dalia's group I did not do badly. During the Scout evening, I danced a lot and was walked home, etc., etc., etc. I also felt that the boy counselor thought I was nice but did not want to show it. Poor guy! And once when I passed him with Mummy, he didn't even say shalom. Also with

---

[109] A kibbutz near Haifa.
[110] Called charoovim, which grew on trees.

Jonathan[111] everything went nicely, and my mother told me after I left that he approved of me. (It could be her imagination. But even if he never said it, I felt that things were okay.)

There was a major Scout gathering and I bumped into Daniel. I must admit I was very, very happy to see him and the feeling was mutual. I wanted to meet him again that evening, but Mummy did not permit me, and because she was ill[112] and tense, I did not have the heart to oppose her. (I was very sorry about it.)

By the way, I got a lovely sweater from an aunt by the name of Teema.[113] She had just come from England. I liked her very much.

Everything I have written up to now is from one angle, but from the other point of view there was a constant grim atmosphere at home [referring to my aunt and uncle's house]. There were days when nothing but Danny was talked about. Whenever I came home from a fun evening, I always played it down, made nothing of it. I never sang or hummed or put on the radio. And also the Seder did not take place.[114] And of course how could you expect a different mood? Apart from that, Danny's photograph captures half the room, and there are times when one simply thinks that he's still alive.

Because I am crazy about my Aunt Etti, I felt compassion for her and her sorrow is also my sorrow.

Daniel has not written me since Pesach. I cannot guess why but let him not think that I will be the first one!...

I think my heart is heavy for two reasons: a) it seems to be that I have fallen in love; and b) it seems to me that without realizing it I am starting to worry about my final exams that are approaching.

As to the first reason I have written that it only "seems" to me, because at the beginning of the year it seemed to me that I had fallen in love with [R]. A lot of his languid charm attracted me. He always reminds me of Henry Wotton (in Oscar Wilde's *The Picture of Dorian Gray*). I always imagine him sitting in the garden of his estate, his long legs crossed, and a beautiful rose held between his long white

---

[111] A second cousin of mine, Jonathan Hyman, who fell in the 1973 war.
[112] She was on her way to the Hadassah hospital to cure a severe skin allergy.
[113] This is the "aunt" I referred to above. I'm not at all sure of the relationship, but to the best of my knowledge she was a cousin of my mother's.
[114] I vividly recall my aunt Esther saying that without her son there was nothing that she felt like celebrating, not even Passover. This was the only Seder I have ever missed.

fingers… . I, of course, did not think I had much of a chance with him. He was new, I never went home with him [in the same direction] and I never exchanged a single word with him, except for looks that he would sometimes send me. As time went on, Dalia, who lived next door to him, fell madly in love with him and caught him. I'm not sure that he is all that in love with her. While he was known to have become her boyfriend, he carried on a relationship of glances with me and Putti. She also tried to flirt with him, but with them also it was a relationship of looks. I know that had he suggested that I become his girlfriend I would have agreed and would have gone on loving him. Seeing that that is not the way things developed, I controlled my feelings and decided that I would not be among his many admirers waiting with fear and trepidation for one of his glances. Apart from this, the fact that he was in America during the time that Jerusalem was under siege repelled me. As things stand right this moment, I would not agree to be his girlfriend, and I have no feelings for him. It might very well be that it was not love at all. I don't know if this is even important enough for me to analyze it.

The youth who has now captured a large part of my heart is Rafi F.[115] How and why, I do not know. A) he is very handsome, b) an honest boy—when I asked him if he's interested in politics, he said no, only in drawing and music. With R., I cannot build for myself an ideal, but with Rafi I can find an ideal. His attitude toward me I do not know. I think it is warm. The fact that at times he doesn't say anything is just like me and strengthens my wondering what he feels. I will cover up my feelings of love as long as the relationship between us is neither clear nor in the open.

What is hidden in the lap of the future I do not know. Right now, I am crazy about him, but I am convinced that if he does not show me a sign that he is mutually interested in me in such a way that I can trust him—and not that the whole time I'll be testing to see if I was right or not—I will then suppress my feelings toward him.

When I started writing at this date, I wrote that Daniel had not written and that I would not respond. Well, a few days afterward, he came to visit me. He was suntanned and handsome. He amazed me by how much older he seemed. According to him, he now looks at girls from a purely "realistic" point of view. He says it's not worth wasting too much time on them. If she "permits," it's fine; if not

---

[115] This was Raphael Freund (Rafi), a boy who later became Ora's husband.

he gives her up. What really seemed strange is that while he was sitting, he was blushing from the beginning of the visit till he left, as if he were repressing feelings and issues, and they were all dying to burst out of him—such as experiences that he had never felt before, etc., etc.

June 30, 1949

The time has come for me to say the blessing Shehecheyanu[16] because I have finished my exams, with the last one, most beloved—mathematics!!!! The rest I passed fine, but about mathematics, I'm not sure. Anyway, there is no point in my worrying about it right now. I'll wait for the results.

In the last few days, I've been having an awfully good time. On Wednesday, Mrs. Rosenblatt telephoned to say that her nephew[117] has appeared, or some sort of relative, 15 years old, who said that he was interested in meeting only girls. She brought him over in the evening, and I must say our first meeting went over very well. He sat around for a few minutes and after that we went down to eat ice cream at Snir's.

Before that I had been expecting one of two different types: either the American popular type with the turned-up nose and so on, or a Diaspora type with glasses. Well, an American appeared with glasses. He is very far from being unattractive. He has a high forehead, beautiful far-apart eyes. His face is open and intelligent. From the minute we left the house we did not stop talking till quarter to one (9:00 to 1:00). He has three important things (I don't know his character yet): mind, tact, and a sense of humor. One can have discussions with him about everything. We talked about politics, about President Truman and his daughter, about his circle of friends. He described with great humor some of the types of [New York] girls and we talked about my group and more and more. He is awfully mature for his age, and his manners are free and easy.

[116] Shehecheyanu—a popular saying, based on a prayer of deep gratitude to God. It is recited in thanks, a Jewish blessing that has been said for two thousand years to celebrate special occasions: Blessed are you, our God, king of the universe, that has kept us alive, sustained us, and has brought us to this very moment. Then we say amen. What strikes me every time I hear this is that it's so existential. It's not about tomorrow but now. It's so affirming, a blessing of being in the moment.

[117] As you'll see and no doubt have figured out from the name, this is the first appearance of the then 15-year-old boy who would be my husband.

Even before we came home, already on our first meeting as we're walking up the hill toward my house, he somehow kept nudging toward me, and I kept edging away, and found myself off the sidewalk literally walking in the thistles. When we got back into the living room, I pointed at one armchair and I sat on an opposite one. About a quarter of an hour later, I guess he got tired of it and he came and sat down on the arm of my chair while one of his arms was stretched across me and leaning on the other arm of the chair, so that if I had wanted to get up he would have had to get up too.

Next morning he picked me up and we went by bus to the beach. It was great, great fun. I had on my American bathing suit[118] and my hair pinned up on top of my head. I simply looked like an American girl (but that was not my intention!). Peter had on bathing trunks and a cotton T-shirt with huge letters on it saying West Point and the emblem of the academy. I, being a girl, was not even aware of it, but Dan Friedland shouted to me, "What is this, are you going out with West Pointers?" We swam, laughed, and talked. After that, we started taking photographs. He had color film, and I wanted to pack into the pictures as much color as possible, so I walked gingerly between the stones till I reached a large rock that was covered with green moss, jutting out amidst the waves. I had many demands. I wanted him to photograph with a wave in the air, with the foam and all. He wanted us to have a picture together. I was hesitant about taking a picture with too intimate a pose. But, to my great relief, by the time he set up the camera and ran to sit next to me, the camera clicked and there was no opportunity to get too close.

On Friday night, after supper, he joined my group for an evening of listening to classical music. He was wearing long gabardine pants. I felt that already then my group began making a great impression on him.

On Shabbat I had the opportunity to get to know him a little better, and especially his ease with people and a capacity to accommodate to them. I have not as yet met a person who can change the color of his skin as easily as he can and who possesses such a dry sense of humor.

Already, for our Scout meeting, he arrived in short khaki pants, a khaki shirt, and socks that came up to his knees. The meeting was cancelled, so a few of us

---

[118] This was a blue-flowered suit that had come in a care package from the United States, sent by American Jews who put together clothes and supplies to help during the period of austerity after the war of Independence.

went off to Jerry's house. Jerry's apartment is quite large according to my standards, but for Peter it was probably all new.

As we entered, all of Jerry's family was still asleep (Shabbat in the afternoon!). His father wandered around in brown plaid slippers and a dressing gown. From afar, we spotted the grandmother resting on an unmade bed. Peter suddenly whispers with a smile, "what have we walked into, a hospital!?!" After this, I took him to a dance workshop with my friends. At first we danced together, but I couldn't concentrate all the time because he kept commenting in English and I had to laugh. After all who comes to this kind of a workshop, not the most graceful of our dancers. We stood on the sidelines and he said he had never seen such peculiar dancing in his whole life. He doesn't understand how one can dance with such a slow rhythm and all of us pointing to one direction. We were practicing the Dabke.[119] He compared [one of my girlfriends] to a lion because she is not tall but square and she has masses of thick hair. I wanted to get rid of him so that he'd be more with the boys, but I did not have to worry, because after a short time he was sitting in the midst of the boys and they were interrogating him about American history. We then came back to my place because in the evening we were supposed to congregate on Mount Carmel with my friends.

We sat down on the balcony, and I brought out a small tray with sandwiches and we drank lemonade. Of course, it took us ages to finish eating because we never stopped talking and laughing. He also sketched a map of N.Y. for me and showed me where he lived. We could have gone on sitting that way for at least another hour because it was so comfortable, so cozy on the balcony. But Nitza came to call us to go. As we're sitting and waiting for the bus, I see that he has messed up his knee socks so that they were around his ankles and not pulled up to his knees as before. I asked him how come? He said they had simply fallen down. I said nothing because I understood what was going on. He had seen that none of my boys wore knee socks, so he very quickly imitated them. Reaching the top [of Mount Carmel], he disappeared among the boys and even Nahum and Schmuel Eiger carried on a conversation and it all went on very nicely. He's already gotten quite close to Jerry and, anyway, I've noticed his ability to become friendly with people, to get along easily with people, and to be liked by them. The day after this, we became very friendly.

---

[119] Dabke—a slow, rhythmic folk dance, based on an Arab folk dance.

During the morning, he went to the beach. I didn't feel like getting up early, so I sent him off with Nitza. He reappeared at the door at 3 p.m., in order to "pick up his watch and some other things." He came in and swirled around and around until he fell into a heap in an armchair. He was simply dead. During the morning, a terrible *khamsin*[120] developed, and the whole time he had been sitting in the sun, his back exposed, which anyway had been burnt from before and now got burnt even more. I had managed already to eat, but, of course, we offered it also to him. From 3:00 he stayed till midnight or even quarter to one. It was an absolutely delicious afternoon.[121]

I wore red gingham shorts[122] and a white blouse hanging out, so that everything was very simple and homey. We both shared the sofa, and I laughed the whole time when he described to me Nitza dragging him in the sweltering heat at 2:00 in the afternoon, on foot climbing the steps [from the German colony to my house]. He told me about the gossip surrounding Cleopatra and how Julius Caesar attacked England. After my parents left, I sat him down on the cool tiled floor, took off his shirt, and covered his burned back with talcum powder.

After that we visited a little bit with Hannah M., my next-door neighbor, and Vicky came and showed us magazines. After that we came back to my place, Peter, Vicky and me, and Vicky photographed us. Everything was simple and nice with no contrivances. I did not even bother to comb my hair before the picture taking.

Of course Peter does not know how to say "shalom," so he also stayed for supper. The whole time he wanted to help, but I, of course, did not allow him to enter the kitchen.[123]

After supper, we went for a walk and sat on a bench near the French Carmel. He talked a lot and we compared American youth with Israeli youth, and I told

[120] Khamsin—a hot, dry desert wind.
[121] That entire day, although more than six decades past, stands out in my mind. I know Peter walked in the hot sun all the way to my place from the beach, rather than hailing a cab or even hopping onto a bus. He had dreaded the long walk, but persevered because he did not want to seem like a spoiled American, to which, when he told me this, I promptly replied, giggling, "which you are of course." He went on in great detail with stories about his "exhausting" trip to the beach while I, sitting behind him, methodically peeled his burnt back like a mother monkey picking out lice from her baby's head, all the time laughing at his self-deprecating humor and egging him on for more hilarious details. When my parents entered the room, he quickly slipped into his shirt and stood up. His manners were always so good and easy.
[122] These had come in a parcel from the South African Jewish community.
[123] Our kitchen was old fashioned.

him the whole story about Danny. (It must be pointed out that I never talked about Danny to Daniel, even though I have known him for so many years.) That of course got us much closer.

When we started going downhill, he kept complaining that his back hurt and that he felt hot and cold. I said I didn't know how to help, when all of a sudden I felt him taking my hand... . At first, I tried to resist. He said that was not very nice of me, because in his present "condition" it makes him feel a lot better. I was petrified and speechless. Every time I saw a person's shadow, or the approaching lights of a car or bus, I abruptly pulled away. He could not understand my behavior and called me a "nervous wreck." That name stuck to me forever, at least till he left the country. He did not want to come home, so we continued walking up Hillel Street and back up toward Panorama [an area above the French Carmel overlooking the whole of Haifa]. We looked at people dancing in the café, and all the time we were holding hands! We then started walking down the narrow donkey path. While walking, I innocently suggested that we sit down on one of the rocks on the path.[124] That suggestion determined my fate, or at least his, for the rest of his stay in Israel. That evening, he seriously fell in love with me. We sat down and he moved closer and closer till we sat very close and he leaned his head on my shoulder. I didn't say or utter a word. The view was breathtaking. The whole of Haifa was lit up with some light from the moon. Simply magic. We'd been sitting for an hour when I said we should move. The whole way home neither of us uttered a word. I did not know how we'd part.

We stood a few minutes, and I, in order to break the tension, suggested we meet the next day and that he should bring the photos—in other words, all about logistics. He never stopped holding my hand the whole time, and when I finished, I was quiet for a minute and then blurted out "shalom," turned around and took off. I was sure he thought the parting would be more dramatic, but I was glad that it wasn't. After all, from my standards, I had already surrendered too much, and I decided there and then that whatever contact we would have for the remainder of the summer, a kiss would remain out of his reach.

My mother shouted at me a little and told me not to do anything stupid so that the neighbors won't say I'm a little tramp or floozy. (I had to smile to

---

[124] The donkey path was a shortcut through the woods from my house to the Merkaz on Mount Carmel.

myself because she said the word in Hebrew [and it sounded funny coming from her]—*pirchachit* or *pirchchit*.)

As a result of my agitation and the new experience I was not able to fall asleep. All night my mother told me that I tossed and turned in my sleep.

I'm going to stop writing now. I have packed these pages with so many details because, if he forgets, or if I do, or if somehow we never see each other again, I should have a memory of a brand-new experience, taking place in such extreme proportions for the very first time.[125]

AUGUST 18, 1949

After the last time that I wrote about, Peter and I went on meeting every day till we went off to camp. We went together to the cinema (Moriah and Ein Dor), and I went up to his hotel [Lev Hacarmel]. I loved sitting in his room, looking at books, etc. I always love the cozy aspect.

When I went up to the Lev Hacarmel before camp, we would go out on the balcony to drink something. So then when we sat down he suddenly turns to me and apologizes because he said it's not comfortable for him to eat and drink in khaki. I laughed and asked him what difference does it make how he's dressed. Anyway, he was not happy, so he went and got on his long gabardine trousers.

Anyway, I didn't know how I'd meet with him after "that" evening. It seemed to me that he also didn't feel comfortable. After we left the house, he asked me what my mother said to me when I came home so late. At home, when I thought about what happened I was very concerned, because, after all, with us we're not used to that kind of behavior after so few meetings. I surrendered as if I were used to it.[126] The surrender symbolized it but not my conduct: a) I was so overwhelmed that I had not uttered a word; b) I sat stiffly; if he needed more closeness or something similar he would have to make the first move. If he was going to hug me, he had to hug both my arms, because I did not move and my arms and my hands were close to my body. I did not make one step toward him. When we were returning

---

[125] I feel lucky to have a personal, eyewitness account of our meeting, and I'm grateful that I was conscious enough of the importance of these times with Peter to take the time to record these days in my diary.

from Lev Hacarmel, I would move away from him when a taxi would come by. Anyway, I am sure that for him my conduct was modest and okay, and different from the conduct of the American girls. Apart from that, I shared with him some of my ideas, and really they came straight from my heart. I told him that girls give everything more meaning, not like the boys that show off as if it were a victory. To my mind, it's nauseating to hug every girl if one does not love her. I asked him, "What's the pleasure of going with one girl when twenty have already groped her?" (As in America.) Those opinions gave him a chance to get to know me better and to see how sensitive I was on these issues, because at the beginning I was terribly worried because he had not as yet said or confessed to me that he loved me. (His daily visits—except for the time we skipped a day, and even then, when I came home he was there and his excuse was that he had "forgotten" his bathing suit— expressed his feelings.) After the visit to the donkey path, he kept saying, "Oh Naomi, I like you so much."[127] And I knew that there was still another word that meant more. Most probably he was afraid to be the only one saying it. After he brought me as a gift his pin (from his fencing group, the one he had promised me on the night that he had held my hand), he began using the word love.

I was not sure if it was worth my while that he should go out to the work camp with me. At that point, I must say I had not yet felt feelings of love. Then my feelings were toward Rafi. I was not sure how Peter would relate to me in the work camp. I feared questions such as, "Where's your American?" "What is it? He's fallen in love with Zehorah or some other girl?" Anyway, I did not invite him and not one word did I say that one could have interpreted as a hint to some sort of relationship. However, he joined us and went out to the camp, a little because the group influenced him to come and I imagine that also because I was going out. Had I not gone out, he also would not have gone.

At the beginning we were not much together, because he didn't know how to get close, but afterward till the end of the camp we were constantly together. When we just arrived at the place,[128] it made a terrible impression.

---

[126] What I'm referring to here is all of our hand-holding. Neither I nor my culture engaged in these kinds of displays of affection.

[127] It's interesting that I was quoting him and I wrote this line in English, rather than writing it in Hebrew. I also wrote the word "love" in English. I clearly heard these important words in his own language and quote him here verbatim.

[128] Kibbutz Ein Zeitim.

All looked barren and hot (they also did not let us take a shower[129]). When we started setting up the tents, I asked Peter how he liked the place. He responded that he had never seen a place with so many rocks in one place. During that day while we worked, we did not talk to each other. I would glance at him from time to time and he would throw me back a glance.

After sundown, after I went crazy with the girls [meaning laughing, giggling, and having a wonderful time] and it was terribly nice, I sat on the bed outside the tent and Peter came and sat next to me. We started talking and within a few minutes I see the whole group of girls sitting around us. I don't know how come it was comfortable to sit around us as if we were a circus.

Slowly, slowly he started to know our customs and slowly, slowly he got closer. (He always came to me. I never went over to him.) We would sit side by side in the communal dining hall and took walks in the evening. I loved sitting next to him. He always poured water first for me and always asked me first where I'd like to sit, and anyway so polite. At the same time, I felt how the others were looking at us. Apart from this, we would sit and laugh about some of the people, being aware of how we saw things the same way.

As for the evening walks, they were a whole other chapter. He got into the habit of coming to my tent. He would sit on Ora's empty cot and I sat on mine. This I loved most of all because the conversation between us was full of laughter and charm. There was nothing in it from the upper spheres, as there was in the evening.[130]

For example, [Naomi says]: "*Oh Peter, I can't wait to see your future wife. Sort of tall, bare shoulders, and yellow hair hanging down half her face. Boy, how I will laugh.*" Then Peter responds: "But you don't have blond hair, and you're not tall." Or, for example, he would tell me that his father and uncle owned shares in the hot baths of Tiberias. Naomi: "*Once you'll be married with children, then I will come to you as your poor friend from many years before, and I will ask for a ticket with a reduced price. Will you remember me?*" Peter: "*You won't have to come to me.*" (The intent is clear.) Or, when I would put on his ring (boy, do I love

---

[129] This was because of the scarcity of water.

[130] What I'm trying to convey here and what I so well remember is that we often talked very seriously and philosophically in the evening. The Hebrew idiom "the upper spheres" refers to spiritual and intellectual subjects, all much deeper than our conversations during the day.

when boys wear rings!)[131] and turn it around [so it would look like a marriage ring], and we would both laugh. There were thousands of these kinds of sweet experiences (those poses[132] to be photographed, like when we would sit on a moonlit night and he would describe us taking a trip together to Europe).

After that came the day we parted. The parting was 100% dramatic. I had no idea how much he loved me till Yosef R., who rode with him to Haifa, told me afterward that at the turn at the bottom of the road from which you can see the kibbutz, he noticed that Peter had tears in his eyes. When he told me this, I simply wanted to cry and began to appreciate the extent of his love for me. Despite all the signs of affection that he showed me (like bringing me bobby pins from Safed), I still did not trust those signs completely—I cannot decide why. I was sure that once he'd leave, the relationship would stop.

A few days passed and to my delight Ora appeared. The joy was really genuine. As I was speaking to her, I suddenly see Riva running toward me and shouting, "Peter has returned... ."

For the first moment, a wave of disappointment swept over me. For a moment the farewell and the closeness that was involved in it, and that was against my will (but I consoled myself that this would not continue the same way because I would not see him for at least another year), seemed to me empty and contrived. I did not have time to think very much when Peter's gleaming face was right in front of me. He stayed for another half a week. During that period I did not see him during the workday or during the night but the rest of time [meaning supper and the evening] we were together.

During that time our whole group got a special treat and we drove down on Shabbat morning to the Kinneret. On the way down, Peter had to be in a constant state of amazement as I kept pointing out every *moshav*[133] and kibbutz that we kept passing by. As we passed by [Kibbutz] Segera and my arm was stretched out under his face, he suddenly kissed my hand. I was sure that everybody saw. But he asked me how could I think that he would be so stupid that he didn't first check to make sure nobody was looking. I must say that this simple and innocent exchange I liked better than all those embraces

---

[131] I meant this facetiously because I never liked rings being worn by boys.

[132] This is how we referred to those special moments worthy in our eyes to be photographed.

[133] A *moshav* is an agricultural village where people have their own private property but share some of the heavy equipment, like tractors.

on our evening walks. Before leaving the second time, he gave me a letter that he wrote two hours before leaving. What a fan-tas-tic letter! With those few and undramatic words, he expressed his feelings exactly.

Before that, in the evening, we walked all the way to Safed.[134] We took lots of pictures, and it was very sweet. As we started our walk, he told me he wanted this to be an American evening. At first my heart sank and I thought that he was referring to something else, but he meant that he would be paying for everything. I agreed and asked that we should plan a lovely evening, in a nice restaurant, and that it should all be sort of grand.[135] He understood me of course, as usual. (I wore a khaki skirt and a Yemenite blouse, even though I wanted to wear my green dress, but I was afraid that there would be too much talk in the camp, because we left despite the fact that Sonia did not give us permission.)

We walked around Safed. We went up to the monument[136] and sat by it, and the scenery was simply astounding. He put his camera and our sweaters on the parapet of the monument. I asked him to remove them. I also did not want to take pictures there, so as not to desecrate the sacredness of the memorial. When he wasn't looking, I kissed the stone. As we were leaving, I kept turning my head and resting my gaze on the engraved names, with all the dignity and holiness that surrounded this monument. (For a moment it seemed to me that I was betraying the brave who had fallen and was passing my time with an American.)

We ate dinner at the Herzlia Hotel and we walked back.[137] In the morning, I missed an hour of work and I walked with him through the tents. Before we left, we came into a corner in his tent, and I rose on the tip of my toes and kissed his forehead! I was sure that this would truly be the last time, but fate wanted it different. With fate's permission, we spent one more beautiful day without having expected it.

I left Ein Zeitim with Nitza and Hadassa in a truck and we reached Haifa about 9:00 a.m., and I showered, ate, and washed my hair that was filthy. Because it was terribly dry there, and the skin gets dry from the sun and wind and dust, I took cream and smeared it all over my face. I wasn't the last word for

---

134 This was a distance of three miles up a curvy, hilly road.
135 Again, it's revealing that I wrote the word "grand" in English.
136 The monument was to the boys who fell defending Safed in the 1948 War of Independence.
137 I vividly recall the walk back in the pitch blackness of night, which took well over an hour between Safed and Ein Zeitim.

beauty.[138] As I was sitting on the balcony and drying my hair, there was a knock at the door…and my "knight" entered. I nearly had a stroke. I quickly put on my mother's robe and with cotton wool took off the cream. On my hair I wrapped a towel turban-like around my head… and appeared. We both split our sides laughing. I told him that not till I get a postcard from Paris, would I believe that he had actually left. (Mother told me that when he arrived in Haifa and he knew that he would not be leaving that same day he telephoned my mother and told her that the minute I arrived home I should telephone him.) We sat in the room chatting… . Afterward, we went over to Hanna [Matzdorf]'s and she played the flute and all was really lovely. We had a nice time all morning till his aunt telephoned and said that his father sent a cable and gave him permission to stay another two weeks. He was so happy that he nearly hugged me… . And everything was taking place at the Zalkins'.[139] He only had to run back and forth, back and forth to Melchett Street and to Chilik Weizmann[140] to see if he could change his ticket. After the poor guy ran back and forth a few times in the heat nothing succeeded and they were not able to change the ticket.

He stayed and ate with us and he wanted us to go back to his hotel so that he could send a cable back to his father. I was dead tired, and if not for my mother, I would have gone up to the hotel. She told him that if he wanted to he could wait, but that I had to go to sleep until 4:00. I just put my head down on the pillow and right away fell asleep. They woke me up two hours later. I slipped on the only dress that I had left and off we went to the Merkaz [the Mount Carmel Center]. We wandered around, entered the café, drank iced coffee, and it was wonderful. After that he picked up the pictures that were developed and we went to the hotel. It was lovely that when the moment arrived to go to the Moriah [Cinema] we didn't feel like it. Nevertheless, we did go. After that, we went over to his place and ate

138 This line, too, I wrote in English; I have no idea why, but maybe because my mother might have used it from time to time and I picked it up from her.

139 We still didn't have our own phone, and had to go next door and rush up three flights of stairs to our other neighbors', the Zalkins, to answer the phone. The Zalkins were our landlords. They owned the apartment building we lived in and the one next door, where they lived.

140 Chilik Weizmann was a younger brother of Chaim Weizmann, who became the first president of Israel. He was also the father of Ezer Weizman (born Weizmann), who became commander of the air force, then defense minister and later Israel's seventh president. Chilik was a good friend of Peter's father. He had visited him at the Plaza Hotel, spreading maps of the 1948 battles on the living room carpet, fascinating Peter. It was Weizmann who invited Peter to visit Israel that first time.

dinner at the hotel. Peter was in a terrible mood. I felt that if I didn't carry on the conversation he would have to speak and then he would simply burst out crying. The whole time he looked at me with such a deep and expressive look, and the tears simply stood in his eyes. The whole way walking home, neither of us uttered a word. My parents were not at home but we entered the house. I wanted to cheer him up, so I told him that I knew that after two seconds "Romeo" will forget me, etc., etc., etc. We parted at midnight without much ceremony, which meant a lot more to me than if the end would have been melodramatic!

At the moment that I said shalom, I did not realize the meaning of that moment as much as afterward; I had not realized that I had gotten so attached to him and that I would miss him so much, and after the end of the work camp I would not feel like going anywhere and certainly not to my Scout group. There were two weeks that I did not leave the house. I simply had no patience for anybody. The Scout group seemed hollow and lacking importance and I waited for the beginning of school. A stream of letters and postcards started arriving. Despite the fact that he expressed his feelings in the letters, I know that if I had seen this kind of letter at Arza's or Ora's or anybody else's, I would have said, "Boy, he is sure nuts about her!" But I don't have that much self-confidence, and all that remains is to wait till next summer and see… .

In the meantime, the more time passes, the more I think about him, and all the incidents float into my memory. The situation is to the point where Rafi is completely out of my thoughts and I can speak about him objectively. At most I am a little more fond of him than of the other boys. I know that my love for him was more superficial, maybe physical, like an attraction to a handsome statue and not more. I always knew that to be his girlfriend would not be among the easiest things, and the more I came in contact with him, his way of speaking and the conversations did not attract me. With Peter I feel that he understands me and we can adjust ourselves to any situation. What at first put me off about Peter was the lack of "*Palmachnikiut*."[141] I could not imagine him with a Sten gun, carrying the responsibility for a whole kibbutz and its welfare on his shoulders, as I could see Rafi in that role very easily. As time passed, that feeling faded until it disappeared completely. I am sure that I don't know him totally, and I'm afraid that there is another side to him that is a little bit hard, but I don't really know. One thing I do know is that those aspects that

---

[141] By which I meant a sabra attitude toward life.

I am familiar with only increase my love for him, and they are many and not found in everybody!!

(When I read again all I have written, I see that I have left out half of it, and that what I wrote is really very inadequate. It is similar to the description of my visit to Poria!!!!)

NOVEMBER 19, 1949

Tomorrow I'm due to get a letter from Peter, but it probably won't arrive for a few days. What I would like most at this moment is that somebody who has just spoken to him, or corresponded with him, will tell me exactly what his attitude is toward me. Does he still love me as he did in the beginning? As for me, what is interesting is that always when I feel low or in a difficult, unpleasant situation, I remember him and want him to be with me. Apart from this, I also would like to meet someone very attractive and then test myself to see if I'm still as attached to Peter.

Last week my group went for an outing and I played hooky. Instead, I went to a movie called *A Date With Judy*.[142] I'd like to see it many more times. One of the leading characters in the movie spoke exactly the way Peter does, and he also gave the girl a pin and is faithful and true to her. The movie so reminded me of everything that had happened, so that every moment I had to bend my head down so that nobody would see me smiling to myself, and especially as Ora kept remarking, "Doesn't he talk just like Peter?" My God, even she felt that.

The business with the pin reminds me of the Sukkot holiday I spent in Jerusalem. It is not news that I love visiting my aunt [Esther] in Jerusalem, and that when I visit her I am so content that simply being in her apartment fills me with satisfaction and I have no wish to go anywhere else.

By the way, there was no running water in Jerusalem, and so each time I had to go to the bathroom, I'd take a long walk into the fields outside the house. To add to all these troubles, I also got my period. We drove in a private car to Mr. Friedgut's.

[142] This was a movie that had just come out the year before, starring, among others, Wallace Beery, Jane Powell, and Elizabeth Taylor. I don't remember them specifically; what I do remember is the boyfriend, whose character's name was Ogden "Oogie" Pringle, and that it was something about a teenager with overprotective parents.

We were: Friedgut[143] and his son, my aunt, my mother, and I. The trip was very pleasant. The son, Norman, is not exactly Tyrone Power, but his face is not bad. (He doesn't have the sweetness and understanding that Peter's face has.)… He is smart and pleasant to talk to. During the trip he showed me pictures of his girlfriend and everything proceeded nicely. When we got to my aunt's, they came in for a cup of tea. I don't understand Norman. If he knows that he is so fragile, why does he keep emphasizing it the whole time? As we went up the stairs to my aunt's, I naturally wanted to help with the suitcases, and he turned around and said, "Do you think I can't carry them because I am so puny?" We then sat down and he settled into a large brown armchair and let his legs swing in the air. He was also wearing his father's jacket that simply covers him completely. When they got up to go, I suddenly heard him invite me to go with them for some supper. Of course his invitation gave me much satisfaction. Already during the trip he had suggested that I go with him to the cinema, but we arrived too late for that, and so I went with them. It was a very pleasant evening. One thing bothered me. From one point of view, after all, he invited me to go with him and I was supposed to behave like a mature human being. From another point of view I was young and I wanted him to relate to me the same way.

His brother, 17, was very nice and I really enjoyed it when the three of us were stretched out on the sofa and listening to the game between Brooklyn and N.Y.[144] In my heart I wanted N.Y. to win, even though I didn't understand very much of the game. When we took the bus to a small café in order to buy some soda bottles for his mother, each time he asked me if I would like to eat or drink something, each time I responded like a girl of three, "no, thank you." I was not used to that and I didn't want to tell them that. He asked me to go to another café. I nearly wanted to answer him that, oh my, if I would be seen with a young man in a café in the evening…but I kept my mouth shut because after all he invited me, and not a baby from nursery school. I wanted to go back to their house and lie on the sofa, joke, and be cozy.[145] We came home and his brother showed me lots of postcards of New York. I was embarrassed

[143] A Canadian Jew whose whole family had immigrated to Israel.
[144] This was, of course, because of Peter.
[145] I wasn't ready yet to take on the mantle of a young woman, which was not the way I related to boys of my own age, with whom I was so absolutely comfortable. None of the boys in my group would have invited me to go to a restaurant and paid for it. We just didn't do that. So it's clear I was having very mixed feelings here. I didn't want to pretend that I was more sophisticated than I really was.

to admit that the only place I recognized was the Plaza Hotel. I was ashamed to say that I know somebody living there.

After that he suddenly asked me how come I'm wearing a fencing club pin. I tried to deny, but they went on trying to guess and the three of us were laughing and all was very pleasant. He took me home in his car, which purred along the road and near my legs there was a small machine that warmed them up. I did not leave the car, till he walked around it to open the door for me. The real reason was that I could not figure out how to open the door. The first time a similar thing happened in Haifa and Norman opened the door, my father commented in his innocence, "Naomi needs a footman." Oh, I was so content.

I visited King David's tomb and Mount Herzl[146] with the two "Abrahamson sisters"—that is how Danny, ZL,[147] used to refer to them [meaning my mother and my Aunt Esther]. These were beautiful and interesting experiences but I have no patience to write about them.

November 26, 1949

On Thursday, I went upstairs to Vicky's to get a *Look* magazine. I wore my blue dress with the small stars and embroidery. I must admit the dark blue is very becoming on me, but that does not justify his falling on top of me. It simply crossed all boundaries. He even tried to kiss me and only managed to kiss my arms. I don't know if this was really the result of a sudden passionate reaction to me, or because he was following a textbook that pointed out the vulnerable areas in the female anatomy in order to arouse them. To my credit, I must point out that it did not arouse anything in me, and I fought to free myself from him. He never stopped trying to seduce me, by saying that after all he's not going to eat me, that we're old neighbors, and that I must have realized that he favors me over all the other girls in the neighborhood. Of course, that left no impression on me! If what he says is true or not, it doesn't impress me, especially when there's a voice inside me that tells me he says it to all the girls. I also added that I can never come for a simple visit

---

[146] This is the military cemetery in Jerusalem.
[147] This is the acronym that stands for "of blessed memory."

without him putting me into all these situations. He promised me that next time he would behave well, but he told me that I was not right and that June Allyson sings "All the Best Things in Life Are Free." Nevertheless, I don't understand the meaning of such an uncontrolled outburst.

This evening there will be a farewell party for Sonia. I must admit that with her leaving, an important stage of life will come to an end, especially for the girls, from all points of view. Aviva Mendel is taking her place. Aviva had been a good friend of Danny's. When she ran our first Scout meeting, I got into a terrible mood with all the memories that were tied into her.

DECEMBER 19, 1949

Today we got our report cards for the first semester. As predicted, it was not outstanding, but after parents' day, where the news was bad, the report card was a great relief. Sweet, lovable Berkov [the English teacher] commented "very diligent."

Now I want to tell about a very pleasant experience the likes of which I've never had before. That is the trip to the immigrant camp in Pardes Chana.[148]

---

[148] Most of the immigrants in this particular camp came from Yemen. In 1948, the new Imam, Ahmad bin Yahya, unexpectedly allowed his Jewish subjects to leave Yemen. The Israeli government launched "Operation Magic Carpet" and evacuated around 44,000 Jews in 1949. At the camp, we slept on the floor and chatted all night long. We tried to help with the children in particular. It was difficult but very satisfying. Among the youth at the kibbutz was a group of Youth Aliya—all of them orphans, no parents. Mothers, fathers, brothers, sisters, grandparents, all had perished in the Holocaust. I got close to one young man, very blond, whose Hebrew was obviously not native to him. He was too blond for me, a little withdrawn, and I could tell immediately by his tentative behavior and soft-sounding vowels that he was not a sabra. We spent a lot of time together, and he behaved in such a way that I knew he cared about me and was badly smitten. We spent a lot of time sitting on the back of big empty barrels in the shade behind the kitchen of the communal dining room, peeling hundreds of potatoes. A dark number was tattooed on his arm as also on the arms of many of his friends. He told me in a monotone unemotionally, about what happened in the death camps. One story I shall never forget was about either him or his father, who had to go over a list of people they knew were being sent to the gas chambers. They came across a name of a very close relative. He had the power to erase the name of the relative and substitute somebody else. I never dared ask what happened, and he did not volunteer an answer. We corresponded for some time, and I kept his letters for quite a long time.

MARCH 4, 1950

I see that the last time that I wrote was about the experience that I really enjoyed very, very much in Pardes Chana and afterwards in Ein Shemer. I had a good time because a) I personally had a marvelous time and b) because I also felt that the satisfaction derived from something a little bit new, original, helpful and that we succeeded in it.

Despite all of this, I did not write about it and I see that now I'm going to write about something totally different. It seems so true, whoever wrote it, "love is the history of a woman's life; with a man it is only an episode."[149] (Andre Maurois—French novelist)

Y.[150] and I have been friends for a long time. I got to know him better through Peter in the summer work camp. But that was the extent of it. After that he started joining the group and became friendly with everybody. I loved to chat with him because he was an easy conversationalist, with a light, clever sense of humor. He went out a bit with Ora after they had worked on a project together. If I want to be totally objective, I don't think he fell in love with her. He has walked me home a few times and once we had a really fun time. He bought me a cake, and then we were caught in an unexpected downpour just as we were walking by the Ezra Hospital. It was a lovely experience and maybe it started then…but I'm not sure. I did not notice any symptoms…. He had invited me twice to the cinema but I could not go. The group hinted that Y. and I were interested in each other.

Last week Purim[151] was approaching. I began bothering people for a hat and the socks [I needed for a Purim outfit]. Y. promised me his sister's socks…. (I must admit, I am sorry lately that I did not go with him to the cinema. After all, there is no reason that I should not have somebody to go with, especially someone as charming and witty as Y. is. I also calculated that at the end of school he is a wonderful jumping

---

[149] At one time I thought this was something said or written by Oscar Wilde, but I learned only later that it was Madame de Stael who wrote "Love is the whole story of a woman's life; it is but an episode in a man's."

[150] Y. was a classmate of mine, a friend in my Scout group.

[151] Year after year, Jewish communities the world over commemorate the actions of a brave young woman, Esther, an exile from Judea living in Persia in the 4th century B.C. An edict was sent out from the Royal Court to annihilate the Jewish minority living in the Persian empire. Esther's beauty and courage saved her people from the disaster. Her triumph is marked by joyous costume parties and the retelling of the Biblical story (*megillah*) on the holiday known as Purim.

board to various places. I thought of this in terms of friendship only. It did not occur to me to cause him to fall in love with me!!!) I was glad when he did invite me again to the cinema, and I did go with him. It turned out that he forgot to bring his sister's socks. After many runnings up and down the steps of his house, I went up with him. It was lots of fun, very comfortable and cozy. He dressed up and pretended to be his grandmother. (It now occurs to me that maybe on purpose he had forgotten the socks?) As a result of the flowing friendship between us, I asked him to photograph me in five different costumes [dressing up for Purim].[152] He right away agreed and decided that he would come to my house before the Purim party.

In the morning I was involved in rehearsals and he spent a lot of time wandering around the rehearsals and it didn't occur to me that it was because of me. If he really did fall in love with me, then it happened during that afternoon.

I showered, combed my hair carefully, and kept changing into the five different costumes, which became me. The afternoon was lovely. Each time he was ready to take a picture, he'd say "bird, bird!!" [which got me to laugh naturally].

In the evening, I was very cute in the nurse costume. I could see him watching me the whole time during the dancing. During the party he was in a terrible mood. Riva, in her innocent way, said in French so that the others wouldn't understand, that it was because of me. At 3:00 p.m. we were ready to go home and I declared in a loud voice that we were about to leave in order that Nitza and Miku would join us. Y. heard this and got ready to go too. He had already left the room and we followed, when Miku began to look for his *tarboosh*,[153] and the search took at least half an hour. When we got to the streetlight near Matty's house, we saw Y. walking. I whistled to him, but he did not turn around, but instead hurried up and went home. My instinct told me that his behavior was because of me.

In the evening I had a lovely time and danced a lot. To my astonishment I saw that Y. has started to learn to dance the hora with the boys to the point of exhaustion. All this actually was in opposition to his state of health. I understood that something has caused this sudden change in him. I tried to get out of dancing with him because he simply doesn't know how. At twelve o'clock he walked me and Nitza home. Since then we tried to keep away from each other.

---

[152] In the end, I decided on a nurse's outfit and went dressed in what I thought looked quite attractive, with a starched nurse's cap with a red Magen David on its front topping off the costume.

[153] This is a hat possibly more familiarly known as a fez.

I must admit that during the Scout meeting, I had a wonderful time. I am in a very good place right now. I never dreamed about it a year ago. And yet, a human being is never satisfied with what is given to him. Anyway, I feel that if Y. continues to love me, then I will be satisfied with that, and anyway I am training myself to be content with that. I want to add a minor detail. At the end of the free evening[154] Nitza taught me the song called "All Roads Lead to Rome." Many of the verses remind me of the evening I spent with Peter on the haystack in Ein Zeitim in which he spoke about a trip we would take together, and of course Rome would be in the plans. I simply fell in love with the song and smiled to myself out of joy.

MARCH 21, 1950

The holiday is continuing to be very pleasant… going to the cinema with a lively group of boys, a walk to the French Carmel in the evening in the company of Nitza, Y., and Z. (of course Begoiler, too), and an excursion to Luna Park and flying on the carousels.

I am constantly fighting with Daddy till my nerves crack—an alarming lack of control on my part…. Hovering over all these scenes is Josephine, pining away nonstop for her Napoleon!!!! And Juliet waiting faithfully for her Romeo!!! When I think that soon the day will come and Peter will knock at the door, and we'll go out together, I simply smile to myself, but at the very same time I don't believe that this date will arrive, so again I sink into a world of dreams and fantasies about imaginary, spontaneous meetings and having a lovely time between us…

APRIL 3, 1950

Nisan N. is about to get married!!! That's all that Sonia wrote us. My first response to the news was similar to Ora's. Most probably an accident. Oy, I was flabbergasted…Nisan N. getting married? At last this Adonis had been caught,

---

[154] This means that we didn't have a prepared program for the evening, but rather just a gathering of the Scouts with no special agenda or program.

and I really don't know how a man like this can at last commit himself to one woman. It seems tragic that an accident of this sort can determine one's life and one's destiny. Anyway, he has become so spoiled and sure of himself that it might be that his "wife" (if she amounts to something) will turn him into a man. He certainly has the raw material. With us, he was a very good, successful counselor and held the boys together. Sometimes people complain to God that He did not endow this or that person with enough good looks. In this case, it would have been much better if the Almighty would have given Nisan instead of a full ten portions of beauty, only five or six!

Now, I will come to write about something very different and of a type of human being that has a bit more weight and importance in society than my dear counselor, and he is Peter's uncle, Laurence Steinhardt.[155] He had been the American ambassador to Russia and now lately to Canada. Peter was extremely proud of him and feels very close to him. He had been hoping that he'd manage to visit him during his summer holiday. A few days ago, his uncle had been flying in a plane that crashed between Canada and America and he was killed. This upset Peter very much, more than I had imagined. I felt that Peter lost a very close and helpful friend. Peter always talked about how he wanted to be in the Foreign Service. I am convinced that even if Peter's and my friendship ends, I shall always care what directions Peter's work takes him. I want him to succeed in whatever career he chooses, a) because that is what he wants and this is where his

---

[155] 154 Laurence Steinhardt was Peter's mother's elder brother. Born in New York City in 1892, he was a graduate of Columbia, where he was Peter's father's classmate. It was he who introduced Peter's father to his sister and future wife. A brilliant lawyer and diplomat, he was appointed by President Roosevelt in 1933 to be U.S. minister to Sweden and later served sequentially as ambassador to Peru (1936–39), Russia (1939–42), Turkey (1942–45), Czechoslovakia (1945–48), and Canada (from 1948 until his death). He was killed in the crash of the Embassy's plane outside of Ottawa as he was flying back to Washington for consultations. Some mystery surrounded the crash and its cause at the time, with some thought that sabotage might have been involved, part of the Cold War tactics. But this idea soon was dropped as having no evidence or merit. Ambassador Steinhardt had planned to take Peter back to Ottawa with him for his school's spring vacation. I was terribly affected by the unexpected tragedy—not a sharp pain, but I felt so for Peter, that he had lost a close and valuable friend, a sort of soul mate, and certainly a valuable mentor. Peter always shared with me that he wanted to be in the diplomatic corps. He and his uncle talked about it, but his uncle had tried to dissuade him, suggesting that the Foreign Service was not a place for Jews, but was a tightly knit old boys' network.

ambition points to; b) because he's a terrific guy, highly intelligent, and also his character helps him to get along with people and to be respected by them. He is so not damaged or spoiled as a result of the background in which he grew up! This I could see in his conduct in Ein Zeitim. He never complained even once. Only when I opened my mouth, he agreed with me, and I am witness to the fact that there was an awful lot to complain about in Ein Zeitim!

We spent the Seder at the Chissicks'. I must point out that I thought that I would be a lot more impacted by Mrs. Chissick's absence[156] at the Seder. Half of my clothes and my confidence in my profile are a result of her friendship with me and are evidence of what good friends we were.

The G family was also present at the Seder. The father is charming, and the son "T" is a klutz! Many times I tried to start a conversation with him but he did not pursue it. Of course, I realize that it's out of shyness. But just as with Nachum,[157] shyness can be a charming characteristic—but with T, it's a character fault. Nachum is bashful but when one starts talking with him the conversation continues easy and interesting. And I have gotten used to Peter's self-confidence and his initiative-taking, which helped solve many issues and made it possible for us to meet so many times and over such a long time that I fell in love with him. (Nevertheless, this is a situation now, and I will test it during the coming summer.)

---

[156] The Chissicks, whom I mentioned earlier in the diary, were English Jews who lived in Haifa and owned the Armon Cinema. Ruth Chissick had lost her whole family in London in a direct hit on the bomb shelter in which they were hiding during the Blitz, and she herself had died during the previous year. When I was first born, Mrs. Chissick had asked my mother what she would wish for me, her baby daughter. "Is it beauty, wealth?" Ruth had asked. My wise, wise mother had thought for a minute and answered resolutely—"no, I want her to have character. In the long run that's the most important thing." Mother told me that story over and over again, and it left a strong impression on me. Ruth Chissick was my introduction to the world of fashion and elegance. She herself was a lovely woman, exceptionally elegant. She wore tweed skirts and a fox fur draped nonchalantly around her shoulders. She was slim and long-legged, and seemed very tall to me. Her skin was pale, her neck long, and she had a narrow, delicate aquiline nose. She had a sense of style that she conveyed to me. It was she who gave me a French silk scarf that I still have today and a Vogue magazine as a gift. I used to spend hours staring at the models in the ads. They looked aloof and bored—not a worry, concern, or sense of obligation marred their faces. I escaped reality by sinking into their faces; they were creatures that inhabited another planet. Mrs. Chissick and I became unlikely comrades despite our differences—in age and many other ways.

[157] A shy, respected boy in my class and Scouts.

I did not have much patience with T. Just as I dislike the exaggerated self-confidence of Ronny R., so I also don't have patience with the exaggerated bashfulness of T; it is simply an exaggerated lack of self-confidence.

This evening, the Gershonis are coming over with their parents. I am so excited. I simply have tears in my eyes when I see this couple! I hope I merit one day such a beautiful married life![158]

In order to prove that my head and heart are not solely into inconsequential matters, I'd like to say that I have finished reading *A Farewell to Arms*, and I'm preparing a book report on it. I also saw the film *Day of Wrath*. I was shaken by it and have not thought of anything else other than that. My father is extremely proud of my good taste, as half the town did not appreciate it. I must add that I would not have appreciated the film had I not read *Kristin Lavransdatter*.[159] It gave me an idea about the period and especially a feel for the Scandinavian countries.

THE EVE OF MAY 1ST

I have three more weeks till my French exam. I feel that if I age, I will age during this month. I simply must buckle down day after day and persevere in work that I have never liked. I find it difficult to concentrate when I know the summer holidays are approaching, and hopes and dreams are tied up with that: work camp (I long for that more than anything else), Peter's arrival with all that connotes… when I think of the minute when he will knock at the door, and we will go out together and it won't be anymore just a dream, trips to Jerusalem and pleasant times together. In other words, a holiday that a 17-year-old girl enjoys.

Last Saturday at 3:00, Daniel came for a visit. The visit was a great success. During the last few visits there were always silent pauses. This time everything flowed, and I was reminded of the good old days when Daniel was a constant

[158] I find it interesting that the Gershonis, whom I so greatly admired as a couple, later divorced. They were a very attractive American family who volunteered to help Israel in the 1948 War. He was an especially handsome, soft-spoken naval officer, having gotten his education in Annapolis. She was a strikingly attractive woman, also soft-spoken. Every time they left our house or at some event at which I was present, I felt very emotional.

[159] This was a lovely trilogy of novels set in 14th century Norway, by Sigrid Undset, who won the Nobel Prize for Literature a couple of decades before I read it.

visitor. Without actually saying it, we both felt happy and content with each other. We are not as open as we used to be. This might be to the good, because in this situation a friendship will grow between a boy and a girl and not merely between friends. Anyway, I cannot approach him this way. When he says to me that there are no cute girls left except me, I shut him up and I do not continue in the same direction as maybe I would with another boy. Also his hair is very long and he does not seem as handsome as before, but even now I have seen boys uglier than him. I hope that our friendship will go on forever.

That afternoon Y. came over so that we could go up to the hotel to pay Peter's aunt [his Aunt Gertrude, whom we were repaying for the photographs]. I felt before we went up to the hotel that he was trying to pretend as if this whole thing were a bother to him and that he was only going up with me because I asked him to. Intuitively, I understood that if his feelings toward me were more neutral that he would not have to behave in such a stiff way. Really, when we walked down to the Hadar, we talked and talked till we hit on the subject of L-O-V-E!!!

He lectured me about some of his philosophical ideas on this matter, like the fact that one can love and enjoy the actual feeling without needing the other side to return the love.

Nevertheless, what became clear was that, despite all of this, as a human being, he would want some measure of reciprocity. Lately he's been struggling and he's trying to rid himself of his feelings. I too talked and talked about "her," with whom he is preoccupied, without him understanding that I know that the whole conversation really revolves around me. Our dialogue was the art of playacting. I am convinced and I tried to convince him that he should understand that I hadn't the remotest idea who the "her" was. And I succeeded. This allows me to be much freer with him. If he frees himself, he will free himself. It is most interesting to watch him work through the process!!!

———————————

This last entry brought me to the end of one actual notebook in which I was keeping my diary. I started a new book to go on with my diary, spending a lot of time writing out the title letters with a great flourish—in Hebrew of course. The saying or phrasing for the title I chose for the second book of my diary is part of Rabbi Hillel's statement in the first century A.D.: If I am not for myself, who will be? If I am only for myself, what kind of a person am I? And if not today, when?

If I am not for myself, who will be?

JULY 6, 1950

It's been about a week since Peter has been here. If I had had to fill up everything that I felt before he came and all my conversations with Y. about his coming, then this scribbler [my notebook] would not suffice. I was convinced that Peter would not come back: a) because of what is going on in Korea, I believed that this issue would get in the way, and b) because I can't believe that to me, Naomi Harris, something like this will happen, that a boy will fall in love with me, and a year later he will leave Europe and an exciting "adventure" (I will come back to this later) and come back to me! The situation has worsened and there are fears of a third world war. The newspapers say that the Americans in Europe are in a state of panic and are returning to the U.S.

However, he appeared. Our first meeting was a little tense, at least from my side. Oy, I don't feel like writing just now!!! Because it seems to me terribly artificial.[160] With the passage of more time, I'll be able to write more clearly. Now it seems to me heavy, and the atmosphere is missing. One thing I feel comfortable writing down right now. This time it won't be as successful as last time, because I will not be able to behave in such a rational way, apart from which I have a feeling that he does not love me with the same intensity as he loved me a year before! A lot of water has run under the bridges,[161] such as the Paris adventure and the like.

---

[160] Here I'm talking about recording it all; nothing was artificial about our relationship.
[161] Interestingly, I wrote the first part of this sentence in English, as if to use that English idiom where I couldn't find an appropriate Hebrew one. As it was, I didn't even know that the English idiom was "water under the dam."

Opposite: Original title page of my second diary in Hebrew, entitled "If I am not for myself, who will be?"

DECEMBER 3, 1950

As I reread the last page in my diary, it seems a little dark. I imagine that if I had
written day after day, then our friendship would appear not so great as it does in
retrospect. I'm glad I did not record my feelings daily, because if I had read that
after some time had elapsed, I would have been mistaken and would not have
appreciated the subtlety, and would have only seen my lack of self-confidence. Our
friendship developed in such a way that when Petrushka[162] left he was in love many
times over, and this time his feelings produced a similar response with his girlfriend
("in subtlety there is wisdom").[163]

Peter was here for two months. I saw him daily, except one day (when I had
to do my French). The most beautiful days that we had were the trip to Eilat on
the last day of our work camp and when we took a trip to Shavei Zion[164] with
his family, the evenings we spent together at my place, in the afternoons when
he would come to my place and we would stay until it got dark and talk without
noticing that time was even passing, the trip on the Yarkon,[165] the first kiss (and
anyway after I tasted them I was nauseated from the attempts of my neighbor, V.,
in the same direction), when we would play Damka[166] together on the hay bales

162 During his very first visit to the country, to blend in with the boys in my youth group Peter
wore a Russian peasant shirt with a high collar and embroidery running down one side of
the shirt. I found it touching because it seemed to me so incongruous that this capitalist boy
was wearing a peasant shirt associated with the Russian revolution, so ever after I called him
Petrushka. I admired Peter for wearing such a shirt in an attempt to fit in.

163 This is a saying from the Talmud. What I think I'm trying to say here—looking back over all these
years—is that after being overly cautious in my expectations, I couldn't believe that even after his
wonderful European adventure that he still wanted to come back to me. In retrospect, I'm seeing
that it's good that I took time and didn't write daily because if I had I might have colored the
relationship itself and not have seen the lack of confidence that my attitude conveyed. In reality
our relationship developed in such a way that he was even more in love with me and I responded
in kind. Maybe if I had tried to write it all down at the time, I might have missed the nuances I
felt and would not have been able to capture accurately the subtle, fragile thread of uncertainty and
watchfulness that ran through all my feelings as Peter and I reconnected a year later.

164 Shavei Zion was a very pretty town that conveyed the sensibilities of the Germans who had
settled there in the 1930s as the persecution became heightened in Germany. It became a
kind of small resort, with all the charm and aesthetics that the German Jews were known and
respected for. We were there with Peter's cousin, David Rosenblatt, and David's wife, Carol.

165 The Yarkon was then a lovely river at the height of its beauty—long before its water were
partially diverted for the Negev—flowing to the sea.

166 The Polish term for checkers.

behind the kibbutz dining room, eating and sitting near the brand-new barn, and afterward coming half-asleep—either because of the late hour or because of having been sitting together for a long time—to the communal dining room and eating together the thick black bread with jam smeared on top and hot tea.

The talks between us were a little bit mixed with sadness relating to his future because I felt it would not be possible for me to have a part in it. Pain mixed with sweetness when we talked about that Parisian woman. When he would roll around laughing when he read an American joke book.[167] All the stories about his family, his brothers, his sister-in-law and his mother, his father, and the nanny. (Today a suspicion awakens in me about the relationship between his father and the nanny.) The writing of the diary together (that afternoon at the Ha-Uga[168]). [I would at times pelt him with inane giggly questions. The diary records some here:] *"Do you like Naomi?"* Peter, *"I love Naomi."* Naomi: *"If I lost all my hair would you still go out with me?" "I would."* The bathing in the morning in the sea of Eilat. When [trying to prove how flexible and agile he was] he had to put the big toe of his foot into his mouth. His response to my stories about women's periods[169] that melted my heart—*"poor Naomi."*

FEBRUARY 13, 1951

I am sick at home with strep throat and so have time to write. The last thing I wrote was about Peter, and so I will continue with him to this date. His letters now are different than the year past. They are a lot more meaty, except for one or two in which he talks a lot about his fencing. When he touches that subject, I totally lose interest in the letter.

Lately he's been writing a lot more about his conflicts. They are as remote from mine in a sense as the East from the West. (Capitalism? constitutional monarchy?) And yet it's not all that strange to me. I understand him very well, but I see no

---

[167] I so remember Peter's great peals of laughter, which could be heard throughout a vast tent area. At times, he'd laugh so hard that tears would roll down his cheeks. It was the kind of laughter that drew me and so many others to him.

[168] Ha-Uga, which means "the cake" in Hebrew, was a popular café on the Carmel.

[169] In Hebrew we call it *orach nashim*, meaning "the way of women," which refers to women getting their periods but not so clinical as defining it as menstruation.

point in strengthening him in his ideas because they have no relevance to the 20th century and nobody more than I would like him to accommodate to present circumstances in order to succeed.

He is impressive in that he instinctively holds back from the world he grew up in—a world which, in its most extreme aspects, is a reflection of this particular century: the modern world that expresses itself most clearly in Russia and America but in different ways. All this he understands even though he has not read Orwell's *1984* or listened to the lessons of our Dr. Schechter—with Peter it is a natural repugnance. I, within myself, believe with my innocence and my faith, that with all the minuses, the most productive way of solving these conflicts is the Land of Israel.[170] If for others this has helped, it would help him too. Under the influence of this country he will not have to look for answers in far-off European history, but rather in the simple and constructive present of this country. (Simple relative to the USA.)

Worries came related to the summer holidays, the work camp, etc., but I don't feel like worrying right now and therefore will not write about it right now but will postpone it to the summer and I shall see…

At this point I am hoping that his father will come for Passover, and my excitement about his coming can produce an enigmatic smile…

A few months ago, I made the acquaintance of the "personality" Danny Kraus. I have referred to him as a "personality" because if nobody else thinks so, at least he does. I met this cute boy one morning. I had guessed that he might come for a visit and wanted to be ready. That's why when I heard the doorbell I knew it was Mrs. Solomon [referring to Sara Salomon, whose American nephew was Danny], I quickly ran out to the balcony and vaulted the low wall into the yard. In order not to arouse suspicion that I had been expecting them, I waited a few moments before ringing the front bell, with my school bag. (That day in school we only had four hours, and I had time to change my school uniform into a flowered skirt and a white blouse, and I introduced myself.)

He made a cute impression. He was wearing [kibbutz] working clothes, khaki, which hinted at a strong body and beautiful grey eyes that seemed slightly magnified through his glasses. I sat on the sofa and he opposite me. I don't know why, but I did not permit myself even to look at him once, even though I took a lively part in the conversation. They left, we said shalom, and Mrs. Solomon managed to shout from her car that Danny thought Mother and I were "two very

---

[170] What I was really saying was that the answer for Peter was to live in Israel.

charming women." I quickly covered my mother's mouth so that she wouldn't respond in kind in a much too complimentary and effusive way.

NOVEMBER 24, 1951

The date on which I am continuing to write is after much time has passed—much, much, much time. The date is 24/11/51 and I am in the Israel Defense Forces, in the navy! ("In the ocean, amongst the waves, Naomi is rowing here and there... .") I have glanced at what I last wrote about, and find it a pity not to continue to describe that last episode in more detail, a pity because that episode was the first of a string of episodes of the same type. The rest didn't leave me with anything and did not tempt me off the path on which I am now walking. All because they are only a variation on the theme of that first episode. That first experience [with Danny Kraus] inoculated me against all situations of that same type. And it's good in the way in which it ended, because from my point of view, nothing positive would have come from it. Maybe because it passed quickly and no difficulty grew out of it, it remained first, amazing, and in a way very innocent.

At the first meeting, in the morning, we did not exchange a word but I was aware that he noticed me. He did not make such an incredible impression on me except for the fact that I felt that he was a masculine presence. He stood there strong in his khaki clothes and those large blue eyes. In the afternoon he came back again, and in the evening I went to the cinema with him, *The Girl from Jones Beach*.[171] He wore an impressive "battle dress" made of leather with fur lining. As we sat in the dark, I was aware of his broad shoulders, but nothing more. (I must comment, that the more I write about him, the more his attraction seems to evaporate. He's getting out of my system!) The whole way walking home, we talked. We talked about the youth movements, Mapam,[172] about dancing, and the conversation flowed and was animated and lively. Most of it, of course, came from me. At the end of the evening we found each other attractive. I came home with the impression of a great guy!!! I was lucky that he remained

---

[171] It turns out that this movie, made in 1949, was a star vehicle for Ronald Reagan, but I certainly don't remember the leading man.

[172] Mapam was a left-wing political party, with a strong, idealistic pioneering youth movement attached to it.

another day and a half [before going back to the kibbutz]. The next day he came early in the afternoon. (This was difficult because it was in the middle of my studies, and Daddy and homework were not a couple that came bonded together from heaven.) We went outside.

It was at the beginning of winter, and the weather was wonderful. The sun caressed one instead of tiring one as it always does. We walked up the donkey path. We hardly talked. It seemed as if our first meeting exhausted all possible topics. Danny K. is one of those silent ones that don't talk much. We walked up and from time to time I responded or he responded. (I wore grey slacks and the blue sweater dotted with flowers that Teema brought from England.) Danny K. brought with him a camera and tried to take a photograph here and there. We sat together for a long time on one of the rocks on the way up along the donkey path. Despite the silence, he embodied a certain masculine atmosphere. His presence managed to convey a tension of something still to come.

As we walked up or came down the path, he would skip from rock to rock, or he would skip over a bush and after a few minutes of quiet walking, he would bend down to pick up a stone and fling it. I sensed that within him there was a restrained, primitive energy seeking an outlet. He had little polish and manners, or wit or the capacity to have a light conversation the way Peter or Yerry were able to. Maybe also he did not have enough education for that, but this idea did not occur to me at all. Maybe I was afraid to acknowledge it, and I explained it to myself that he was a rough diamond. And I believed in this explanation wholeheartedly. After all, it was enough that he had picked a new way of life in which he fully believed and loved. There was in him an earthiness, something very basic… . During that time that we sat on the rock something was woven between us. We walked down and sat a little bit in my room, chatted, laughed. I don't remember it much. I only know that suddenly he blurted, "You are very lovely… ."

The next day I accompanied him to the Hadar because I had to go to the reading room.[173] The walk down was sweet, and the parting was short and to the point. As I walked away, I felt him staring at my back and I knew that he would not forget me very quickly. I went walking for quite a bit with a smile on my face.

---

[173] I'm referring here to my school library, because at the time of episode, I was still in school. This entry is written with me looking back on time spent with Danny K.

The beginning of our acquaintance was stormier than what I had thought. Two days had not gone by when I was called to the telephone with a call from Rehovot.[174] In short, there were lots of phone calls from Rehovot and many hurried visits. We would sit on that same sofa until two or three in the morning. We would talk, we'd be silent, and again we would talk. We felt very comfortable together. We'd be walking back from the cinema, cold outside, it was winter, chilly and damp, both of us in raincoats and he would always put his arm through mine. That's how we always walked. Specifically in this movement, there was nothing of tension, only an easy affectionate friendship and that was what I found so nice about it. Because of this reason, I was not ashamed to walk with him this way, and I liked it and found it comfortable.

---

[174] This is a town south of Tel Aviv, where today the Weizmann Institute is located, one of the premier scientific institutes in the world. And, again, I mentioned being "called" to the phone because we still didn't have one and always had to go to the Matzdorfs to receive calls.

When All is Said and Done

Part III

Go Forth and Fear Not!

THIS BOOK IS NOT MEANT TO BE NOSTALGIC AND WISTFUL—but rather reflective and evocative. I love the way I was reared, but I don't yearn to return to the long-ago past.

My starting point was the diary I kept as an adolescent from 1947 to 1952—key teenage years for me and the founding years of the country. I wrote *In the Beginning*, my introduction, to provide background and context. At times it was painful but also rewarding and funny. As emotions buried for so many years began to surface, I re-lived the bitter and the sweet. These backward glances, with all of the accompanying laughter and pain, illuminate experiences I have not thought about for a long time, and bring back vivid reminders of those who peopled the past. These memories will enrich our lives and those of generations that follow.

Now, having attained the age of 81 and having reached my 62nd wedding anniversary I want to share a few ideas.

For reasons not all that clear to me, I was fearful of rereading my diary, and so for a very long time I didn't. When I turned to it again, a wave of sadness swept over me initially, gradually replaced with gratitude and amusement. The diary made it clear that my home and school armed me with a can-do attitude that has served me well, and helped me get through life's ups and downs. I had felt a deep sense of belonging—to my family, my community, and country. I internalized the overriding Israeli belief that when there is no choice, one must simply cope and prevail. It was a wholesome adolescence and youth, that combined innocence with a measure of sensuality. I was aware even then—and certainly now—of the pull of history, of the unique slice of time into which I was privileged to be born. My parents were unusual people who made unusual choices at an unusual time in history. They left the sought-after English-speaking havens of their birth and settled in a special piece of land. I was the beneficiary. My love for the land was real, visceral and binding. I remember once stealing away from my hiking group, crouching and spitting onto the parched earth—my way of watering that thirsty, neglected, dry and barren terrain.

Opposite: Barren land on the way to Jerusalem.

The values of the sabra culture, honed for me at the Reali School and embedded in the kibbutz and Palmach cultures, are part and parcel of my bedrock beliefs. I realize these values must inevitably evolve and change with time, but I have found none better. Even though I was too young to actually be a member of the Palmach, its standards and ethics shaped my generation. My closeness to my cousin Danny, a commander in the Palmach, reinforced those values, and I fervently pray that his name will never, ever be forgotten and will be passed on from generation to generation of the family. If the stories from our past are not carried forward, the chain of history is broken and identity is diminished.

In many ways, my leave-taking from Israel was abrupt, and accompanied by certain losses—spiritual and psychological. I felt these strongly later on, but began to taste them almost as soon as I said goodbye to my mother and father at Lod airport and boarded the plane with Peter. The enormity of my actions dawned on me ever so slowly. Only in retrospect have I seen that leaving my family was more traumatic than I realized at the time and that leaving Israel produced a sense of dislocation and loss. Especially at the time I left, just four years after the 1948 War of Independence, leaving Israel was like abandoning a growing child in need of care and support.

One recollection that particularly upsets me and that has taken on a sense of sadness and regret is thinking of my mother putting on an exaggerated, cheerful expression when we said goodbye at the airport a few weeks after my wedding.

At the time, I was unaware of the effect of my departure on those I was leaving behind. Was I so selfish, self-absorbed, and self-centered? With the profound joy of a very young, lighthearted bride I must have been blithely looking ahead, but it was also in the belief that Peter and I would surely return to Israel when he finished his studies at Yale. The idea of not living in Israel was too painful and incomprehensible to contemplate, so I didn't.

It's clear that I was basking in my own happiness, but I'm dismayed at not having given a second thought to how my mother, especially, might have felt, and to the hole I was leaving behind in the lives of both of my parents—ours was a full and close companionship that had grown and solidified over the years. I know today that if even the slightest cloud had crossed Mother's face, I would not have been able to say goodbye, but she wore only a smile, conveying nothing but her love for me and her best wishes for my happiness.

However, I realize that my parents trusted Peter implicitly and I carried that feeling deep within me. It was not as if I was leaving her and my father the way the daughter in Shalom Aleichem's story "Tevye and his Daughters"—later written into *Fiddler on the Roof*—ran off with a young revolutionary never to be seen again. It is clear to me that my parents loved me more than they loved themselves.

On my last visit before she died, Mother gave me an extraordinary, extravagant gift, one that I have always cherished. "Naomi," she said, "when I die, do not cry for me. I have lived a full and rich life. I would not have wanted to live in any country other than Israel. I had you, of whom I am very proud. For that I am thankful. Cry about the young soldiers who have given their lives, but not for me."

An episode that occurred while Peter and I were on our way to the United States is especially reflective of feelings I began to discover after leaving Israel. During our honeymoon in France, Peter and I took a side trip from Paris to the beautiful medieval cathedral of Chartres. While walking on worn, centuries-old stones on which countless worshipers had knelt, we listened to our guide as she took us around the cathedral. I can still recall how she looked and what she was wearing— a small, pious, gray-haired woman, her hair pulled tightly into a thin bun. She had a sharp nose and chin, thin lips and wore a black cotton dress with a white Peter Pan collar. Suddenly, in the middle of our tour, she stunned me when she stopped and pointed to several stained glass windows, explaining that the light-colored windows represented love and the God of the New Testament, while the dark windows signified rage and the God of the Old Testament. I was dumbfounded! Was I hearing her correctly? She, on whose European soil the Holocaust, the Inquisition, the blood libels, the Crusades, the pogroms, and the endless Jewish expulsions had taken place, was telling *me* that her "new" God represented love and light, and my "old" God was characterized by the anger implied in the dark colors of the windows? How dare she put down and impugn what she referred to as "the God of the Old Testament"! Only my disciplined upbringing stopped me from flying at her scrawny throat. It was such a shock to me that anybody could think this way, a real blast of cold air. I knew I had to leave the tour then and there, and we did. The experience was a rude awakening, though a necessary one.

The immediacy of leaving my parents and land took on more meaning in the new world I found in America, one that I embraced and have loved for all of these decades. I will always miss Israel and its absolute uniqueness, but this land is mine as well. Marrying Peter was the best decision I ever made, and our 62 years of marriage have reinforced the wisdom of our choice of each other. Looking back I realize that from the very start we were committed to a lifelong bond. We have protected feelings of tenderness from dying out and were conscious not to use language that "hit below the belt," even during stressful and angry times. I never viewed my marital relationship as entailing hard work, but rather as requiring ongoing awareness of the other.

These years in America, despite their richness and achievements, children and grandchildren, have not been without some regrets. Possibly the biggest one is not having put into practice the jewel in the crown, the observance of the Sabbath. How amazing that the 4th commandment—"Honor the Sabbath and keep it holy"—which helped rescue humans from becoming beasts of burden working seven days a week thousands of years ago, would be just as vital and precious a pause for us today when an ever-faster pace and ever-present technology have taken over so many aspects of our personal lives.

I am deeply disappointed with my passivity for not marking at least Friday evening, the Eve of the Sabbath. To paraphrase Eric Fromm, it's not the Jewish people who have protected the Sabbath, but rather the Sabbath that has protected the Jewish people. I believe it also protects the institution of marriage and family. For one evening or even part of it, the outside world is shut out while individuals and families pause from the daily rush and mania of the week. For one evening the family unit takes precedence over cell phones, television, and iPads. Family members face each other around the table, light the candles, bless the wine and the challah, talk, laugh and express thanks and gratitude.

Is observing the Sabbath a perfect panacea for the modern-day family? Does it guarantee harmony and only good feelings between siblings, between children and parents, between friends, between husbands and wives? Of course not, but it goes a long way toward healing by focusing on the ties that bind us, rather than on what divides us. It is a weekly tradition that threads through its prism the spiritual values of hospitality, joy, gratitude and love. Had I marked the Sabbath with my family,

I know I would have enriched our lives, allowing for even greater closeness by observing a powerful and wise tradition.

Our identity resides in the deepest crevices of our being, and like the turtle's shell, we carry it with us wherever we go. Identity affords us self-confidence, passions, beliefs, and a home. Without it we have no anchor, no compass, no roots. I'm concerned about how my grandchildren and their children will forge a sense of their identity, will protect it and transmit it to the next generation. How do we Jews, always so small in number, accomplish this? As I see it, community and the study of the Hebrew Bible are essential. Regardless of one's level of observance or the nature of one's relationship with Providence, if one is a Jew by birth or by choice, the Bible is part of our DNA, containing historical and spiritual stories—our roots. It offers a brilliant and comprehensive picture of the human condition, its triumphs and downfalls. It is our narrative, holding up a mirror for us to see ourselves.

There is a price for any dislocation, both for oneself and for one's children. From time to time my children might have preferred a mother more at home with American customs and attitudes. I never could get excited about Halloween, a day that helps fill the coffers of a good many dentists, or the gushing commercial cards created for Valentine's Day. As to what benefits my children may have derived from my background and attitudes, I will leave it to them to decide.

I fear the world of my descendants will become even more complicated and dangerous. I therefore hope that they draw inspiration and guidance from this diary through the stories and memories of another generation, whose fortitude gave birth to a renewed people.

Life is indeed made up of the bitter and the sweet. I didn't come to the United States for a better life. I already had a good one. I came because I followed a young man with whom I fell in love and continue to love deeply. We are blessed and proud of our three independent, strong-minded children, their like-minded spouses, and our seven grandchildren, for each of whom I am deeply grateful. I urge them to study and seek purpose and meaning in their lives. After all, every day is another paragraph to be written, of which they will be the authors. I end by repeating to them what was said to Sara and Abraham at the very beginning of a long-ago journey: "Go forth and fear not."

Naomi Harris Rosenblatt

260

Naomi is a psychotherapist, speaker, adult Bible class teacher and the author of *Wrestling with Angels* and *After the Apple*, psychological and spiritual analyses of the Biblical narrative. She has spoken and taught in forums across the U.S., including seminars on Capitol Hill for U.S. senators, and has been featured in newspaper and magazine articles and TV appearances including Bill Moyer's PBS broadcast series *Genesis: A Living Conversation*. Born in Haifa, Israel, Naomi attended the Reali School and majored in biblical studies and Literature. After service in the Israeli Navy, she married American-born Peter R. Rosenblatt, now a practicing lawyer and former U.S. ambassador. She earned her master's degree in Clinical Social Work from Catholic University and has a private psychotherapy practice. Naomi is the mother of three children and grandmother of seven. She resides with Peter in Washington, DC.

View of contemporary Haifa, Israel.